PELICAN BOOKS

A542

PRIMITIVE GOVERNMENT

LUCY MAIR

44
47
55
62
67
78-9
82
96
99-100
101
113-4
121-2
157-8

ibs Bibls

7 87
191
200
215

211-215
225
277

Primitive Government

LUCY MAIR

PENGUIN BOOKS

Penguin Books Ltd, Harmondsworth, Middlesex
U.S.A.: Penguin Books Inc., 3300 Clipper Mill Road, Baltimore 11, Md
AUSTRALIA: Penguin Books Pty Ltd, 762 Whitehorse Road,
Mitcham, Victoria

—

Published in Penguin Books 1962

—

Copyright © Lucy Mair, 1962

—

Made and printed in Great Britain
by Hazell Watson & Viney Ltd
Aylesbury and Slough

Contents

Grateful acknowledgement is made to Dr N. Dyson-Hudson and Dr Martin Southwold for allowing me to use unpublished material.

L. M.

Introduction

WHAT is primitive government?

The words in the title of this book deserve some examination: we may start with the adjective. What does it mean to call people or their institutions primitive? The word has implied a good many different things from the time when people in western Europe first began to ask questions about the manners and customs of people in Africa and the Americas, and later the Pacific Islands. It is a fact of history that it was the European peoples who discovered the others, and in most cases established political domination over them, and not vice versa, and the reason is not difficult to find. The European peoples had ships and methods of navigation which enabled them to travel further, and weapons which generally enabled them to win any battles in which they were involved, and the inventions which began in the eighteenth century greatly increased this advantage. These peoples were organized politically in a manner which made it practicable to extend their authority over areas far wider than any controlled by peoples in the countries they discovered; and this was largely because they had writing as a means of communicating over distances and of keeping records, and because they had monetary systems as a means of organizing trade and production. That is to say, they possessed technical superiority in a number of fields; indeed, in the very fields in which the technical superiority of the Romans had enabled them some centuries earlier to extend their domination over the Mediterranean basin. In all these fields, the techniques of the peoples who came under European rule were rudimentary, and in consequence their systems of government might also be called rudimentary. This is one of the senses of the word 'primitive', and it is the only sense in which a modern anthropologist would use the word.

It is necessary to emphasize this point because people belonging to the societies which are called 'primitive' often regard the word as offensive, and it is used by persons other than anthropologists in a manner which may justly cause offence. This happens when it is applied, not to institutions, but to persons. People very commonly confuse the technical superiority of a nation with the moral and intellectual superiority of the population who make it up. Europeans are apt to talk about devices such as the internal combustion engine, or even the atomic reactor, as if they had all had a share in inventing them, whereas in fact most of us simply take advantage of inventions which we could not possibly have made and do not begin to understand. From this it is an easy step to seeing the peoples where these inventions were made as in some way more adult than those whose technical outfit does not include them. And this popular attitude gains support from the Jungian theory of psychology, which at the same time describes as 'primitive' the irrational elements in all human minds and holds that people who get through life with a primitive technical outfit have minds in which the irrational elements predominate.

Let me make it clear, then, that if I write of primitive societies I am not implying anything about the characteristics of the persons who compose them – least of all that such persons have remained in the childhood stage of a human race whose maturity is represented by the 'western' nations. It is *ways of doing things* which can be described as primitive or otherwise. The development of more complicated and efficient ways of doing things is a matter of discoveries and inventions which simply cannot be credited to the superiority of certain total populations over others. But the possession of a complex technology is what enables a modern state to control, and to a large extent organize, the lives of populations of many millions.

The purpose of this book is to examine the way in which

government is carried on among peoples of simple technology. Many anthropologists have classed as 'primitive' the peoples who do not have writing. This makes a useful broad division, because, as has just been said, where people cannot keep records or send written messages the range over which any government can exercise power has to be relatively narrow. Also, where people cannot keep records they can only carry out very simple economic transactions.

Where writing is not known, the number of persons who can be said to have a common government – if we may beg the question for a moment and assume that there always is such a thing – is small, rarely more than a few hundred thousand. So anthropologists sometimes refer to 'small-scale' societies. 'Pre-literate' is another word which does not have the offensive connotations of 'primitive'. But neither of these words goes very well with 'government'. So let us keep 'primitive', but remember that when it is used it refers to the outfit of techniques available to the members of a given society, and not to their mental characteristics.

Do all primitive societies have government? Here again we immediately come up against another of the unfortunate interpretations of the word 'primitive'. Some writers, particularly in the nineteenth century, have thought that many of the institutions which are fundamental to western society developed fairly late in the history of mankind, so that we might expect not to find them among peoples who had not advanced along the path of civilization as far as ourselves. Government and law are among these, and if politics is defined as that which pertains to government, those who hold this view would consider that primitive societies pursue no activities which deserve the name of politics.

But there is another way of looking at politics, according to which it indubitably does exist in primitive societies. One definition of politics is the struggle for power; and even if one is not willing to agree that power is the only thing that men struggle for, one must admit that in every society there are conflicts which must somehow be reconciled if the society is not to split into separate independent parts. Conflict and competition begin within the family, however little we care to admit it; in fact, this is recognized in such phrases as 'fraternal enmity'. But every society has an ideal of family unity such that disputes between kinsmen are expected to be settled without any outside intervention. So some anthropologists would hold that the sphere of politics begins where that of kinship ends. In the case of primitive societies it is not always easy to say where this line comes, for in such societies people trace the links of kinship much further than they do in the western world. But what one can say is that between people who are in close daily contact throughout their lives, sentiments are expected to develop (and often do) which limit the expression of conflict, whereas outside these narrow circles one cannot rely on sentiment alone to reconcile conflicting interests. In these wider fields of social relationships there are always and everywhere persons with conflicting and competing interests, seeking to have disputes settled in their favour and to influence community decisions ('policy') in accordance with their interests. This is politics.

The seventeenth-century philosopher Hobbes contrasted the state of nature, in which every man's hand was against his neighbour, with civil society, in which authority had been surrendered to a sovereign ruler (not necessarily a single man). This was a logical rather than a historical argument; it followed from Hobbes's assumptions about human nature that if there were no supreme authority there could only be a war of each against all. But he did refer to 'savage people in many places of America' whose condition he thought approached this. We shall see that in a number of primitive societies fighting is recognized as a legitimate means of obtaining redress for an injury, though in those cases it is not, as Hobbes imagined, a means of dominating others. The question whether societies of this kind can or cannot be said to have government or law is an interesting one, and contemporary anthropologists have answered it in different ways.

Many modern writers have assumed that government must be carried on through the type of organization which we call the state – a body of persons authorized to make and enforce rules binding on everyone who comes under their jurisdiction, to settle disputes arising between them, to organize their defence against external enemies, and to impose taxes or other economic contributions upon them, not to mention the multifarious new functions which the state has undertaken in the present century. Some primitive societies have this kind of organization, but others do not, and the question then arises whether they can be said to have government.

*

There are two ways of trying to answer this question. One is to start with an idea of what a government ought to look like. Text-books about government say it has legislative, executive, and judicial functions. When you see a parliament and a cabinet, or a congress and a president, you know you are looking at a government, and it is this kind of government, or the country which has a government of this kind, that is called a state. Governments of this familiar kind make laws which they enforce within whatever territory comes within their authority. The whole world is divided today between governments each exercising authority over a territory with its recognized boundaries (of course there are sometimes quarrels about just where the boundaries are). Thus everyone in the United Kingdom has to obey its laws and do what its policemen tell him, no matter whether he was born in the United Kingdom or somewhere else. If an Englishman goes to France he is subject to French law; he can do some things that he could not do in England, and he may be punished for doing others that he would be free to do in England.

The authority of a state, then, extends over a fixed territory. Some writers have said that primitive societies did not recognize territorial authority, and that the appearance of this idea, the idea of a ruler or a government controlling a territory and claiming obedience from all the people in it, marked an important stage in the evolution of government.

According to this view, primitive peoples do not have any notion of a 'country' with laws that apply to everyone in it. In the early stages of society, these writers suppose, people recognize that they have certain duties towards their kinsmen wherever they may be, but they do not recognize a ruler whom they must obey because they are in his territory. The first form of society, they assume, is a 'tribe' consisting of people who believe that they are all descended from one ancestor. They may obey a chief or headman because they think of him as the head of a family (which may be a pretty large family) but not because he is the ruler of the land or makes the law of the land.

The most famous exponent of this theory was Sir Henry Maine, the founder of comparative jurisprudence. He thought the change from the 'tribe' based on blood relationship to the state based on 'local contiguity' was so important that he called it one of 'those subversions of feeling which we term emphatically revolutions'.*

The question that Maine is considering here is what a body of people accept as a reason why they should all obey the same laws. In primitive conditions, he says, the only reason is that they are *really* brothers, or at least cousins; or they think they are. Later on it comes to be regarded as a sufficient reason to obey 'the law of the land' that you are in the land.

Maine points out that where the first of these principles is the basis of common citizenship, the belief in common descent is by no means always true. The different divisions of a people may have legends telling how they joined its original members at some point in time. Many primitive peoples are indeed organized on the principle that everyone

* *Ancient Law* (Everyman Edition, 1959), p. 76.

can be theoretically fitted into a genealogical tree, though some got there by adoption and not by birth. Maine calls this 'the earliest and most extensively employed of legal fictions', and adds that 'there is none to which I conceive mankind to be more deeply indebted. If it had never existed, I do not see how any one of the primitive groups, whatever were their nature, could have absorbed another, or on what terms any two of them could have combined, except those of absolute superiority on one side and absolute subjection on the other.' But later, says Maine, 'probably as soon as they felt themselves strong enough to resist extrinsic pressure, all these states ceased to recruit themselves by factitious extensions of consanguinity. They necessarily, therefore, became Aristocracies, in all cases where a fresh population from any cause collected around them which could put in no claim of community of origin.'

This conjecture comes remarkably near to the kind of development that the instances in this book will illustrate. In fact those peoples who believe that they are all kin do not have the type of political structure that we call the state. The state itself in its simplest form entails the recognition that *one* body of kin have an exclusive claim to provide the ruler from among themselves. This can happen among very small populations; we can observe societies where certain kin groups have a privileged position (are aristocrats, if you like), but their privileges are so slight that it is difficult to speak of them as ruling, as aristocrats are supposed to do. The examples to be quoted seem to suggest that states arise when such privileged kin groups are able to command the services of followers through whom they can impose their will on the rest of the people. But, at any rate in some instances, this process has begun on such a small scale and developed so gradually that it does not seem realistic to speak of a revolutionary change in ideas.

A contemporary writer, MacIver,* goes further than Maine and argues that membership of primitive polities is

* *The Web of Government* (1947).

based *solely* on kinship, and that in this respect, 'tribal government differs from all other political forms'. Its 'territorial basis is not sharply defined'. 'Not sharply defined' is a rather slippery phrase. People who cannot write do not draw maps, and so they may not know where their boundaries are until there is a fight about them. But they may still have a strong conviction that certain territory is theirs and nobody else's. Schapera, who used the phrase 'political community' to mean any body of people who have laws, rulers, or government in common, has shown that the smallest and simplest political communities have their recognized territory. Moreover, even these small communities do not consist entirely of people descended from one ancestor. In all primitive societies the rules of marriage forbid people to marry close relatives. So, in a very small political community where all the men are actually kinsmen, all their wives must be women who have been brought in from other communities. But of course these women become part of the community into which they marry and subject to its authorities, whoever they are; and the converse of this is that when a woman marries she loses her political allegiance to the group in which she was born. In larger political communities people who believe they had a common ancestor in the distant past are divided into *exogamous* lineages. The members of each such lineage must find their wives in other lineages; they believe that their common ancestry is too far back to be a bar to marriage. But these larger communities do not usually suppose that *all* their members have a common ancestor.

This is a convenient place to consider how the word 'tribe' can be useful in discussion. It has come to be used by people who consider that they are civilized, as a way of describing societies which they do not regard as civilized, and so it is very naturally thought to be an offensive word by educated members of the peoples who are called tribes. But when anthropologists use it, they are not concerned at all with levels of civilization. In writing about Africa they use it to describe political divisions of certain large populations which call themselves by one name and speak one language, but do not recognize one common chief or other type of government. These larger populations could be called nations; but today more and more of them are, politically, divisions of still larger populations, each with an independent government which is seeking to make a single nation out of all the people under its authority.

Nevertheless, we seem to be driven at present to use the word 'nation' in two ways. In the first sense the Tswana of southern Africa, the Nuer of the southern part of Sudan, and the Ibo of the Eastern Region of Nigeria are nations. The Nuer number about 200,000; they call themselves by a common name which distinguishes them from their neighbours; they have a common language; their 'culture' – the way they get their living, their rules of conduct, their religion – is the same for all Nuer. But all Nuer never act in common. They are divided into sections each with its own territory, which act independently and are often engaged in actual fighting. The Ibo are a much larger nation, numbering over four million. They too are divided into territorial units, independent of each other and often hostile. It is units of this kind which anthropologists call 'tribes'. In the case of the eight major divisions of the Tswana in Bechuanaland, each of which has a chief formally recognized by the Protectorate government and a territory allotted to it by this government, the word 'tribe' is an indispensable part of the official language of the Protectorate. But anyone who wants to use it as a technical term, and not a term of abuse, should be clear that it simply means an independent political division of a population with a common culture.

The nations in the second sense are the new ones which have attained independence in this century by the rejection or withdrawal of colonial rule. In each of these new nations there are many sub-divisions, each with its own language and culture, which cannot be called nations without confusion, and indeed are not seeking to be independent nations. For them too the word 'tribe' is convenient, though one can often avoid it by saying 'people', which is actually vaguer.

*

The political community, then, has its own territory whether or not it is organized in the form of a state. Next, we have to ask whether we can say that those political communities which are not states have, or do not have, government or law. Now that we are talking about political communities that do not have any of the institutions by which we are used to recognizing a government, we must ask the question differently. Instead of saying 'What ought a government to look like?' we must ask 'What does a government do?' or 'What is government?' From there we can go on to see whether the *functions* of government, or at any rate some of them, may not be performed in simple societies even though they do not have the institutions of the state.

What then does government do? It protects members of the political community against lawlessness within and enemies without; and it takes decisions on behalf of the community in matters which concern them all, and in which they have to act together.

A collection of studies was published in 1940 by two anthropologists, Fortes and Evans-Pritchard, now professors of anthropology at Cambridge and Oxford respectively, called *African Political Systems*. This made the first attempt to answer the question whether there were in Africa any societies which could not be said to have political systems. The answer, of course, depended on what a political system was taken to be. The authors said the political system of any society was concerned with the regulation of the use of force. Every political community (though they did not use that phrase) recognizes some rules about when force may legitimately be used and when not, and this it what makes it a political community. But though all societies have political systems, some, they said, do not have governments. In the societies without government, the people were divided into groups based on kinship, which were independent for most purposes (but, unlike Maine's 'tribes', these kin groups had their own land, and this was perhaps the most important thing that they had in common). The head of a lineage, as these corporate kin groups are called, might have the right to give orders to members of the lineage, but nobody could give orders to him. If a man was wronged, his lineage supported him in seeking redress by force. When they got tired of fighting they invited an influential man to mediate between the two sides. An outsider who arrived at the right moment might well take such a situation as a manifestation of Hobbes's war of each against all. The classical example of such a society are the Nuer, whom we shall be considering at length later on. There are other influences to make people keep the peace – or enough peace – in societies which have no policemen. For instance the people described by Fortes in *African Political Systems* – the Tallensi in Ghana – believed that their land could not prosper unless all were at peace when it was time for them to join together in their great religious festivals, and at these times they felt compelled to make up their quarrels.

The writers who contributed to that book were concerned particularly with the function of government in maintaining law and order. They did not consider the question who took communal decisions or what such decisions were about. Schapera, in a survey of the peoples (or tribes) of South Africa, has shown that in that region the smallest community, with the most rudimentary technical knowledge – the Bushman bands of ten to thirty men with their families, living by hunting small animals and gathering wild plants – recognizes that certain of its members have authority to take communal decisions. This, in Schapera's view, is enough to count as government. In some of the larger populations who are described in *African Political Systems* it might be harder to identify the persons who could be called the government. This is a question which will have to be discussed later.

How do we know whether people have law? If there is no law that is not expressly enacted, very few, if any, non-literate peoples have law, for enactments which are not recorded are apt to be forgotten, or at best become matter of dispute. The chiefs of the Tswana of southern Africa are said to have legislated for their people before the introduction of writing, but few of these earlier laws are remembered.

To Hobbes, where there was no law there must be anarchy, and the Nuer have been described by Evans-Pritchard, to whom we owe our knowledge of them, as living in an 'ordered anarchy'. Even a casual observation of actual primitive peoples shows that they are not constantly engaged in internecine fighting; that they recognize rules of conduct which they can state, and that these rules are obeyed sufficiently often for people to know what they are entitled to, and can expect of others, in any of the recurrent situations of life. Why? One popular explanation has been that primitive peoples are too dull-witted, or else too superstitious, or nowadays the more romantic word is 'community-minded', to question the rules of conduct which they learn as they grow up, and so the force of 'custom' is sufficient to maintain the social order. This interpretation was finally exploded by Malinowski's work in the Trobriand Islands off the coast of New Guinea. Malinowski lived three years in a Trobriand village, and so had plenty of opportunities of seeing people who were angry because their rights had been infringed, and of watching what they did about it. From his day anthropologists have studied quarrels with particular interest for the sake of the light that they throw on the reaction of a society to breaches of its rules.

It is agreed, then, that there is no society where rules are automatically obeyed, and that every society has some means of securing obedience as well as of dealing with offenders. The question remains, however, whether all ways of dealing with offenders are to be described as legal, and if not, what rules are to count as laws and what procedures are to be considered legal.

Floods of ink have been wasted on this subject. No writer has gone so far as to say that every rule which a person feels constrained to obey is a legal rule; the rules of etiquette, for example, obviously fall in a different category. Malinowski, however, would have brought nearly everything else under the heading of law; he hated formal definitions, and he regarded as formal the definition which says that laws are rules enforced by the authority of the state. A 'functional' definition, seeking for the type of contribution which an institution makes to the totality of social life, would in his view have found law in every society, and he offered several such definitions.

Malinowski's leading contemporary, Radcliffe-Brown, in the introduction to *African Political Systems*, described law as 'the application of direct or indirect penal sanctions ... the settlement of disputes and the provision of just satisfaction for injuries'. He would not, therefore, refuse to find law where there were not courts or judges. He gave as an example of legal action the 'lynching' by the whole community of a heinous offender, which used to occur among some Kenya tribes. But he would not give the name of law to what he calls 'regulated vengeance' or feud, in which one section of a community, with the approval of the rest, fight another section because a member of it has injured one of their members. Radcliffe-Brown recognized that the right to resort to feud supports the law against killing, since people will separate men who are quarrelling if they can, so as to prevent a feud from starting. But he would not consider the feud as a legal action.

*

Radcliffe-Brown's definition of political organization, which is followed in *African Political Systems*, is intended to apply to all societies, whether or not they have a state form of government. He says it is 'that part of the total organization which is concerned with the maintenance or establishment of social order, within a territorial framework, by the organized exercise of coercive authority through the use, or the possibility of use, of physical force'. The wider definition given by Schapera* is 'that aspect of the total organization which is concerned with the establishment and maintenance of internal cooperation and external independence'. This definition covers both the means of maintaining the order on which cooperation depends, and also the organization of cooperation itself.

*

The examples of primitive government given in this book will be taken from that part of East Africa which is included within Kenya, Uganda, Tanganyika, and the southern part of Sudan. Within the limits of this area there are a number of very different kinds of political system, but there are also groups of neighbours who have broadly similar systems with interesting differences between them. The peoples of the area live in very different kinds of environment, and one of the questions to be asked will be whether, and where, differences in environment seem to account for differences in political systems.

These peoples have been classified by the language groups to which they belong, as Nilotes, Nilo-Hamites, and Bantu. Among the Nilotes and Nilo-Hamites we find peoples with less of what *looks like* government than elsewhere in this region. Some of the Bantu peoples have states with an apparatus of authority that would be recognized as government at a glance. Indeed when Speke arrived in Buganda in 1862 he was struck at once by the contrast between it and all the rest of the territory he had traversed on his journey. Here was a well laid-out capital several miles in extent in which lived a ruler surrounded by his senior officials, dispensing justice, hearing emissaries from foreign lands, amid a constant movement to and fro of messengers coming in

* *Government and Politics in Tribal Society* (1956), p. 218.

with reports or going out with orders to other parts of the country. Speke later came to regard the Kabaka of Buganda as an irresponsible despot. But there was never any doubt that he had real political power. However, one cannot make a simple classification into 'peoples with chiefs' and 'peoples without chiefs'. Several of the Nilotic peoples have chiefs or kings – words which, as we shall see, may mean many different things – and some Bantu are governed in ways which do not entail the recognition of a single ruler.

Kenya, Tanganyika, and Uganda surround Lake Victoria, the great lake whence the Nile flows northward. The lake is held as in a pair of pincers between the escarpments of the African Rift Valley on the east and those of its western branch, which runs from Lake Albert to the northern shore of Lake Tanganyika. Its shores rise gradually westward from the low-lying Kavirondo gulf, which falls within the frontiers of Kenya; they are not precipitous, as are those of the lakes within the Rift valleys, and so can be – and are – thickly settled.

Where it flows north from the Sudan-Uganda boundary the White Nile falls so gradually that its course is choked by floating weeds, and the nearly level country which surrounds it is largely covered by floods in the rainy season. This is the country of the Nilotic peoples, of whom those we know best are the Nuer, numbering about 200,000, Dinka (900,000), Shilluk (110,000), and Anuak (40,000). I give the figures as they were at the time when they were studied by anthropologists. Changes in population may lead to changes in political structure, and what is important is the size of the population which has the political structure we are talking about.

The Sudan Nilotes live on the banks of the White Nile and its tributaries and the land between them. Much of this land is under water at the height of the rainy season, and then gradually changes from swamp to parched clay, in which water collects here and there in the deep cracks and so provides enough pasture to keep cattle alive. The country nearest to the rivers is savannah with long grass and a few trees. On slightly higher ground grass alternates with forests of thorn trees. .

Now, the ways in which people are distributed on the ground must obviously affect the way in which their government is organized, particularly when they have no means of long-distance communication. The 'pattern of settlement', as it is sometimes called, is rather different in the case of each of these four peoples, and the differences show how important for peoples of simple technology are slight differences in the geographical environment. It would be wrong to assume that differences in settlement patterns are the most important reasons for differences in political systems. But they are particularly important in the case of pastoral peoples living in an environment which obliges them to be constantly moving their herds. Such peoples cannot live an ordered life at all unless they can move in peace through certain territory, and live at peace when they are gathered together around the limited sources of water. The kind of arrangements by which peace is secured among them depend very much on how far the herdsmen have to move and in what conditions numbers have to congregate together.

Nuer country is all savannah. The Nuer build their villages on sandy ridges out of reach of the flood water; this is obviously necessary for people and houses, even if the houses are only huts of wattle and daub with roofs of straw thatch, and it is equally important for cattle, because cattle become sick if their feet are constantly wet. The villages are built on the tops of these ridges, strung out over a mile or two, with grazing land on one side and fields of millet or maize on the other, for the Nuer do grow grain, although they regard it as an inferior kind of food; they also catch fish in the pools which are left when the floods recede. In the dry season they have to leave the villages so as to be within reach of water and of grazing for their cattle. As the water sinks lower, more and more people have to gather together within reach of the pools that have not dried up. They congregate at these places in camps of grass huts. People who live in the same village do not necessarily go to the same cattle camp, so that different sets of people are in constant contact at different seasons of the year. In the wet season it is the people of neighbouring villages who need to be able to count on peaceable relations among them if normal life is to be carried on; in the dry season it is a much larger number of people. During the time when the cattle are being driven across the country in search of water, what is important is that the herdsmen should be able to count on being able to travel without being attacked by other people moving through the same country.

The Dinka surround the Nuer on the north, south, and west. Like the Nuer they are herdsmen who supplement the meat and milk of their cattle with grain and fish. Their country is very like Nuer country, but less of it is under water in the rainy season. Whereas the Nuer villages in the rains are isolated on their ridges, the Dinka herds can still move about, though they have to keep to higher ground. Just as the pools get fewer in the dry season, so the dry ground gets less in the wet season; and for the Dinka the important concentrations of population are those of the wet season. The same people expect to finish the wet season every year at the same camp, on higher ground in the savannah forest. These are the herdsmen of a division of a tribe (sub-tribe) who also organize a number of other activities together. Because they join together in the wet-season camp, they think of themselves as forming the body within which peace ought to be preserved. But the size of such a body is limited in a way that the concentration of people at a dry-season camp is not. The wet-season camps are places where cattle can be tethered for the night on well-drained ground. If there are too many cattle, some herdsmen will find, as the floods rise, that there is nowhere to tether their herds except on ground that is waterlogged. Then they may decide to move away and find camping-ground some-where else. A group of kinsmen who herd their cattle to-gether will break off and look for a new camping site where they, as first occupants, will claim the highest ground. As time goes on and their numbers increase they will be recog-nized as a new sub-tribe, and no longer feel any particular obligation to maintain peace with the rest of their original sub-tribe. This kind of division seems to be the reason why the Dinka have spread over such an immense area. But in the dry season, when herds have to range more widely, a sort of truce is made between sub-tribes who would expect to treat one another as enemies at other times.

The Anuak live further up the same rivers which water the eastern part of the Nuer country. They depend for live-stock on sheep and goats rather than cattle; they have cattle, but, as they themselves admit, they slaughter them for food with reckless disregard for the maintenance of the herd. Also, between 1932 and 1939 a large number of cattle were taken from them as a collective punishment for a raid on a neighbouring people. In the western part of the country the rivers flood in the rainy season. The Anuak build villages which are out of reach of the floods, but some of these places in the dry season are short of water even for drinking. When this happens the villagers move to the edge of the marshes and camp on mounds which seem – like those beloved of archaeologists in the Middle East – to have been built up out of the rubbish left by many generations. A village may be from five to twenty miles from its nearest neighbour, and those that have to move in the dry season go independently, each to its own mound. There is no problem here of peaceful passage for herdsmen in territory where they may meet others. The villages are completely self-con-tained as far as the necessities of economic life are con-cerned. Of course marriages are often made between people of different villages, and there are other friendly contacts. But a village in western Anuakland is a distinct political community. There is also often fighting between villages.

In the extreme east of the country, where the forest begins, the river banks are higher and the land is never flooded. The villages are built close together on the river banks, with their cultivated land carved out of the forest behind them. They are protected from surprise attack by impenetrable growths of tall reeds on the riverside, and by the forest on their other sides, as well as by strong stockades. But it is never impossible to travel from one village to another.

Eastern Anuakland can be said to form a single political community; but this has come about not as a result of any actual need for peaceful cooperation between the villages, but because the greater ease of communications has made it possible for all to combine in a single system.

The Shilluk live along the west bank of the Nile to the north and south of Malakal. At this point the ground rises fairly steeply from the river, and houses can be built at a height which is permanently out of the reach of floods. Moreover, the Shilluk do not keep many cattle – a circumstance which leads their neighbours to despise them – and so their lives are not centred in the quest for water and grazing. If the cattle have to be moved in the dry season, boys take them to islands in the river or to pools in dry water-courses. The bulk of the population live all the year round in houses that stretch almost continuously along the river bank, with their cultivated land behind them. The Shilluk recognize a division of their country into eleven 'settlements', each under its own head, but these are not clusters of houses with spaces between them. It is not usually easy to see where one settlement ends and the next begins. In the rainy season it may be difficult to get about on land, but people can always travel by river, so that no part of Shillukland is ever isolated from the rest. Some people think this is why the Shilluk are sufficiently united to recognize a single king; they are the only Nilotic people to do so. Even the Shilluk king does not have much authority. His capital is almost in the middle of the long line of settlements.

There are other Nilotic peoples to the south, whose political systems have not been described in detail. Their furthest outliers, the Alur, numbering about 200,000, live across the boundary between Uganda and the ex-Belgian Congo. The Alur are unlike the peoples that have been mentioned up to now in that they have chiefs with functions which could readily be recognized by political scientists as those of government, and these chiefs have been extending their authority over neighbouring areas in a manner which will be discussed later on.

The area occupied by Nilo-Hamitic peoples begins south of the main block of the Nilotes, and extends south-eastwards roughly along the line of the high ground to the east of Lake Victoria, thus covering the Kenya Highlands and their extension southwards into Tanganyika. In general it coincides with the good cattle country – high ground with short grass and adequate rainfall. But some Nilo-Hamites, notably the Turkana of northern Kenya, live in country of which the best that can be said is that whereas agriculture is nearly impossible, nomads can live there on their stock.

The most northerly of the Nilo-Hamites are the Mandari, of whom only the western section, some ninety miles from the Nile and numbering about 10,000, has been adequately described. Although their dominant interest is in cattle, they grow millet, groundnuts, and pulses as well as maize, cassava, and tobacco, and as they are out of reach of the floods they do not have to move to and fro every year. They live in small groups near streams or rivers, and move within a fixed area as the soil they have most recently been cultivating becomes exhausted. Each of these areas recognizes a chief who claims to be descended from the first immigrants to that part of the country, and no chiefdom recognizes the head of any other as its superior. But herdsmen from many different chiefdoms have to graze their cattle together in the dry season, and at these times there has to be peace between them.

The central Nilo-Hamites are represented in this book by

the Karimojong (55,000) in the north-east of Uganda and the Turkana (80,000) across the frontier in Kenya. For these peoples the problem is never excess of water, but always the difficulty of finding enough. Karimojong country is a high plateau above which isolated steep hills rise in the east. The rain which falls there flows down the steep slopes in narrow rocky river beds, which widen and become sandy as they reach the more level country and eventually lose themselves in the swamps to the south-west. Most of the year's rain falls in a few heavy showers. After such a shower the steep parts of the river beds are dry again within a few hours. The water rushes down, and for two or three days the river banks lower down are flooded. On the plain the rivers flow for about thirty days; then the water sinks into the sand and they too are apparently dry. The Karimojong have an elaborate vocabulary to distinguish different sources of water, and one of their words refers to water which flows continuously, a word that would be unnecessary in countries where the rivers are never expected to dry up. It seems to be unnecessary for the Karimojong too, because there are not in fact any permanently flowing watercourses in their country. They depend for household water on what collects below the surface of the sandy river beds; they reach this by digging as far as they have to through the sand. Their homes are built by these river beds, and their womenfolk grow crops on the alluvial soil.

When water supplies are short the permanent settlements have only enough for human use, and the cattle must be taken elsewhere. The herdsmen move to places where they expect, or know, there is water: pools on rocky ground in the hills, depressions in the clay soil on the edge of the swamps. They must be constantly moving on as the water at each source is exhausted. Each herd owner has certain water courses that he knows, and will assert a prior claim to when supplies are short; but most herdsmen do not know where they may expect to be from one dry season to another. At any one time herdsmen who meet at one watering place will come from many different settlements, and no one will expect to meet the same people each year (in other words, the people who are in close contact during the dry season do not form a permanent social group). The Karimojong recognize this and say, 'The sun mixes us up.' They are most mixed up at the height of the drought, when a number of herds and their herdsmen combine to use the same water and grazing and to keep others out of it. If a conflict of this kind occurs, loyalties are clear. The 'insiders' in this temporary group must stand together against outsiders, whatever ties of kinship or neighbourhood may bind them to the outsiders at other times.

The Turkana organize their life in much the same way; their difficulties are, if anything, greater. It can be said of both these peoples that since in any case the conditions of life make it undesirable for people to congregate anywhere in large numbers, the best way for small groups to avoid friction is to move out of each other's reach. It could be argued that if the Turkana have any government at all, they have less than any other people in East Africa, and possibly anywhere. The Karimojong have rather more government than the Turkana.

The southern Nilo-Hamites (Nandi, Kipsigis, Masai) share with Bantu peoples that part of the Kenya Highlands which has not been allotted to European settlement. Of the Kenya Nilo-Hamites, those that have been best described are the closely related Nandi (about 120,000) and Kipsigis (80,000) who now occupy small areas near the western escarpment of the Highlands, and the Masai, who although they have lost half the territory that they formerly controlled – and the most fertile half – still occupy 80,000 square miles in a wide belt stretching from a point north-west of Nairobi southwards into Tanganyika. Like the Turkana the Masai move constantly with their cattle in search of grazing. But with the Masai we come to a people for whom the need for an area within which they can go to and fro in peace is not the most important political consideration. In their enthusiasm for raiding the cattle of their neighbours, the Masai do not differ from other cattle peoples; but they differ from those already described in that the keystone of their political system is an organization for doing so. The Nandi and Kipsigis have had a similar organization, though they never succeeded in making themselves feared over so wide an area. Their system is that known as 'age-organization', the central feature of which is a fairly prolonged period of military service for every man in the population.

All the Bantu peoples of East Africa are settled agriculturists, and I will venture the proposition that the less a people are dependent on herding, the less significant is the connexion between their pattern of settlement and their political system. In much of the hilly region surrounding Lake Victoria the characteristic terrain consists of ridges divided by clefts in high mountains or swampy valleys in lower ones, and the characteristic unit of settlement is a village strung out along the ridge. This would be equally true of the country to the north of Nairobi inhabited by the Kikuyu (with the closely related Meru) and that of the Soga and Ganda along the northern shore of Lake Victoria. But the million and a quarter Kikuyu had in the past a system of age-organization which was rather more elaborate than that of the Nilo-Hamites and was not directed predominantly to the making of war, in which the Kikuyu could never compete with the Masai. The 500,000 Soga have a number of small-scale state systems, while the 856,000 Ganda have a state system embracing a total population, including conquered populations and immigrants, of 1,300,000, and form the largest political community in East Africa.

As regards the Bantu peoples, then, all that need concern us at this preliminary stage is where they live and certain very broad characteristics by which the reader can identify them. The Kikuyu have been mentioned; other Kenya Bantu are the Gusii and Luhya (200,000), peoples of the lower-lying country to the west of the escarpment, who have neither age-organization nor state systems. It is characteristic of the Kikuyu that their livestock consists of goats rather than cattle.

In Uganda the peoples known as the Interlacustrine Bantu have a tradition that the first inhabitants of the country were agriculturists who were conquered by cattle people from the north, and this is made probable by the evidence that we have of the southward migration of Nilotes who have kept their Nilotic languages. In the south-west of the country there are four states, each under a single ruler, which have been recognized as distinct political entities in treaties made with the British authorities. These are Toro, Bunyoro, Ankole, and Buganda. In all except Buganda the cattle owners (Hima) until recent times maintained their position as a dominant aristocracy and refused to intermarry with the cultivators (Iru). In Ankole (population 540,000) they do so to this day, but in Toro (860,000) and Bunyoro (110,000) the distinctions are disappearing, largely because people are ceasing to rely solely on cattle and many of them no longer have cattle. In Buganda there had already ceased to be any distinction when the first recorded descriptions of the country were made; this again may be due to the fact that on the lower ground near the lake there is less good grazing and more good agricultural land.

The Ganda staple food is the banana, which needs a well-distributed rainfall, but, provided there is no exceptional drought, will ripen at any time of the year. Thus the Ganda do not suffer the annual period of hunger, when one year's supplies are nearly exhausted and the new harvest is not yet ripe, that is the experience of most African peoples. But recently it was found that children brought up on this diet often suffer from a serious nutritional disease.

East of the Nile the most important Bantu people are the Soga, who do not, like the four 'Agreement States', form a single political community, but comprise a number of small states each under its own chief. Similar groups of small states south of Lake Victoria are the Ha, Haya, and Zinza.

Since trade was opened up between Africa and the rest of

the world, not only the Bantu, but some of the Nilo-Hamites who live in suitable country, have taken up the cultivation of crops for sale. The Kikuyu grow coffee and wattles; the Kipsigis maize; the Ganda coffee; and everyone in the low-lying area around Lake Victoria grows cotton. These changes in modes of subsistence have been related to many changes in political systems, and we shall have to devote some attention to these modern developments. But the main topic of this book is the type of governments which primitive peoples developed for themselves, and to follow this out we have to transfer ourselves in imagination to a past before their countries were brought under foreign control. This applies particularly to the settled cultivators, who were easily brought within the sphere of new rules and institutions just because they were settled; the more elusive pastoralists can be seen even today as living examples of political systems which do not depend upon a state organization. Whether, how far, and in what sense, they may be said to have government will be a matter for a later chapter.

*

Anthropologists often find it difficult to decide whether they should write in the present tense or the past, particularly when they are quoting from books by other anthropologists. Every anthropologist writes of the people he works among as he finds them, and so uses the present tense. But some of the books I am using here were written twenty years ago or more, and Africa is changing so quickly that what they say may not be true any longer. On the other hand, some things about African society have been very slow to change, and it cannot be taken for granted that everything in these books is now past history.

Moreover, the interest of the present book is to describe kinds of government which have existed at some time – and not so very long ago – among simple societies. In a study of the different ways of organizing government, it does not matter whether we are talking about something that exists today or something that only existed yesterday. Readers of this book will find that both tenses are used. The past tense signifies that I am pretty sure I am describing institutions that do not exist any more, but what is sometimes called the 'ethnographic present' does not guarantee that people are still behaving in the way described.

PART ONE

Government Without
the State

CHAPTER I

Redress for Wrongs

PEOPLE argue whether primitive societies have government. They also argue whether they have law. But nobody questions that they have rules of some kind which everyone thinks it is right to obey. Indeed, a very large part of the violence that does characterize many primitive societies occurs because the rules to which everyone subscribes in principle are broken in particular cases. This is where Hobbes was wrong.

We have to consider in this chapter how rules are upheld in societies such as those of the Nilotes where there is nothing to correspond with courts and policemen.

Every primitive society recognizes in some way that fellow citizens have mutual obligations which do not extend to aliens, and in the societies which have the least government these obligations are concerned with the limits of the use of force. If we give a very broad meaning to the word 'law' we can express this fact in the proposition that there are social groups which recognize the rule of law among themselves, but do not consider that outsiders come within it; and if we give the very broadest meaning to the phrase 'the rule of law', we can say it is a situation in which peaceful relations are regarded as normal, and there has to be something to justify a breach of these relations. It must be added that among the Nilotic peoples not much justification is needed.

In the Introduction we noted that the transhumant pastoralists of the Nile swamps have to have some confidence that they will be able, when they have to, to move at peace with their herds, and that there is a close connexion between this need and the nature of the group within which the rule of law is recognized. If there were no group within which peaceful relations were regarded as normal and fighting as exceptional, we should really have the war of each against all as Hobbes conceived it.

The minimum that people expect from peaceful relations is security of life and property. Another way of putting this is to say that what people mean by living in amity with their neighbours is that nobody should seek to kill or maim them, or to make off with their possessions. Everyone now recognizes that all societies, however simple their inventory of material goods, have clear rules of property, and in those societies where there are few or no formal institutions of government, the most significant social groups are concerned with the control and protection of property. If a people are predominantly pastoralists, their property consists of beasts; if they are predominantly agriculturalists, it consists of land. Many peoples, of course, have both kinds of property.

Let us recall Radcliffe-Brown's definition of political organization. It is 'concerned', he says, 'with the control and regulation of the use of physical force'. Radcliffe-Brown would not call the use of physical force *legal*, even where it is permitted, unless it is applied by persons authorized to act on behalf of a whole community. But it is typical of the Nilotes that either they recognize no such persons or, if they do, the persons who are authorized to act on behalf of the community command so little force that they are very rarely able to use it effectively.

If there are to be both government and *a* government, there should be persons who are recognized as having the authority to govern. By this criterion the Nuer can certainly be said, if they have government at all, to have as little of it as any human society anywhere. What they have is the principle that certain actions are offences, and that a person who has suffered an offence is entitled to redress.

In order to understand how people go about obtaining the redress due to them, we need to understand something about the part played in East African societies by *descent* as a principle of organization. Descent in the male line (*patrilineal* or *agnatic*) is the basis of important social groups everywhere, and of the most important social groups among peoples which have no chiefs. A group of persons related through males, who can actually trace their relationship, is commonly known as a *lineage*. Lineages have corporate rights in property; they consider themselves to be injured as a body if one of their members is injured, they support him in seeking compensation, and the compensation is shared among them. On the other side the lineage kin of a wrongdoer, or at least those most closely related to him, are liable to help him pay the compensation which he has incurred.

Compensation is paid in cattle, but it is seldom offered. The injured party usually has to go and take the cattle due to him. He may do this after there has been a public discussion of the question how many cattle are due, or he may not wait for the discussion. An unpaid debt is collected in the same way. People trying to collect a debt may be resisted. This depends, in the first place, on whether the other party acknowledges the debt, and in the second, on how many of the injured person's agnates will support him. This second question depends on the strength of his lineage, since it is the duty of all lineage kin to support a just claim, and on the views of individual members as to whether the claim is just. If there is resistance, somebody may be killed, and then the dispute takes a new turn, for when a man has been killed it is both the right and the duty of the members of his lineage to seek vengeance. They are entitled to kill the slayer or one of his close agnatic kin – brother or son. If, however, they do not carry out the retaliation which is their right very soon after the first killing, it is possible in this case, too, for compensation in stock to be offered and accepted. But the acceptance of compensation is not an alternative to vengeance; it is a means of putting an end to hostilities when people have had enough of the disorganization that they cause. However, both the vengeance and the compensation are ways of recognizing that killing is the breach of a rule. Thus, if we say that the political community are the people who accept a common rule of law, we can agree with Evans-Pritchard that the Nuer political community is that group within which compensation is payable for homicide. In fighting between tribes no payment is accepted in atonement for a killing, and this is what justifies us in describing such fighting as war.

If, however, we were to take Schapera's definition of a political community as the people for whom decisions are taken in common by some person or persons with authority to decide, we should find ourselves in a difficulty; for if the Nuer have any such authority, it belongs to much smaller groups than the one which recognizes a common rule of law. We shall have to consider later how far the Nuer can be said to have government in Schapera's sense. At present we are concerned with the means by which their apparent disorder serves to maintain order.

The political system of the Nuer, as it is analysed by Evans-Pritchard,* consists in the rules deciding who is to join in, and on which side, in any situation where there has been a resort to force. The people who are called Nuer by their neighbours also call themselves by a common name, speak a common language, observe common customs, and regard themselves as different from other peoples. But they are divided into tribes, and these again are further subdivided. Members of a tribe consider it their duty to support any of their fellow-members who are involved in fighting against outsiders, and this fighting would be properly classified as warfare, even if the enemy were another Nuer tribe, for two reasons. First, in these wars, as in all wars, killing is legitimate; it may, as in all wars, arouse a desire for revenge, but the revenge is not conceived as redress for the infringement of a right, nor can compensation be offered. Wars could be defensive or offensive. One cause of war might be the encroachment of herdsmen of one tribe on the grazing grounds of another; if the intruders won, this was a con-

* *The Nuer* (1940).

quest of new territory. They were contests over the corporate rights of autonomous political communities, not over the individual rights of members of one community. It is interesting, however, that in wars between Nuer and Nuer houses were not destroyed, women and children injured, nor captives taken, though all these actions were permissible in wars against other peoples.

We must then look within the tribe for the kind of fighting that can be fairly, if paradoxically, described as a means of maintaining law and order; and to see how this result is produced we must ask what happens when a Nuer considers that he has been wronged.

Between members of a single tribe the use of force is governed by what might be called rules and conventions. Of course, one cannot make the distinction between law and convention that is made in societies which have written laws. But one can say that there are recognized claims and obligations, and conventions as to the extent to which these are acted upon. The rule, then, is that if a fight has started or even threatens to start, certain persons are in duty bound to rally to the support of the person already involved. This depends upon their position in the total *structure* of Nuer society – that is its division into corporate groups.

Every tribe is divided into sections, each with its own name and territory, these into smaller sections, and these again into villages. These divisions are called after the men who are supposed to have founded them, descendants of the founder of the whole tribe, and so they are thought to be grouped in a genealogical relationship. The people who belong to one of the smallest sections are in a sense brothers; they fit into a larger section of metaphorical cousins and this into a yet larger one of second cousins. The people who actually live in these territorial divisions are not related in this way, because there is no rule that people must live in the territory that is associated with their own ancestors. But this picture of a kin relationship sets the pattern of obligations of mutual support in fighting.

All the men of fighting age in one village should support any one of their number in a quarrel with a neighbouring village. But if someone in this second village has a quarrel with a member of the neighbouring tribal section, both villages will unite against the outsiders. And if a member of a more distant section attacks one of these new enemies, again what is thought of as an internal quarrel is dropped and the ranks closed against the enemy from outside.

It is an ideal standard of conduct, rather than a rule, that every man should be quick to retaliate against an offence, either to his honour or to his rights. It is taken for granted that a man who was afraid to fight for his rights need not hope that they would be respected. Yet the knowledge that a man who considers himself wronged will not hesitate to fight, though at first sight it may seem to indicate a condition of lawlessness, is in fact what maintains the law. People know what actions are infringements of others' rights, although they may not agree in particular cases that someone's rights have in fact been infringed.

The rule or principle, then, that every Nuer would state is that it is incumbent on a man of honour to fight on very slight provocation, and on his kinsmen and village-mates and, if the occasion arises, the inhabitants of wider areas, to support him when called upon. But yet the Nuer value peace among neighbours as much as all men do, and the existence of a state of hostility can cause so much general inconvenience that the people who are not directly involved in a quarrel will do all they can to prevent it from reaching this point. This is where one might see the conventions that modify the operation of the rule. Also, although there is no way in which anyone can be *compelled* to settle a quarrel peaceably, there are recognized procedures of peaceful settlement for those who wish to bring one to an end.

There are two ways in which a Nuer can deal with an infringement of his rights. If cattle are owed him he can seize them; if they are owed him by someone outside his own village, he will try to take them by stealth while they are out at pasture, so as not to get involved in a fight. If his claim is against a man within the village, he will simply go to the man's cattle byre and take them. Everyone will know what he is doing and why, and, if most people think his claim is just, his action will not be resisted. If it is resisted, other people will try to persuade the disputants to invoke the good offices of a man who may be described as a professional mediator. This is a person with special ritual powers, including that of performing the rite of reconciliation to end a feud which has been started by the killing of a man. The Nuer call this man by a name that is translated 'leopard-skin chief', but this name does not imply that he has any right to command obedience. The right to wear a leopard-skin cloak is the privilege and the symbol of his position.

The second way of reacting to a wrong is to challenge the perpetrator to single combat. This is the appropriate reaction to adultery; or to an insult, such as may well be received in the course of an argument about a disputed claim. When two men have begun a fight, honour prevents either from giving in until he is too badly damaged to go on. But even in this restricted field of hostilities, there are ways of reducing the risk that every fight will end in somebody's death. The deadliest of Nuer weapons, the spear, is not used against close neighbours; if the fight is between two men of the same village or cattle camp, they use only clubs, and bystanders will do what they can to separate them. The older men, who are not expected to be so fiery in quarrels, exert their influence here.

Outside the limits of this convention, however, fighting is more serious. In a quarrel between members of neighbouring villages, all the village-mates of both men should join in. Visiting between villages goes on at the time of year when the floods have subsided but it is not yet time to move to the cattle camps. Young men go courting in bands, and vie with one another in dancing. In the massed dances the youths of one village stand shoulder to shoulder, spears always in their hands, ready to support one another if any quarrel should start. The spears are as sharp as a butcher's knife, and an accidental movement may draw blood.

At the cattle camps, the men of several villages are collected, and within a camp people are as anxious to prevent serious fighting as they are in a village. But men from neighbouring camps may get involved in quarrels when they are out herding – perhaps over some such question as whose cattle arrived first at a water-hole. Other men from the two camps will come to back them up until there is a confrontation of miniature armies.

Now we have a situation where, if fighting does start, it will be serious; spears will be used, and men killed, and their deaths will call for revenge. But the massing of forces takes time, and this also leaves time for intervention. It may well be that in the opposing lines there are many people who intend the gathering to be no more than a demonstration, and hope that such intervention may enable them to call off the fight without loss of face. This is another case for action by the leopard-skin chief; one of the older men would bring him the news of the impending battle, and he would rush between the lines and hoe up the ground so as to make a boundary which neither side must cross.

However, men are sometimes killed in fights, and a killing has to be avenged by the agnates of the dead man; his ghost is believed to demand this, and it may plague his kinsmen if they fail in this duty. Also, the act of killing, even in circumstances where it is held to be justified, involves the killer in supernatural dangers. Both these considerations lead people whose interests and honour are not directly involved to do what they can to prevent quarrels from reaching the point where there is likely to be killing.

Although a killing calls for revenge, it does not of itself commonly lead to a general fight. It does not even lead the agnates of the dead man to give up all their normal avocations until they have secured revenge; if they do this, it will be for a few days at most. But the act of killing, whatever may be the response to it of the people whom it has injured, creates, by its supernatural consequences, a barrier between the kinsmen of the killer and those of the victim which cannot be broken down until the killing has been paid for and a rite of reconciliation performed. Hence, it is necessary, if normal life is to go on, that feuds be brought to an end. A further killing in vengeance, although this is theoretically the only satisfaction that self-respecting people would accept, would not end the feud by evening the scores, but would begin a new one. Here we see in its acutest form the contradiction between the immediate interests of the injured party and those of the persons less directly concerned, and the contrast – if it may be put this way – between the rule that vengeance is every man's right and the convention that the injured side can be persuaded to accept compensation. When it comes to making peace, the people who are asked to accept compensation in cattle and forgo their right to take a life make it very clear that they are yielding only to persuasion, and keep up a show of intransigence to the last moment. Nor do they then forget their injury and let bygones be bygones. The memory may be recalled in the course of any quarrel between persons who were once involved in a feud, or their children – and again to avoid the risk of further fighting, when the warriors from two villages dance in opposing lines, men between whom there is such a grudge will take care to place themselves far apart, so that they will not knock against one another and so be provoked to an exchange of insults.

What are the inconveniences of a feud? Not primarily danger to life from the avengers. They are only entitled to kill the killer or a close agnate – brother or son; and the killer takes sanctuary with the leopard-skin chief, to whom he has to go to be rid of the supernatural pollution caused by the killing. One way of seeking vengeance is to make an all-out attack on the enemy's village, and in this case the avengers would have the support of all their village-mates, as has been explained. But this does not seem ever to have been common. It is the supernatural consequences of the killing which create a situation that cannot be maintained between close neighbours for long. Persons between whom there is a blood feud cannot eat or drink from the same vessels. If they do, it is believed they will die.

Now in a Nuer village people eat and drink in every homestead, so that one cannot avoid this mystical danger merely by avoiding the homesteads of one's opponents in the feud. So whole villages have to break off relations as long as this situation lasts. This creates an uncomfortable situation, not so much because the people in one village cannot get on without the people of the next, as because people have relations in other villages from whom they do not like to be cut off, particularly married sisters and daughters and the children of these women. Moreover, some of these women may actually be married to men of the lineage against whom their brothers are prosecuting the feud; and through these marriages the enemies themselves are kin, though not kin by lineage. There is supposed to be a particularly close relationship between a man and the children of his sisters; yet a feud may place them in opposing camps. Therefore, although the lineage kin of a man who has been killed are expected to show implacable resentment against the killer and *his* lineage kin, and do in fact often maintain this resentment for years, many other people are always anxious to persuade them to accept compensation for the injury that they have suffered, and let the appropriate ceremonies be performed to end the feud and purify the villages from the taint of death.

A point which should be made here is that, in accepting compensation, the kinsmen of the dead man are not implying that their loss is something that a payment can make good. On the contrary, when they do accept cattle as a settlement of the feud, they use them to make a marriage whereby the lineage may gain more sons. They are not reckoning the value of human lives in cattle.

While on the one hand people are more likely to get involved in fighting the more often they come into contact, on the other hand it is the people who are most frequently in contact who find a state of hostility most irksome, and so it is near neighbours who seek to avoid fatal quarrels and put an end fairly quickly to feuds. Indeed if a man kills a really near neighbour, his kinsmen sometimes hand over a cow at once as a token of their willingness to make good the offence, and this can be accepted as making it unnecessary to embark on a feud.

Up to now we have been thinking in terms of the claims of individuals, and of injuries done by and to individuals. Larger units fight – or fought in the past – for collective interests, over issues which may have been expressed in the form of claims but were settled purely by superior force. One of the commonest was the right to grazing grounds. Some tribal sections have had to move considerable distances because they lost such fights; and there was no rule that fighting of this kind could take place only between members of different tribes. However, it could hardly happen between members of that smallest section who held their grazing land in common; nor could it happen between sections which were not neighbours and so could only reach one another across somebody else's territory.

In such fighting men were killed, and these killings created a state of feud and a duty of vengeance. Fighting of this kind, too, brought into play a system of obligations of mutual aid which might be likened to alliances, were it not that they did not depend upon deliberate choice. We have noted that the Nuer perceive their tribal divisions as though they were on a genealogical tree, each division having a fixed relationship to the rest; the subdivisions of a larger division are conceived as brothers, who must sink their differences and combine against an attack from somebody more distantly related. But since this more distant relative is himself a kinsman, the occasion may arise when the brothers must join with him against a remoter cousin. This obligation may not always have been honoured in fact; the action people took in a given case might depend on such considerations as the brother's chances of defending himself successfully without their aid. But this is the ideal rule, and plenty of cases of its operation are remembered.

Let us recall again that political organization as defined by Radcliffe-Brown is concerned with the use of force, both within the community and against its external enemies. In a system of shifting alignments such as we have described, who is inside and who is outside? It might be argued that the prosecution of a feud, since it is a matter of upholding a law which all acknowledge, is an internal matter, but it is not so easy to see contests for the control of territory in this light. Among the nations with government of state type, the state is by definition the war-making unit, and a modern state is so organized that divisions within it *cannot* carry on war; if we find they are doing so, we have to say that the state organization has broken down. Among the Nuer, by contrast, groups which in one sense are members of one political community may carry on hostile relations of a kind that might make them seem to be obviously separate politi-cally. This shows how indefinite the boundaries of a polity can be where the means of political control are as slender as they are in this example.

But the large tribal sections do not carry on continuous warfare, even when there are unsettled feuds between their members. Rather, relations between them appear to be for much of the time in a condition of uneasy armistice. Killings are neither avenged nor atoned. There is nothing to make these sections part of a wider whole except the recognition of the principle that to kill is an offence. Sometimes a tribe may formally split in two, and thus recognize that the hostilities which have accumulated between its sections have become irreconcilable.

We might perhaps say that the Nuer recognize two kinds of political community. Every Nuer believes that if he kills any other member of his tribe he has done a wrong which ought to be paid for. But if a Nuer kills a fellow-tribesman whose home is so far away that his friends cannot make any trouble, nothing much may happen. The people who have to avoid the pollution of death will not be on visiting terms anyway, and the people who ought to pursue vengeance will be out of reach. Still, here is a rule which everyone recognizes, and it is a rule that applies to the relations between members of the same tribe and not to their relations with members of other tribes. It is a rule about what ought to be done if one man, by using force in defence of his own interests, kills another. The duty of vengeance and the duty of standing by your fellow are rules about how force is to be used to meet this situation. Radcliffe-Brown would have agreed that these were political rules, though he would not have allowed that they were any kind of law. So the tribe, throughout which such rules hold good, can be recognized as the widest political community to which any Nuer belongs.

But there exists also the community of people whom a Nuer expects to be meeting constantly, and which includes his close kin and their spouses and children. These are the people among whom it is important that peace should be kept, and between them the conventions come into play which prevent people from ruthlessly pursuing their rights even when their cause is clearly just. This might possibly be seen as a political community of narrower range, and if we take this view we must say that every Nuer belongs to two political communities with different values, even if not with different rules.

But these political communities do *not* have the characteristic that their members recognize a common authority. Among the Nuer no individual anywhere has authority to say whether fighting is permissible or to command that it should cease. The general conclusion of Evans-Pritchard is that it is useless for a leopard-skin chief to offer his mediation unless it is clear that the injured side are willing to accept a settlement. Even then their dignity requires them to appear to refuse up to the last moment. At such a juncture a leopard-skin chief might invoke his supernatural powers to threaten them with a curse. But if this can be regarded as the exercise of authority, it is the barest minimum of authority.

*

We know a good deal less about the way in which wrongs are redressed and order maintained among other Nilotes – the Dinka, Anuak, and Shilluk. Before they were brought under the Sudan Government bands of Dinka* fought over the pasture-lands, those which claimed the best and widest grazing areas seeking to defend them against encroachment, and fights broke out too between herdsmen belonging to different sections within a tribe. But in the latter case the same precaution was observed as in Nuer villages – only clubs were used. If a man was killed by someone belonging to another tribe, it was his kinsmen's duty to seek vengeance. But it was thought right that between members of the same tribe redress for injuries should be sought by the peaceful process of mediation and the payment of compensation. The men whose mediation was sought were ritual specialists, as they were among the Nuer. Such men among the Dinka were called 'masters of the fishing spear', and it was they also who were expected by means of their ritual powers to secure success for the tribal armies. Some of them were regarded with great respect, and they are described in ideal terms as if they were rulers who commanded obedience. But one has to take such descriptions with some scepticism because, in a world as wicked as the one we live in, it is rarely possible to command obedience without commanding force.

If we are trying to assign scores to different peoples for the quantity of government that they have, it would be hard to decide whether the Nuer or the Anuak had less. Each Anuak† village has a headman, but the headman can hardly

* G. Lienhardt, 'The Western Dinka' in *Tribes Without Rulers*, ed. J. Middleton (1958).

† G. Lienhardt, 'Anuak Village Headmen' in *Africa*, October 1957, January 1958.

do anything that could be called governing. Nuer have no persons who even claim to be headmen, but they have arrangements for combining to assert their rights through the demand for vengeance or compensation which extend over considerable distances and quite large populations.

Within an Anuak village, disputes are settled by recourse to the headman, though this does not mean that he acts as judge. But between villages, political relations seem rather to resemble those of independent states. If someone is killed by a man from another village, either his kin can seek revenge or the headmen and elders of the two villages will discuss the matter and try to effect a reconciliation. But there is no individual with the special function of ritually ending a feud, as there are among the Nuer and Dinka.

Disputes in an Anuak village are talked out in the presence of the headman and elders, and the nearest approach to a verdict is the consensus of opinion reached in this public discussion. A headman is entitled to formal respect, and this imposes a certain order upon the proceedings. The idea that revenge for killing could be pursued within the limits of so small a community as an Anuak village is as unthinkable there as anywhere else, but the Anuak way of preventing this is for the killer and his kin to leave the village till the anger of his victims has had time to cool. During this period, of course, they must live somewhere; as we shall see later, one way in which relationships are established between Anuak villages is through the movement of people who, for political reasons in the widest sense, find it expedient to change their residence.

The Shilluk* differ from the other Nilotes, in that they recognize the ritual superiority of a single individual – the Reth, as he is called – over the whole people. Have we then come to a people who recognize a final authority? The question is hard to answer, because, not only during the period of British rule, but before that under the Turks, the Reth had government backing and the foreign overlord expected him

* E. E. Evans-Pritchard, *The Divine Kingship of the Shilluk* (1948).

to keep the peace among his people. Some authorities who have written about him even describe him as a ruler whose word was law. Nevertheless, feuds were still being pursued in this century, and they often lasted a long time. It seems that within any one settlement the need to maintain friendly relations led people to compose their differences quickly; the rules of ritual separation between people engaged in a feud were the same as they were among the Nuer, and formal rites of reconciliation were performed by the settlement heads. But a feud between two settlements might be maintained for years, and it might be prosecuted by the total armed forces on both sides. One such feud was said in 1932 to have caused about fifty deaths in twenty years – a figure that might not seem very shocking to a modern army commander or road safety authority, but was so to a District Commissioner in the Sudan. In 1932 it was brought to an end, at least for the time, by the Reth at a peace ceremony which all the warriors on both sides attended. A description of this ceremony which was written at the time shows that it was by no means certain that the ritual would actually be performed. On previous occasions quarrelling had broken out and fighting started again even at this solemn moment. This leads to the conclusion that here, too, we are still in the realm where respect for rights is ensured principally by the recognition that people are entitled to fight for them and the knowledge that they are prepared to do so.

*

The Nilo-Hamites are illustrated in this context by the Turkana, who have as little government as the Nuer and possibly even less, the Kipsigis, who have procedures for discussing matters in dispute that are more formal than any we have considered so far, and the Mandari, who alone in this language group recognize chiefs over the dozen or so sections into which they are divided.

The Turkana* recognize the right of self-help, but there

* P. Gulliver, *A Preliminary Survey of the Turkana* (1951).

is no defined body of kin, as there is among the Nilotes, who have an obligation to support one another in pursuing it. We can see that this is related to the fact that there is no body of people in constant touch either because their homes are close at hand or because they join together at dry-season cattle camps. People need allies, but every man has his own, some of them kinsmen and some personal friends who express and maintain their friendship by giving each other stock from time to time, the 'stock group', as Gulliver calls them.

The Turkana have no recognized mediators and no recognized rates of compensation. People who think they have been injured take stock by force from the herd of the guilty party, until they themselves judge that they have made the damage good. If this does not lead to prolonged or large-scale fighting, it is principally because it is impossible for any considerable number of Turkana, with their herds, to stay long in one place at the same time. The Turkana believe that the oldest men, in virtue of their close contact with the ancestor spirits, whom they may be expected soon to join, have power to curse people whose actions displease them, and possibly they may use this power to insist on the settlement of a quarrel. But these old men can in any case only influence events in their immediate neighbourhood.

The Kipsigis may have pursued the blood feud in the past, but at the time when Peristiany* visited them, shortly before the last war, they dealt with the right of reprisal in a different way. This may be the result of the imposition of the *pax Britannica*. The Kipsigis recognized that the kinsmen of a murdered man were entitled to seize compensation in cattle; but if the kin of the slayer quickly gave them one beast in token of willingness to pay, then they would discuss the matter before the elders and not simply take reprisals by force. But even here, it is stated that 'the judges are only there to help in minor matters and do not have to adjudicate damages or to punish the culprit'. They are mainly con-

* *Social Institutions of the Kipsigis* (1939).

cerned to see that the beasts due are handed over in an orderly way and then to perform a rite of reconciliation.

The Mandari chiefs,* though, as we shall see later, they performed on a small scale most of the activities that are characteristic of more famous powerful rulers, nevertheless did not enforce the settlement of disputes. With their elders they sat at a known meeting place under a shade-tree and waited for cases to be brought to them. If it was agreed that an offence should be made good by a payment in cattle, these were formally handed over in their presence. Actually the cattle might not be handed over at all unless the injured party were strong enough to back up their claim by force. But if they took upon themselves to seize the cattle due to them, they would have the moral support of a public decision by the elders that they were justified. Sometimes, however, the chief might send the young men who consti-tuted his following to seize the cattle due to an injured party who had failed to get them by his own efforts; this is a police function in embryo form.

Among the peoples that have been described up to now, we can see how a modicum of respect for recognized rights is secured because all members of the political community know that those who violate the rules must expect retalia-tion; and at the same time the perseverance with which retaliation is pursued is tempered by the general desire that people should be able to pursue their normal avocations in peace. In discussing this subject we are handicapped by the fact that feuding is one of the first activities which colonial governments make it their business to suppress, so that many ethnographers have had to rely very largely for their information on memories of the past.

*

In Kenya, among the southern Nilo-Hamites and the Bantu, we begin to find persons who are expected to be able to

* Jean Buxton, 'The Mandari of the Southern Sudan' in *Tribes Without Rulers*, ed. Middleton (1958).

mediate in disputes over rights; who, an anthropologist would say, have the *social role* of mediators. This is a beginning of government conceived as an activity of persons whom the community authorizes to take action on its behalf. But we are still a long way from anything that could be called law enforcement, either in the sense of compelling disputants to refer their quarrels to a judge or in that of compelling the party in the wrong to accept a verdict.

Still taking the reaction to murder as our critical example, we find, first, that some peoples recognize vengeance and settlement by compensation as permissible alternatives, but yet do not approve of the prosecution of a feud over time; according to this view, if revenge is not taken at once, then it should not be taken at all, and if the kin of a murderer at once admit their responsibility and offer payment, this ought to be accepted. This is what Evans-Pritchard describes as happening among the Nuer if slayer and slain belong to the same village; but in our present examples the rule is of wider application, and it does not seem that honour is held to call for a show of intransigence.

Among the Bantu we shall begin to find institutions that would readily be recognized as judicial bodies. There are elders in some cases, and individual chiefs in others, to whom persons who consider themselves wronged should take their complaints before they act to obtain redress. But there is one good example among the Bantu of Kenya of a people who, like those whom we have been discussing, recognized in principle that every man was entitled to redress for wrongs against himself, but in practice had more effective means for a settlement of claims than we have found among the Nilotes. This is the group of tribes living to the east of the Kavirondo Gulf who used to be known as the Bantu Kavirondo, but today are officially called by their own name of Luhya.

Like the Nilotic Nuer and Dinka, the 800,000 Luhya* are divided into tribes, each claiming a territory of its own.

* G. Wagner, *The Bantu of Kavirondo*, vol. I (1949).

There are about twenty of these, and the normal relationship between them is hostile and was expressed, up to the time when colonial rule put a stop to this, in warfare. The Luhya are both farmers and cattle keepers, and their climate allows them to live permanently in the same place. Hence their warfare had two objects, to increase their herds and to extend the area available to them for cultivation. The more powerful tribes did not achieve the latter aim by formal conquest leading to the recognition of new boundaries, but rather by intimidating their neighbours so that they would think it safer to keep their homes and fields at a distance. Hence they regarded the killing of enemies as an important part of warfare, and it was not thought to entail supernatural danger, nor did it give rise to claims for compensation.

Each Luhya tribe was divided into patrilineal descent groups, and each of these had its own territory in which the members of a descent group normally lived together. Rights to land for cultivation still go today with membership of a descent group, and such rights are much more important in the economy of the Bantu than they are in that of the pastoral Nilotes. Wagner calls these groups 'clans' and 'sub-clans'; most modern anthropologists would call the latter division a lineage. Each clan and sub-clan recognizes for certain purposes the authority of its older men, the elders; the way in which people become elders in this sense will be discussed later. The elders of each territorial division are recognized as its spokesmen in dealing with outsiders. They do not command any force, but they are able to exercise considerable influence, and it is thought to be one of the most important qualities of an elder that he knows how to calm down angry feelings and prevent quarrels leading to fighting. Here we can fairly say that we see an identifiable political office.

Nevertheless, it is still recognized that an injured person is entitled to right his own wrongs. If someone owes him a cow and will not hand it over, he can seize it by force; if someone encroaches on his land he can root up the crops that have been planted there; and if someone kills or seriously injures his brother he can retaliate by force.

What happens in this last, most serious, case depends upon whether the offender and the injured family belong to the same or different clans. In the first case, as Wagner tells us, as soon as the news of the original offence becomes known, 'the elders of the different sub-clans would rush to the scene of the offence and hold a meeting to prevent fighting and discuss the situation'. He adds 'give judgement'; but it might be argued that an opinion on the rights and wrongs of a dispute which the parties could not be forced to accept was something short of a judgement. However, the elders' view on the right way to end the quarrel would often be accepted. But sometimes the elders themselves did not agree; each of them would be the head of a different division of the clan, and those whose kinsmen were in the conflict might each consider the right was on his side. In that case, however, there would not be fighting. What would happen would be that the section that could expect to lose a fight would split off, move out of the clan territory and either join another clan or establish itself as an independent unit.

If the parties to a dispute belonged to two different clans, the people who considered themselves wronged went to the elders of the offender's clan. If the offence was a serious one, particularly if someone had been killed, they would be backed up by their own elders and also their fighting men, and they would state what compensation they thought they deserved. Again it would be for the elders to try and reach a compromise. In this case if they failed, there would be fighting, which would go on until those involved in it wanted to stop. This would probably be when scores were considered to be about even. But the elders on both sides were expected to intervene as soon as the opportunity offered, and urge the enemies to make formal reconciliation.

In the case of disputes within a subdivision of one clan, it seems that people would not go to the length of fighting for their rights. If they could seize the cow that was owed to them, well and good. If the possessors of the cow resisted, they took the quarrel to the elders, who could be found every morning sitting in their meeting place in the pasture land. The parties came before them, stated their case and called witnesses, and if no one could decide who was speaking the truth, an ordeal was administered. This was believed magically to punish the offender. Here we can certainly see the beginning of political institutions.

Among the Kikuyu, direct vengeance and judgement by persons speaking for the community as a whole existed side by side. Jomo Kenyatta, who, before he became famous in the political field, earned some distinction as the first member of any East African people to write an account of their social organization,* describes how the kinsmen of a murdered man would attack the murderer's homestead, and either take a life in vengeance for the one their group had lost or lay waste the crops. But then the elders on both sides were expected to intervene and persuade the injured group to accept compensation.

But we are still in a field in which government, whatever it is, is not an organization of people able to enforce a peaceful settlement. It is the duty of the elders to do what they can to persuade enemies to agree, but it is nobody's duty to take a quarrel to them rather than fight it out. Nor is it anyone's duty to accept a particular decision, since the side which is not satisfied will go to another elder and see if his idea of the right settlement is more acceptable.

Although homicide is the most serious offence, and the one which calls for immediate vengeance, there are more disputes over claims for property – debts which may have been incurred as part of a settlement of an earlier quarrel or in other ways. The Kikuyu are unlike the Nuer in that they would not proceed directly to seize what was owing to them; they would get the elders of their kin group to go and claim it on their behalf, and if the claim was disputed,

* *Facing Mount Kenya* (1930).

then it would be argued out before such elders as the parties chose. There does not seem to have been any fixed body of councillors all of whom were entitled and expected to hear all disputes. The parties would come to the discussion with the elders of their choice, who would be regarded more as advocates or ambassadors than as impartial arbiters; and the same dispute might be argued more than once before different elders if both sides were not satisfied with the original proposal. However, when the elders had agreed among themselves on the amount that should be paid, the successful claimant would be held to be justified in taking what was due to him, by force if necessary. The elders might even expressly authorize him to do so, and they could do this also if one party had refused to come to the discussion, since this was taken as evidence that he was in the wrong; but, as a British official remarked of the state of affairs some fifty years ago, in that case he was also unlikely to accept a decision against him. The same official wrote, 'I have more than once ... known the whole assembly to be driven away by a truculent litigant.'* The elders themselves, he added, did not consider that their duty was to pass judgement and sentence, but simply to put an end to strife.

Of one section of the Kamba of Machakos, however, it was recorded only a few years later that if an accused person refused to appear before the elders, they would send a band of young men to fetch him, and that these young men could also be employed to seize the stock due in compensation from an owner who did not voluntarily hand them over. Yet if the offence was that of homicide, it was open to the kin of the victim to take a life for a life. It seems from this account, however, that the Kamba, unlike the Nuer, were expected to be willing to accept compensation and not to pursue the feud unless it was refused.

* C. Dundas, 'The Organization and Laws of some Bantu Tribes in East Africa' in *J.R.A.I.* (1915), p. 260.

*

Two examples in which both the authority of the chiefs and the right of vengeance are recognized may be quoted from Uganda. One is that of the Nilotic Alur, whose chiefly clan were extending their domination over neighbouring peoples up to a period so recent that it has been possible for an anthropologist* to reconstruct the process. The peoples who became subject to Alur chiefs recognized the right of retaliation for wrongs and, as they now remember their own past, did not have any formal means of bringing hostilities to an end. They were not conquered in battle by the Alur. They acquiesced in the extension of Alur rule, and some of them even asked an Alur chief to give them one of his sons as their ruler; and one of their principal reasons for wanting a ruler was so that he could settle their quarrels.

Nevertheless, these new chiefs did not bring with them a complete apparatus for the enforcement of law and order. People who were not immediately under their eye could still fight out their quarrels if they wished to, and they only appealed to the chief if they failed to get by their own efforts the redress that they believed was due to them. In the eyes of a chief, however, fighting within the area which he claimed as his domain was a defiance of his authority, and the actual extent of his authority was measured by his ability to put an end to such fighting. Moreover, fighting between the subjects of different chiefs might lead each to appeal to his own chief for protection. It would then rest with the chiefs to decide whether the matter should be settled by war or diplomacy, and a chief who preferred the latter could force his subject to pay compensation.

A chief had both moral and material means of enforcing the settlement of disputes, even if these were not always effective throughout the area which he claimed as his domain. Alur chiefs were greatly respected, and brawling and bloodshed in their near neighbourhood was regarded as an offence against the respect due to them. This applied also to the wives of chiefs, and a chief's wife was sometimes

* A. W. Southall, *Alur Society* (1954).

sent to live in an outlying part of his territory so as to keep
the peace there by her mere presence. The killing of a chief's
subject was also regarded as an offence against the chief –
as well as against the dead man's lineage – for which a fine
was due to him; and where his authority was effective, he
would send messengers to collect the fine and order the
enemies to make peace. If the order was not obeyed the
chief himself would appear on the scene with all his retainers, a band of followers who were neutral in the dispute
at issue, and powerful enough to give decisive support to
the side adjudged by the chief to be in the right. Also, while
they were engaged in the business of settling the quarrel,
they expected to be well fed from the herds and granaries
of the disputants, so that the cost of letting fighting get out
of hand was high. This was the procedure among the Alur
themselves. On the borders of Alur authority, among subject peoples, the way of dealing with sections who flouted
the chief by refusing his orders to settle a dispute was to
authorize more loyal subjects to plunder their possessions.

Finally, we must mention the Nkole and Ganda, where,
although the ruler was recognized as a supreme authority
and was in a position to punish people who disobeyed him,
he still dealt with cases of homicide by granting to the
victim's kin the right of blood revenge. But here it was not
permissible to pursue revenge until the case had been
brought before him.

*

There are certain circumstances in which it is held to be
permissible for a person to be put to death, not in revenge
for murder by the persons who have lost a kinsman, but
by the community as a whole on account of some other
offence. We know most about the Kikuyu and Kamba institution for this purpose. It has been described as 'organized
lynching', but although the word 'lynching' conveys the
idea of combined action by a mob, it also suggests action
taken against somebody whom the officers of the law would

not have condemned to death. The procedure which the Kamba* called '*Kingolle*' could not be carried out without the approval of the elders. It was essentially a means of ridding the community of a person whose presence had become intolerable to a large number of his fellows. This might be because he had accumulated a large score of offences such as theft or refusal to pay due debts, or he might be held to be injuring the community by the exercise of witchcraft. The decision to put him to death was taken by the elders after they had heard the charges against him, and before he was killed his nearest relative had to give his consent, and so agree in advance that he would not demand vengeance or compensation for the death. This relative also had to give a symbolic authorization for the attack on the guilty person by throwing a handful of earth at him, a symbolic way of cursing him. Then the people he had offended would attack him with weapons, and no blood guilt would lie upon his killer. Indeed, one of the reasons for the concerted attack may well have been that the actual killer would not be identified. Even in this case of concerted action, however, the initiative does not come from any authority; the elders do not order it, they merely permit it.

This again is a subject about which there is no direct evidence. There is no record of such a scene by any eye-witness. The existence of a name for this proceeding is enough to show that it is not a figment of somebody's imagination. What is quite uncertain is how often such slayings actually took place. It is possible that guilty persons were sometimes simply turned out and left to fend for themselves, a hard enough fate in the African bush, and that such people managed to get accepted in other villages as hangers-on of leading men there.

* J. F. M. Middleton, *The Kikuyu and Kamba of Kenya* (1953).

CHAPTER 2

Minimal Government

WE have seen how among the peoples of East Africa the redressing of wrongs is left largely to the efforts of the injured party and his kinsmen, but yet this does not lead to mere anarchy and indiscriminate violence. Public opinion distinguishes between cases in which fighting is and is not justified, and the general need, and desire, for peaceful relations is strong enough and effective enough to prevent people keeping up hostilities till they destroy the community. If this result is achieved without any of the organizations which we are accustomed to call by the name of government, it nevertheless cannot be denied that it is one of the results which government is expected to achieve.

What of the aspect of government that consists in taking those decisions that must be taken if the normal life of the political community is to be carried on? Where decisions are reached informally, and there is no mechanism for enforcing them, some people might think it preferable to speak of leadership rather than government. But then we should merely have to change a word and say, looking at this question as we have looked at the redress of wrongs, that in societies where there is no single authority able to enforce obedience, there are nevertheless leaders of some kind who are looked to in matters where decisions involving numbers of people have to be taken.

For the purpose of this discussion, we can take it that the inhabitants of a single homestead always recognize the authority of their senior member. One might argue the question whether such authority is to be called political. Some anthropologists hold that we do not enter the field of politics until we are concerned with larger units. If we take the definition of a political community as one which will join in fighting outsiders, the homestead is not a political community, and authority within it is not of a political nature. Others would add that the homestead head is obeyed for reasons that do not normally operate in the political field – through the direct personal relationships that grow up between people who are in close daily contact throughout most of their lives. But there is certainly an element of this personal respect, affection, and fear of anger rather than punishment present in the attitudes towards their leaders of very small political communities, such as island populations of a thousand or so. I do not propose to draw the line separating domestic from political authority, but merely to note that the existence of authority within domestic groups can be taken as given and is not treated as part of the subject of this book.

Government can be 'minimal' in a number of different ways. The political community, the aggregate of people who look to a common source for decisions as to how they shall act, may be very small. The number of recognized positions of leadership may be very small. The extent to which people holding such positions can in fact exercise either leadership or authority may be very small. East Africa offers examples of minimal government in all three senses.

For the first we may take the Tindiga from the neighbourhood of Lake Eyasi in Tanganyika. They live mainly by hunting small game and collecting edible wild grasses, fruits, and roots, roaming the country in bands, the largest of which numbers about 150. The size of the band that can move together is strictly limited by the amount of food that can be found at one time in any given place; and if people wish to move as a band, they must reach some effective decision every day on the question whether they shall move on next day, and if so in what direction. Thus, although their way of life keeps the independent community small, it makes some form of government in this sense indispensable. The band does, in fact, recognize a leader or headman, whose position is hereditary in the male line. We know little of his functions, but it appears that, when a large animal is killed, it falls to him to apportion the meat, and also that if a member of the band is guilty of theft, the leader, after discussing the matter with a few of the senior men, can require the thief or his close kinsmen to make reparation. Our authorities do not tell us how the band actually decides where to go and what to do.

The Nuer provide the supreme example of minimal government of the second type. Among them certain persons are leaders in the sense that they are respected, and people will wait to see what they do and then follow suit; others have ritual powers that are not shared by all members of the community, and certain ceremonies can be performed only by these men. But none of these persons can claim to give orders, nor do they even announce decisions which have been taken collectively. We have seen that the Nuer attach importance to the maintenance of peaceful relations between neighbouring villages, and over the territory through which they drive their cattle to and from the dry-season pastures and watering places. But they do not seem to attach importance to any concerted action at all, except perhaps in warfare. When they were confronted with Arab and later British forces seeking to bring them under foreign rule they seem to have taken such action on a considerable scale. Some coordination was necessary too for inter-tribal warfare and for raids on the Dinka.

What then gives a man a position of leadership among the Nuer? To answer this question we must consider the constitution of a Nuer village. It has a small population of a few hundred. It does not consist, as do many villages among people who are primarily cultivators, of persons who have a claim by virtue of their descent to the land which surrounds it. It is thought right for men to live among their lineage kin, but in practice they may live in any place where they are related by any kin tie to someone already there — a mother's brother, brother-in-law, or father-in-law. In any village the bulk of the inhabitants will be living there because of their relationship to one or two leading men. The kind of man who attracts people to attach themselves to him will probably be, to start with, the eldest of a group of brothers who themselves have adult children living in the village. He will be a man who has kept on good terms with his brothers, so that they did not separate when their father died. Other people will have come to his village because a less harmonious family has broken up on the death of its head; his widowed sisters or daughters may have brought their children to live at his village; or a sister's or daughter's son whose father is dead and who thinks he is not being well treated by his father's heir – or whose father's brothers have few cattle – may choose to attach himself to the head of his mother's family.

Thus the village is not a permanent group whose leaders succeed one another; it is a changing group held together by the strength of personal attachments to particular individuals. What qualities should such persons have? It appears to be an advantage to be an aristocrat – though this is another of the words which have a minimum of meaning for the Nuer. We have seen that all Nuer territory is divided into sections associated with particular lineages. A Nuer is an aristocrat when he is in the territory of his own lineage. The privileges which this involves are so few that many Nuer do not mind losing them, and actually live outside their lineage land. However, a member of the aristocratic lineage in any given place has slightly more chance than a non-member of becoming the 'bull' of a village. It is more important to have cattle, since if a man can help his daughters' and sisters' sons when they need cattle they are likely to prefer his village to those of their own lineage kin. He will not become a leader unless his personality commands prestige; this he may gain from a reputation for prowess in fighting in his youth, for skill in debate, or for ritual powers (which are believed to be inherited). A man who has gained prestige in these various ways may be able to build it up further by marriage alliances with similarly placed men in other villages; others may attain their position in the first instance through such alliances.

What the 'bull' gets out of his position is another question. No Nuer will let any other address an order to him. The leadership of the 'bull' is recognized only in the sense that people wait for him to give a lead. Moving with the cattle from camp to camp in the dry season may be compared with the movement of the Tindiga band in search of food. The people in a Nuer camp do not discuss and reach a decision. They wait till the leading man moves and then follow when it suits them.

In every Nuer tribe there is also one individual who can be said to have a position of authority in relation to the activities of the whole community. This man would be called 'an officer of government' if we follow Schapera's usage. He is concerned with the organization of all the men of the tribe into sets based on age or, more strictly, on the time when they were formally initiated into manhood. The age-sets do not have great political importance among the Nuer. They rank people in order of seniority, so that wherever a man may be he knows what other men he must treat with formal respect and from what other men he should receive this respect. For this to be possible there must be a clear line drawn between successive sets. In the past this was done by having 'closed periods' of several years during which there could be no initiations. The responsibility of proclaiming the beginning and end of these periods rested with a person who was called the 'Man of the Cattle', because he belonged to one of a number of lineages who were believed to have special magical powers for treating cattle diseases. Later the Nuer gave up the closed periods, so that boys could be initiated at any time, but it still rests with the 'Man of the Cattle' to say when an age-set is to be considered complete and the next initiates are to be grouped in a new one. The completion or 'closing' of a set is effected by a ceremony which only one 'Man of the Cattle' can perform for each tribe. The 'Man of the Cattle' inherits his position from his father.

If we try to find among the Nuer a political community defined as a unit which manages its public affairs collectively, and is not subject to the command of any person external to it, we are in some difficulty. For the purposes of daily life there hardly seems to be any such unit; if there is, it must be the village in the rainy season, and the cattle camp, where the population of several villages congregates, in the dry season. But for the one purpose of the organization of the age-sets a whole tribe is a unit, and accepts a time-table decreed by one authority. What gives this man authority is the belief that only he, by virtue of his inherited powers, can perform a rite which is indispensable to the well-being of the recently initiated youths. We shall find that the kind of authority which rests on such beliefs in the inheritance of special powers is particularly important among peoples where government is minimal. It is also characteristic of such peoples that the initiation of the youths into age-sets brings together more people than will combine for any other purpose. In East Africa the Anuak, who do not have any initiation ceremonies, provide the only exception to this generalization.

Another example of leadership which is informal, in the sense that the leader is neither designated by his birth nor expressly chosen, comes from the Luhya in Kenya. The men who attain leadership there do so through very much the same qualities as have been described among the Nuer. They need to have wealth, and while this may depend to some extent on their own skill in cattle management, it does depend largely on the accident of birth and the advantages which this gives to an eldest son. An eldest son is always married as early as possible, and then can build up his own homestead and gather dependents around him. He will begin while still a relatively young man to receive cattle for the marriage of his daughters, and he may then be able to take additional wives for himself, and so increase the area of his fields and his supply of grain. Further, he will succeed to the management of his father's herd. Each son should inherit an equal number of cattle, but the herd is not divided until it is considered that there are enough to make an equal division practicable. In the meantime, the eldest controls them and can use this position to increase his own wealth.

In homesteads where there is plenty of grain there is usually beer to offer to visitors, and visitors frequent the homesteads where they can expect to be offered beer. When they are there it is polite for them to listen with deference to the views of their host. A man with many cattle can afford to kill one now and then for a feast, and he can use this occasion to distribute the meat so as to favour people who have supported him in the discussion of public affairs. He can also make loans to his poorer neighbours, who may be in need at the time of scarcity before harvest, or because a contribution to somebody's marriage cattle is outstanding, or because the diviner has told somebody to make a sacrifice. If people cannot repay these loans, they will be willing instead to work for their benefactor when he needs extra labour. In some cases a man who has become indebted in this way attaches himself completely to his benefactor's homestead. (This is *not* a form of 'debt-slavery', nor is there any strict calculation of equivalence between the value of the object lent and the labour given; the principle that operates is rather the social one that every service deserves a return.)

It is the men who have attained eminence through their wealth and reputation who are listened to when disputes are brought before the elders at their meeting-place under the tree, as was described in the last chapter. The oldest of these men have a special duty. The Luhya, like many other peoples, believe that sickness and death may be due to the malevolence of enemies practising witchcraft or sorcery, and when someone dies his kinsmen look for such a cause. At funeral ceremonies accusations of witchcraft may be publicly made, and these may lead to quarrelling and fighting.

It is the duty of the specially revered elder, the *omuseni*, to check such quarrelling by pacificatory speeches, reminding the kin of the dead person that we must all die, that quarrels weaken the community and throw it open to its enemies. It is also his duty to try to bring to agreement people who are quarrelling about the division of the estate. Wagner gives him the title of 'public comforter'.

But there is no presumption that any given unit *must* have a leader of the type just described. Where no one man is pre-eminent, the elders all take an equal share in public discussions, which, as far as our information goes, are concerned mainly with the settlement of disputes.

The Dinka are an example of a people where certain positions of authority are hereditary but the authority attached to them is very slight. Among them certain clans have the monopoly of ritual powers, which are symbolized by the fact that they own sacred fishing spears. People who do not belong to these lineages are called collectively 'people of the war spear', and this phrase signifies that they go to war, while the clans of the fishing spear provide the priests who ensure victory by their prayers. Every division of a tribe should recognize a single 'master of the fishing spear' as superior to all such men who may be in its territory, and one of these should be acknowledged as pre-eminent throughout the tribe in virtue of the pre-eminence of his lineage. Similarly, each tribe should recognize a pre-eminent warrior lineage from which its war leader should come. The 'masters of the fishing spear' are important in peace as well as in war, since it is their duty to reconcile the disputants in quarrels which might otherwise lead to brawling or feuds. They also perform ceremonies for the general prosperity of their people, and their reputation varies with the success which is held to attend these rites. There is no question of removing an unsuccessful 'spear-master' from his office, but in practice sections of the warrior population may turn to others than the one who should theoretically be theirs, and so the actual political divisions of the Dinka do not always accord with the traditional idea of what they should be.

Perhaps the most paradoxical example of minimal government of this kind is the Reth, or 'Divine King' of the Shilluk. The Reth, so the myths say, is the incarnation of Nyikang, the deified first leader of the Shilluk who brought them to their present country. At the ceremony of his installation the spirit of Nyikang is thought to enter into him, and he is treated thenceforward with extreme respect. His office is hereditary; it may be held only by a man whose father has himself been Reth. At his capital, at the centre of his long narrow river-side country, retainers wholly dependent upon him keep up the state of his court.

But his most important functions are in the field of ritual and not in that of command. The sacredness of his person is not merely a matter of the respect due to him; his physical welfare is believed to be directly related to that of his people, their cattle, and their crops. His first duty, in a sense, is to remain in a condition of physical health and vigour; he has also to perform the necessary sacrifices to make the rain fall and secure victory in war; and he is responsible for the upkeep of the shrines of Nyikang. In addition he has a similar ritual function to that of the leopard-skin chief among the Nuer, of performing the rite of reconciliation to end a blood feud.

Some writers have interpreted his position as if his divinity gave him the kind of divine right that was claimed by the Stuart kings of England. It is difficult to be sure what his position was before the Shilluk came under Turkish and then under British rule. It is possible that before he had the backing of a foreign government, the Reth could use his palace retainers to overawe people who refused to agree to the settlement of a feud; but it is pretty certain that he could not do more, and there are enough recent records to show that even under British administration he did not, and was not expected to, prevent the outbreak of feuds. Nor did he command his subjects in any other field.

Yet he was something more than a priest, more than a leopard-skin chief or a tribal spearmaster, and this something more derives from the uniqueness of his position. Because there can be only one Reth of all the Shilluk, all Shilluk have a common interest in the Reth – in the choice of his successor, in his installation, in his continued health. This is what makes the Shilluk nation one, and so it deserves to be called a political fact. It is particularly when a new Reth has to be chosen that this fact is brought home to them. All sections of Shilluk country are represented in the discussions, and after the choice has been made all the different settlements are represented, through their heads, in the ritual of accession, each having some special duty which is the prerogative of his lineage. Competition between claimants to the succession has sometimes been fierce enough to cause fighting between different sections of the kingdom – another indication of its great importance to all Shilluk.

The Anuak provide two examples of minimal government of different kinds. We have seen that they are divided into isolated villages which are self-sufficient in the affairs of daily life, so that there is no need for any arrangement to ensure peaceful relations between the inhabitants of different villages. They do not have large herds of cattle, and so there is no need for them to control wide areas of grazing land or to gather with people from other villages in times of drought. Although the populations of different villages are linked by ties of kinship and marriage, each village is autonomous as far as the recognition of authority and of mutual rights and obligations is concerned. A village may contain perhaps two to five hundred people.

In the greater part of the Anuak country, every village is held to have been created by a section of a single clan, to whom in the course of time other people have attached themselves, and the right to the office of headman is held by one lineage of this sub-clan. Only a man whose own father has held this office can be a headman. Consequently in every generation some grandchildren of a headman are likely to be disqualified from the succession because their father has not held the office. It is the duty of the line – that is the brothers and their sons – who have been most recently disqualified, to take charge of the regalia of headmanship, and to install a new headman when the occasion arises. These occasions are frequent, because the Anuak do not ascribe any divine right to their headmen, but on the contrary claim the right to dismiss them at will. One might well ask what advantage they see in having a headman.

The answer is that, as we have seen, the headman provides a place where disputes can be publicly discussed and so settled without fighting. This is the place outside the gate of his homestead, where a fire is kindled in the evening and people gather to talk until it is time to sleep. Every Anuak homestead has such an 'exterior hearth' where men welcome their friends. Visitors to the village are brought to that of the headman, which, in virtue of his position as the man of highest rank in the village, may be called his court. Indeed, this is the first meaning of the word 'court'. At one time there was no distinction between the place where the sovereign confers honours on his subjects and entertains foreign ambassadors and the place where the judge tries cases; the sovereign and judge were one. This is what we shall find among all the peoples discussed in this book, and we shall also find that judging cases is thought of as the first duty of a ruler.

The Anuak headman is also expected to be a source of benefits to his fellow-villagers. His court, if it is properly kept up, is a source of prestige to the village as a whole, and there is keen rivalry for prestige between Anuak villages. It is the young men of the village who maintain it; in particular they decorate the fence of his dwelling with poles carved to look like the horns of wild deer. But this is not regarded as their duty; they give their services in recognition of the generosity which the headman shows to them. He has no claim on their wealth, such as is made on their subjects by the chiefs of states, and so he is not likely to be able to keep up for very long the standard of generosity which his villagers expect. The young men may band together for a time as his retainers, and they may clear fields for him and so enable him to have a large grain supply for brewing beer, but they will only do this as long as he slaughters cattle and sheep to feast them, and these he must supply from his own resources.

While he is popular, however, he is treated with very great respect. People are expected to take off their shoes when they approach his court, and when they walk past him to crouch low so as not to cross his line of vision. The headman's dignity is the dignity of the village, and if any person does not respect it, his fellow villagers may fall on him and take a beast from him as a fine. They may do this spontaneously, or at a hint from the headman; but the headman cannot order this punishment, and he does not get the beast – the villagers do, and make a feast with it.

Every headman has his friends and his enemies, as does each of his rivals. His friends are his kin outside his own lineage – sisters' and daughters' husbands and children – who have preferred to live in his village rather than in villages of their own clan. His enemies are people who have not got what they wanted in the discussion of disputes at his court, and others who have been punished for disrespect in the days of his power. There are also some neutrals – people who have no close attachment to a rival claimant, but will transfer their allegiance if the headman's generosity seems to be falling off. The supporters of a rival claimant have to capture this 'floating vote'. If they can also secure the approval of the guardians of the regalia, the unpopular headman may simply accept the position and leave the village. In other cases, there may be a fight. But it is not expected that the headman will be killed; he just goes with his family, and perhaps his principal supporters, to another village, probably that of his mother's kin, possibly that of a relative-in-law, and awaits an opportunity to mend his fortunes and return when his friends in the village send for him. He has not received a sentence of banishment; he is more like somebody who has lost an election, for this ostracism or expulsion is a formal procedure, with its own name, *agem*. It is not regarded by the Anuak as revolution but as a part of normal political life. Nor is a deposed head-man like a refugee in a foreign country. He is still within the bounds of a population that regards itself as one people; he merely moves outside that political community in which he has a claim to a special position. It has been remarked that the frequent moving of deposed headmen creates the links which effectively bind these Anuak villages into a wider unity.

At the eastern end of Anuak country a different system prevails.* Here a single clan claims pre-eminence over an area which is still not very large, but which does include a considerable number of villages. This claim is based on the possession of certain emblems which have been handed down through the generations and are regarded as sacred. The most important of these, a necklace of ancient beads and a spear, are believed to have been brought with him by Ukiro, the mythical founder of the clan, when he emerged from a river and begot the first king of this section of the Anuak. We do not know how many people accepted his kingship. At the outset, perhaps, his claims were no more than are made by the headmen who, as we have seen, also must be invested with hereditary regalia in order to hold their position.

Rivals competed for the emblems as they did for the village regalia. But in the case of the heirlooms of Ukiro, at the time when traditions begin to be clear and consistent, they could not be taken from the holder without a fight to the death. This was not a single combat, but a pitched battle between the supporters of the emblem-holder and those of his rival, who in this case was a man of a different village. To hold the emblems, the most sacred objects that

* E. E. Evans-Pritchard, *The Political System of the Anuak* (1940).

existed in this part of the country, was a matter of prestige for the village where they were kept as well as for the individual holder, and gradually, in a manner that will be described later, more and more villages came to be linked by their rivalry for this prize.

The emblem-holder is generally called the king of the eastern Anuak. Those to whom the word 'king' suggests the rather different word 'monarch', which literally means 'sole ruler', may find this an incongruous name for a person whose special status gives him no special power. This, however, is a good reason for not calling him a chief, since that word, in the great majority of contexts where it is used, does imply power and the right to command. The Anuak king was not himself sacred like the Reth of the Shilluk, but he was the holder of sacred objects and thus held a unique position, as all kings do.

Some six generations ago, nine persons in turn became king by killing their predecessors. This series began with the killing of a king by his younger brother. But in most cases the rivals were cousins – sons of the two brothers with whom the story began. The rule that only a man whose father had held the emblems could contend for them restricted the contest to these two lines. As long as the emblems were transferred in this way, at any given time there could only be one emblem-holder living.

However, there came a time when the holders did not think the privileges of kingship, whatever they were, worth defending with their lives. Sometimes a man who saw that his side was losing would run away while the battle was on; sometimes he would put up a token show of force or even hand the emblems over with no resistance at all. The followers of contenders preferred that there should be a fight, since it increased their prestige to have won a victory in battle.

Now the emblems began to circulate very quickly, and many persons who had held them were alive at any one time. Everyone whose father had ever held them sought to hold them himself so as to be able to pass the right to hold them to his sons. To do this it was still necessary to have a following, since a token challenge still had to be made. Contenders established themselves, or were established by their fathers while they were children, in the villages of their mother's kin, and thus the area within which the significance of the emblems was recognized was constantly being extended. Every man who had held the emblems established thereby his claim to noble rank, to be treated with deference, and live in a house of special type with his retainers (only a small body). At this stage the actual holder was in no way superior in authority or privileges to his predecessors; the uniqueness of his position consisted simply in the fact that only one man could hold the emblems at any one time, and for the moment he was the man.

Later still, three members of the two noble lineages managed to obtain rifles from Ethiopia, and thus consolidated positions of real power resting on armed force. At this period the man who held the emblems would allow claimants to be invested with them on payment of a fee, and the fee was raised by the same followers who previously would have formed the claimant's fighting force.

This appears to be the present situation. At the present time nobility confers considerable privileges; nobles claim, successfully, the right to fall upon commoners who offend them and despoil them of their possessions, and sometimes a noble punishes in this way a man who has wronged another commoner. But they still do not perform any of the functions of government. This position of privilege without responsibility would be hard to parallel among peoples living at such a simple technical level, and perhaps it is to be explained as a result of the introduction of fire-arms.

The political significance of the traditional system was, in part, that a claimant to investiture had to have a following – in the old days to fight for his claim, and later to amass the gifts that had to be made to the emblem-holder. In a more abstract way, it links those Anuak in the part of the country where members of the noble lineages live, by the fact that they are all competitors within a single system for a single prize. Moreover, the commoners appear to value the prize enough to put up with the nobles' behaviour. The system has gradually been spreading into the region further west in most of which village headmen were autonomous, by a process which will be described later when we come to consider how government can be built up and extended.

The Karimojong and Turkana also illustrate minimal government. The Turkana belief that the very oldest men can curse offenders, which has already been mentioned, appears to be the only approach to government that they have. If it is to be called so, the justification would be that there are two old men, each the senior in one division of the people, who have a unique position in relation to the maintenance of social order. But this is stretching language as far as it will go.

The Karimojong* have rather more government. Like the Turkana, and like the Nuer, they are organized into age-sets in such a way that every man knows whom he must treat with respect as his senior and who ought to behave with respect to him. But the Karimojong elders claim obedience as well as respect, and are able to enforce it in certain circumstances. The elders are not the very oldest men, because these formally retire from authority at a solemn ceremony, and after that are no longer consulted in public matters, though of course they are still treated with respect. They are roughly between forty-five and seventy.

They wield authority because no man whose father is alive has independent control of the cattle belonging to the family group, and so the younger men are dependent on the elder; because they are believed to be the wisest section of the community – as is likely in a society which is not changing; and because they are believed to have the power of blessing and cursing. On their orders the younger men will combine to punish those who disobey them.

* N. Dyson-Hudson, *The Karimojong* (unpublished thesis).

The elders regulate the movement of the herds to an extent that is not paralleled among the Nilotes or the other Nilo-Hamitic peoples. For this purpose they do not act as a government of the whole country; indeed this would hardly be desirable in a country where local differences in rainfall may be so important. But in each of the ten sections of the Karimojong people (consisting of up to 4,000 men) the herdsmen must wait until the elders have performed a ceremony called 'freeing the cattle' before they can take them away from the permanent settlements for their dry-season grazing. Those who go out too soon, and begin to use up the scarce dry-season pastures and water while it is still possible for the cattle to graze near the river-beds, are brought back and punished. Their own self-interest would make the law-abiding young men willing to do this. This was being done as late as the 1940s.

The Karimojong, like the Nuer and like their neighbours the Turkana, take it for granted that they will have to fight for their rights, and to that end rely not only on their lineage kin but also on those friends whose alliance they have won by gifts of cattle. But members of very small local groups do refer quarrels among themselves to public decision. Within a 'neighbourhood' of two or three to a dozen settlements, numbering a few hundred people, disputes are talked out in a gathering of all the adult men; and at the end the elders of this small political community pronounce a decision which probably represents a general consensus of opinion.

CHAPTER 3

Diffused Government

SOME of the peoples of the Kenya Highlands have a government which can be said to consist of the whole adult male population, for the duties of public service fall, in theory, equally upon them all. There is no chief or head of the whole people, though there may be persons who have offices allowing them to exercise authority at certain points in the system. These are the peoples whose organization is based on the division of the population according to age; the best known are the Nilo-Hamitic Masai, Nandi, and Kipsigis and the Bantu Kikuyu with the related Meru. The Karimojong in north-eastern Uganda also have an organization of this type.

In every society a person's status depends to some extent on his age. In western countries people have to reach a specified age before they can marry, before they can vote, before they can legally contract debts; the qualifying age may be different for different activities and is different in different countries. Where people record the dates of their births it is easy to know how old they are. After they have attained to full citizenship rights their actual age does not matter very much until the time comes when they are entitled to retire from active work and draw pensions.

In non-literate societies people do not know exactly how old they are, and so one cannot claim to be adult simply by saying that one has reached a given age. But in nearly all East African societies, boys (and sometimes also girls, though girls are not usually important in political matters) are counted as adult after they have gone through a ceremony known as *initiation*. This includes a test of manhood. Among a very few peoples, such as the Karimojong and Turkana, the test is to kill an ox with one blow of a spear.

More usually it consists in enduring a physical operation with courage. Nuer boys have six long cuts made on their foreheads. For other peoples the operation is circumcision.

Among the Kenya peoples to be described in this chapter the traditional ceremonies of initiation were prolonged and elaborate. The boys who were being initiated into manhood were taken away from their homes to live in camps in the bush, made to endure ordeals of various kinds, instructed in tribal lore, and treated with substances that were believed magically to give them courage and other desirable qualities. A number of boys who were roughly contemporary were initiated together, and from that time they were regarded as contemporaries whatever their actual age. The initiation process divided the whole male population into batches in order of seniority. What kept these batches clearly separate was the fact that initiation did not go on all the time. Periods during which boys could be initiated alternated with 'closed' periods during which no ceremonies might be held. Consequently there might be considerable differences in age between members of the same age-set. A boy could not be initiated before puberty, but if something prevented his being initiated at the same time as his contemporaries, he might have to wait several years after he was physically mature.

At present there is little left of initiation among Kenya peoples except the operation of circumcision, which is performed privately for individual boys as they reach the appropriate age. The Nuer initiation, which does not include any elaborate ceremonial, still continues. It has very little significance for the government, or lack of government, of the Nuer. But it does place every Nuer man in a batch of persons who count as being the same age, and as being younger than batches initiated before them and older than batches initiated after them. This may even contribute something to the keeping of the peace. For example, when a large number of people are gathered together drinking beer they should be served in order of seniority. The division into age-sets establishes this order, and at least obviates one reason for quarrelling.

But for the Kenya peoples who have just been mentioned the division into age-sets was important primarily as a means of organizing government. The batches of men who were initiated together had public duties to perform of different kinds according to the stage in life they had reached.

The basis of a politically significant organization by age is the division of the male population into those of fighting age (warriors), those too young to fight (boys), and those who are too old (elders). But this does not mean in practice that the entire male population between puberty and middle age is continuously under arms and so debarred from ordinary domestic life. Although each set formally enters and leaves the warrior grade in a body after a solemn ceremony, the actual ordering of individual lives is a good deal more flexible.

In discussing systems of this kind it is useful to distinguish certain technical terms. An *age-group* is any division of a population by age, such as that made by demographers and used for census purposes. *Age-mates* are fellow members of any recognized division based on age. An *age-set* are the persons who have been initiated during the successive annual ceremonies of a single initiation period; this may be divided into *sub-sets* consisting of those who have gone through the same ceremony together. Where the allocation of duties in the political community is based on age, the *age-sets* pass through the successive *age-grades* of warrior and elder, or there may be subdivisions of these.

Of all the political systems which have come under European rule, this type is least capable of adaptation to the purposes of the rulers. It offers them no identifiable individuals who can be invested with authority as their agents and held responsible for what happens in fixed areas. Also it lays more emphasis on warlike activities than colonial rulers like.

Where the warriors have been suppressed, or nearly so, and the elders disregarded, age organizations have lost all political significance.

The Masai are often thought of as the classic example of an age-set system of this kind. But the most satisfactory description of government based on organization by age is Huntingford's* of the Nandi. With the Nandi (as also with the Masai) boys are initiated over a period of four years. The time for this process to begin is indicated by the flowering of a bush, called *setiot* in Nandi, which is believed to flower every seven years. Each alternate flowering of this tree marks the opening of an initiation period. According to such records as have been preserved, the actual periods seem to have varied during the present century between fourteen and seventeen years, so that the intervals between the completion of one set and the opening of the next were of ten to fifteen years.

To understand a system the working of which is so remote from the experience of the readers of this book, the easiest way may be to follow an imaginary individual through it; we may give him the Nandi name of Kiprono. When the last four-year initiation period closed, Kiprono was eleven years old – just too young to be initiated; so that by the time the next was due to open he was in his early twenties. There were a few men even older who had not yet been initiated because they were ill at the appropriate time, or because through some misfortune their fathers were not able to provide the gifts of beer which are due from the father of an initiate to the elders and the master of ceremonies. All the youths who were old enough for initiation were watching eagerly to find a *setiot* bush in flower; and as soon as one was seen they brought the news, and arrangements were made for new initiations to begin. Most of the youths who were well past puberty were initiated in the first of the four years; in the remaining three were those who for some reason missed the first year, with the younger boys as they

* *The Nandi of Kenya* (1953).

came to puberty. People did not know their exact ages, but the youngest of these would probably be twelve.

During their initiation the boys lived together in a hut in the bush, and were secluded from contact with anyone except those responsible for the ceremony; most especially they could not be seen by women or uninitiated boys. The proceedings began with the physical operation of circumcision, and while they were recovering from this the youths were given instruction bearing on their duties as adult members of society. Their seclusion lasted several months, and the experience they shared in it was expected to create a strong and permanent bond between them.

Among some African peoples who have an age organization the most recently initiated young men used to spend a period of two or three years' military service comparable with the conscription period in western societies. During this time they lived together in a kind of barracks, and they were not allowed to marry until it was over. The Zulu provide the most famous example of this system, but it also existed among the Meru of Kenya. But it is a mistake to suppose, as many people have, that men could not marry until they had left the warrior grade. One need only try seriously to imagine a society in which no man could marry for at least fifteen years after he became adult to see how unworkable it would be. The Nandi youths attained full adult status as soon as their seclusion ended – that is, one sub-set at a time. They did not have to wait for the formal completion of the four-year set. And the first consequence of the attainment of adulthood was the right to marry. To Kiprono and his contemporaries this was a matter of considerable significance, and some of them married very soon after their initiation. This made them less enthusiastic about going on raids, but it was not considered inconsistent with their status as warriors. Married or not, they were entitled to the warrior's privilege of making love to unmarried girls.

Initiation technically made Kiprono and his contemporaries into warriors; that is to say that even the little boys of twelve who were circumcised in the last year of the set now had, as it were, their professional qualifications. But these little boys did not actually begin going on raids until later. They did not have to, because the younger members of the age-set initiated in the previous period were still available for fighting; and moreover, the previous age-set were still regarded as the occupants of the warrior age-grade. As time went on more and more of Kiprono's set married and settled down, and more and more of the fighting was done by the younger members. Eventually came the time for the previous set formally to move out of the warriors' into the elders' grade and 'hand over power', in the inaccurate phrase which is commonly used to describe this event, to Kiprono's set. A good many of the members of this older set had already given up the active life of a warrior, just as Kiprono himself had done long before the time came for *his* set to hand over to its successors. To the younger members of the set the handing over may have put an end to a fighting life that they were not yet tired of; to the older ones its main practical importance was that they were now debarred from playing with the unmarried girls, if they still wanted to. As a compensation their entry into the elder grade gave them the right to drink beer, an indulgence not permitted to warriors.

The handing over was the occasion of a great ceremony which brought together all the men of fighting age of the tribe, and so made the Nandi clearly a political community, in a sense in which we have not been able to use the word of the Nilotes. The military significance of this was obvious, and indeed on one occasion plans were made to use it for the start of a rising against the Europeans in Kenya (or so their police informants told them). This ceremony should be held every fifteen years, about eight years after the completion of a new age-set, but the Kenya government has, not surprisingly, taken an unsympathetic view of it, and it has not been held at any time during this century. To interpret it correctly it should be realized that what is handed over is not power, in the sense of authority in internal affairs, but responsibility for the conduct of war, defensive and offensive.

A political system of this kind is clearly focused on military organization, and the first thing to notice about it is that this organization embraces a larger number of people than any that was considered in the preceding chapter – all the males of fighting age in a population of 50,000. The Nandi country is divided into sections which arrange their initiations separately, but the times are fixed for the whole country, as also are the seven names of sets which follow one another in a fixed order. And the handing-over ceremony, when it was held, was held for all Nandi.

*

We must also ask, however, what is done to regulate the internal affairs of the Nandi and by whom, and here we are concerned with arrangements which are probably still maintained. This is the function of the old men in council – those who have moved out of the warrior grade. Nandi country is divided into named areas, which could be called villages provided this is not taken to mean that all the houses in such an area are close together. Each of these areas contains half a dozen clusters of anything from two to five houses, each cluster with its own fields in a compact block, and a distance of a mile or two between the clusters which are furthest apart. Somewhere accessible to them all is a large shade-tree under which the elders gather. One man is their acknowledged leader, and since there is a name for him (*poiyot*) his position may be regarded as a governmental office. He sits against the tree and so is the focus of the group; he lays before the elders in council the matters which they must discuss, and when he has, as Quakers say, 'taken the sense of the meeting', he gives a decision in its name. Such a man attains his position by the kind of qualities that we have already described as necessary for leadership; among the Nandi there is no ranking of clans or lineages, so that birth confers no advantage, and ritual powers do not seem to give any claim either. The *poiyot* must be able to entertain visitors with appropriate hospitality, be regarded as a man of sound judgement and an authority on tribal custom, and have the confidence in his own views, as well as the powers of persuasion, that will lead the other elders to listen to him. The way of attaining this position is not purely informal; he is designated for it while his predecessor is still *poiyot*, partly by this man's choice and partly by the general feeling that he is next in standing. The position of the designated successor also has a name (*mistoat*).

The importance of councils of elders in securing the redress of wrongs has been discussed. They also take decisions on the way to deal with disasters such as drought, invasion of locusts, and diseases of cattle, and, nowadays, the demands of the Kenya government.

For military purposes the village areas in the past formed part of larger sections of Nandi territory, of which there were about sixteen. In each of these sixteen sections the warriors might be described as forming a separate regiment. Initiation ceremonies were held separately in each, as has been mentioned. In each there was a council consisting of the presidents of the village councils. The leaders of the warriors took part in this council, which was traditionally concerned primarily with the timing and direction of raids on the cattle of the neighbouring peoples. But this council also made known the times for initiation ceremonies and for beginning to plant the crops.

*

A functionary who was indispensable to the deliberations of this council, although he did not take part in them, was the *orkoiyot*, a name which in some contexts might be translated 'magician' or 'diviner', but in this connexion is perhaps better represented by 'prophet'. There was only one *orkoiyot* in this sense for all Nandi. This man was the senior member of a lineage all of whom were believed to have hereditary powers of divination, and he was supposed to be a master in all the branches of his art. His person was regarded as sacred, and the name of his office could not be used in addressing him (just as it is only in comic stories about Americans that anyone addresses high European dignitaries as 'King' or 'Pope'). His assurance that the time was propitious was necessary for all major community activities – warfare, the age-grade ceremonies, or the planting of the crops. In addition to giving this guidance he was expected to perform rites to ensure the success of these enterprises – in the case of planting by causing the rain to fall at the right time.

Planting was of course not in any way organized; all that was involved there was an announcement that the time had come. The handing-over ceremony brought all Nandi together, but the initiations were organized separately by the elders of each division, and the cattle raids by the warriors of each. Since all the bands of warriors had to get one man to approve their plans for raids, there may have been rather more coordination between them than could have been achieved without him. The *orkoiyot* of 1923 is said to have had a well-calculated plan for the deployment of the whole Nandi force against the Europeans.

The *orkoiyot* did not himself take part in public deliberations. Huntingford tells us that two members of each council, chosen by it, acted as his representatives, and that when he pleased he could summon all these to a council of his own. This is an arrangement about which it would be interesting to know more.

The warrior leaders clearly form a class of officers of government with definite tasks to perform. We do not know much about the way in which they were chosen among the Nandi, but we know what was done by their neighbours the Kipsigis, who call them 'brothers', and also by the Masai.

Among the Kipsigis the warrior captains were selected by

the elders at the time of the handing-over ceremony. Among the Masai,* when the time for a new initiation period was coming near, the elders who would be responsible for organizing it began to look out for promising boys, and allowed them to listen to their deliberations in council, and so learn something about the principles on which decisions were taken and the kind of demeanour in council which gained support for a man's views. These boys would become a sort of prefect body in their age-set, and would choose their own leader subject to the elders' approval. Sometimes this seems to have been done even before the initiations began. There was no formal election, and the actual process is a little difficult to picture, since the boy who was chosen, who must have been one of this select body, was not supposed to know of the discussions lest he should refuse a position which was supposed to be more arduous than rewarding. The choice was made known at a public ceremony, when the young leader was given a special club as the sign of his position. There was a leader of the whole age-set, and others for territorial divisions; the age-set leader had formal precedence, but no authority, over the others. Each had an assistant, chosen in the same way though without any formal ceremony, and was expected to consult with him before taking any decision. Now that the Masai can no longer raid their neighbours, these leaders seem to be mainly concerned with the age ceremonies, which were traditionally rather more elaborate among the Masai than they are among the Nandi.

Corresponding to the Nandi *orkoiyot* was the Masai prophet or *laibon*. Indeed the Nandi *orkoiyot* and the *orkoiyot* of the neighbouring Kipsigis trace their descent from a Masai *laibon* who was driven out of his own country about a century ago. The Masai *laibon* too held his position by virtue of descent; brothers succeeded one another in order of age, then the son of the eldest brother. He was the

* H. A. Fosbrooke, 'An Administrative Survey of the Masai Social System' in *Tanganyika Notes and Records*, December 1948.

leading authority in all fields of ritual, but his political importance rested on his relationship with the warriors. He fixed the times for the opening and closing of initiation periods, and when a raid on any scale was planned the warriors sent to him to seek charms to ensure their victory. He was not supposed to take the initiative in suggesting that a raid should be carried out, and certainly he could not order that it should be. The initiative lay with the warriors themselves. But the *laibon's* duty was to give them all the encouragement and aid that he could, and he certainly was not expected to restrain them in any way. The warrior leaders visited him frequently, and little boys who had been picked out as possible leaders were taken to see him. He was entitled to receive a good share of the spoils of a victorious raid, and it is possible that a *laibon* might actually instigate a raid if he thought the warriors were not being active enough. Certainly colonial officials have thought they did, and *laibons* have sometimes been regarded as troublemakers and removed from among their people.

*

Although the Karimojong are today as enthusiastic cattle-raiders as the Masai and Nandi have ever been, their age organization is strikingly different in its emphasis. Whereas the Nandi and Masai seem, according to the descriptions that we have of them, to be concerned first and foremost with the recruiting of warriors and the defence of their country, the essence of the Karimojong system seems to be that it defines the people who, as elders, are qualified to exercise authority, to keep the peace, to decide public matters, and to perform rituals for the general welfare.

In drawing comparisons of this kind one must always allow for the possibility that differences are due to the point of view of different observers. The trained anthropologists of today try to look out for everything, and since they talk with their colleagues, they probably have in mind, when making their observations, the problems that are of general interest at the time they are working. So we can have some confidence that the differences between neighbouring peoples that they describe are genuine. And yet a coming generation may very likely lament that they failed to note just the points that it wants to know. However, professional anthropologists do live among the people they propose to describe, and it is to one of them, Dyson-Hudson, that we owe an account of the Karimojong as they were between 1956 and 1958.

For the Nandi and Masai, in contrast, we have to rely on early accounts which have been obtained by questioning individuals but without direct observation of their life, or later ones collected when the war-making organization was largely a thing of the past. In both these situations informants are likely to have spread themselves on the aspect of their tradition that they remember with most pride. After all, if the Nandi elders mediated in quarrels, as we are told the Kipsigis elders did, there must often have been quarrels between warriors. On the other hand, the position of the *orkoiyot* or *laibon* with his special relationship to the warriors is a well-established fact which is not paralleled among the Karimojong.

Among the Karimojong, boys were initiated in small numbers and could be initiated into manhood at any time. The ceremony was a simple one and did not include ordeals or any period of instruction. It did include a sacrifice to God and the blessing of the new initiates. The elders of the neighbourhood – a dozen or fewer stockaded settlements, each comprising two or three households – whose boys were initiated together were responsible for this. The crucial act for the initiate was the spearing of the ox to be sacrificed on his behalf; the rest of the ceremony emphasized his junior status in that all the youths about to be initiated together prepared the ceremonial place, made and tended the fire, and roasted the sacrificial meat which was eaten by their elders.

All the boys initiated within a period of five or six years

form a set with a distinctive name. There is no rigid time-table which indicates to everyone exactly when it is time to consider one set complete and begin recruiting boys to the next one. People look to the division of Karimojong country which they regard as the oldest – that where 'the people of the partridge' live – and follow its lead in this and in the choice of name. Within the sets there is no ranking of individuals by the year of their initiation, but successive sets are ranked in strict order. The sets are grouped into 'generations'. Five sets make a generation, and at any time the adult men of all Karimojong are grouped, for practical purposes, into a senior and a junior generation; there may also be a few old men, survivors of a preceding generation which has ceased to play any part in the government of Karimojong. The sets do not move up separately from the junior to the senior division; the whole group of five move up together at a great tribal ceremony which should be held every thirty years. This is the one occasion that has ever brought all Karimojong together, or at least as many as were not kept away by the necessity of finding grazing for their herds. The scene is a spot in the north-east of the country which is never used for any other ceremony; but at all initiations the presiding elder gazes towards it.

Thus, at different times, the actual age and composition of the senior generation is very different. At the moment when it is just about to retire and let the next generation take its place, the majority of its members are likely to be already dead. This was the situation in 1957, when only twenty members of the senior generation were still alive and even all the senior set of the junior generation had died. In some parts of the country important rituals had been in abeyance for two or three years because there was no one to conduct them, and young men could not be initiated for the same reason.

At the 'succession' ceremony held in that year the four extant sets of the junior generation moved up to the senior grade. But some of these were quite young men who had only been initiated in the past few years. They did not automatically become elders; nobody called them so or expected them to assume the duties of elders. To be an elder a man must *both* belong formally to the senior generation *and* have attained an age which commands respect.

But younger men expect to obey the elders as they expect to obey their own fathers, and of course nearly every man of the junior generation has his own father in the senior one. The duty of respect for seniors – for one's immediate seniors as well as for the senior generation – is impressed on people on all kinds of occasions. There are types of ornament that a new age-set are not allowed to wear until they have the permission of their seniors. At initiation ceremonies all those who are already initiated sit in the order of their age-sets. When men go out on cattle raids they are grouped in age-sets. When disputes have been brought before a public gathering for discussion, the senior men give the final decision; their juniors may only offer comment and opinion. Proverbs remind people that those who obey the elders may expect to prosper, while to treat them with disrespect may cause general calamity: that is to say, if there *were* a calamity, the explanation given would be that people were not treating the elders with due respect.

In Karimojong the elders collectively are responsible for the performance of the rituals that are held to be necessary for the general welfare; these are not left to ritual specialists as they are among so many peoples. The elders, because they are nearer death, are believed also to be nearer to God than their juniors are, and their blessing is an essential part of the initiation and other ceremonies. Their nearness to God also gives them the power to curse people who do wrong. But most people obey them willingly, as happens in any society where everyone has been brought up to recognize certain persons as having authority.

But of course the elders do not constitute *a* government for all Karimojong. This would be impossible, since they are never all together in one place except at the great succession ceremony. Different elders perform the functions of government for different sections of the country. It is normally within the 'neighbourhood' that disputes arise, since this is the area within which people are in constant contact. Such disputes are discussed before all the men of the neighbourhood, and the elders of the neighbourhood decide what should be done.

The neighbourhood is the most important community for the relationships of everyday life. But larger divisions of Karimojong country take common action on special occasions. There are ten named divisions or 'sections' of the country, each with its recognized boundaries, and certain important rituals are performed on behalf of a whole section by all its elders. One of these, the 'freeing of the cattle', has immediate and important practical consequences. It is performed near the beginning of the dry season, when the herdsmen want to go away from the permanent settlements to look for grazing. No one may move out until this ceremony has been held, and when people begin to be anxious to move, members of the junior generation beg the elders to hold it. When they are agreed that the time has come, a man of standing is sent round blowing a horn to summon the cattle to the ceremonial place to be blessed. When all have been blessed, the 'spokesman', still blowing his horn, leads away his own herd, the others follow, and other herd owners who may not have brought their cattle to the blessing join in the procession away from the settlements. Thus the move away from the home pastures is coordinated, and the time fixed and publicly made known. In this way the elders are made responsible for protecting the limited grazing grounds from being used prematurely, and also for preventing competition between individual herdsmen to steal a march on their neighbours. If anyone does, the elders send the men of the junior generation to bring him back, and he is beaten and obliged to sacrifice an ox in atonement for his disobedience. His fellows are the readier to coerce him since their own interests are involved. In the period before the succession ceremony in 1957 this control was in abeyance over much of the country for lack of elders.

Every year or two the section also holds a 'beseeching' ceremony, at which the junior generation kill cattle to make a feast for the seniors and formally beg for their blessing on people and herds. Each elder in turn pronounces a general blessing, and the senior elder of all blesses each individual by splashing him with a mixture of water and sacred clay.

In the days when there was nothing to stop the Karimojong from making large-scale raids on their enemies, these also were initiated by the elders. Again, as with the freeing of the cattle, their action took the form of a ritual of blessing. An army could not – or perhaps was afraid to – take the field without this blessing, given to the assembled warriors at the appropriate place of ceremony. Individuals were not forbidden to make small raids on their own initiative, however, so that this ceremony was not a way of imposing the control of the elders on all warfare. We do not know what commonly happened in the past. Probably the warriors begged the elders to hold the ceremony, as the herdsmen begged them to free the cattle, and we cannot tell whether in fact they were unable to refuse, as is said to have been the position of the elders when Nandi warriors wanted to take the field. Dyson-Hudson does say, however, that 'it is the elders who exhort the junior generation-set to raid the stock and kill the members of foreign groups encroaching on their grazing; or to take retribution against outside groups which have raided Karimojong herds or settlements.'

Thus one might say that the Karimojong, like the Nuer, have political communities of different sizes for different purposes. But there is a feature of their society which can be said to make them one political community for general purposes. This is that *any* member of a senior age-set can adjudicate in a dispute between *any* persons junior to him, whether they belong to the same neighbourhood or section as himself or not. This happens, for example, in the temporary herdsmen's camps in the dry season, where people have been 'mixed up by the sun'. In such a camp there will probably be no elders present, but the principle is followed that the same rules of seniority operate between all Karimojong. The ranking of an individual in the system is known not only by the name of his age-set, which could not be learned from a stranger without questioning, but also by the ornaments that he is entitled to wear as a member of a particular set in a particular generation.

It should not be supposed that the Karimojong are more law-abiding than the other peoples described, and turn to the elders as soon as a claim of any kind is disputed. The kin of a homicide have the recognized right to take a life or cattle in compensation, and it is for them to judge how many cattle they should take. The matter would only come before the elders if the killer's kin claimed that the wronged lineage had seized an unreasonable number. A person who has suffered any other wrong first tries to get redress for himself, and if he fails may go no further. He may get what is due to him by threats, notably the threat involved in going to the offender's home with all his brothers armed with sticks. He may try to seize it, and either succeed or think no more about his claim. Often he can complain to the head of a household and get this man to pay compensation on behalf of one of its members. But when one party is determined on its rights and the other equally determined to dispute them, the matter goes before a public meeting for discussion by everyone and decision by the elders. The decision usually involves some payment in stock, and if the man who has been told to pay does not do so, the elders send the younger men to take it. They may also require him to sacrifice an ox, and have him beaten if he refuses.

It is also possible for the elders to send young men to seize an ox for sacrifice at a public ritual from a member of the community who is unwilling to give it when they judge that he should.

*

Dyson-Hudson's description of the Karimojong succession ritual is the only account of such a ceremony which is contemporary with the events it records. He has noted certain features in it that are not mentioned in the accounts of the handing-over ceremonies of the Kenya peoples. What is most interesting to the student of political systems is less the ceremony itself than the way in which the major divisions of the people and their relationships are mirrored in it – a feature which we are more used to seeing in the accession rites of kings.

Ideally all Karimojong should meet for this ceremony, which is held at the most sacred place of the whole tribe. It is essential for all the surviving members of the retiring generation to be there, even if they have to be carried. But others have to consider such questions as the length of the march, whether they have enough cattle to bring with them for milk and blood to live on and for sacrifice, and who will look after the cattle that are left at home.

There is a meeting place in each of the ten sections of the territory where its people assemble. If they have to halt on the way they camp in a strict order, the sections and their sub-divisions in the same relationship as that in which their homes stand geographically. This is also the order in which they camp at the sacred place, and there particular sections each have their special contribution to make to the great ceremony. One collects wood to make firesticks from which the fire will be kindled to roast the sacrificed oxen; another gets thorn branches and builds a hedge to protect the whole encampment from attack by wild animals; and so on. The section to which the senior surviving elder belongs provides the specially made spear with which the sacrificed animals are divided. Thus the separateness of the sections, the relations between them, and the unity of them all in a ceremony in which tasks are shared, are all the time brought home to them. Even the fact that this is essentially a ceremony for Karimojong is emphasized by the allocation of a special place to people who are descended from prisoners taken in war; they have to provide the slaughter oxen to feed all the assembly. This is the only occasion on which their separate origin is remembered.

The rules of behaviour on the journey to the sacred place are interesting too. No one must make a noise, still less fight; no one must steal, no one must rake up old disputes by asking for the repayment of debts; no one must even beg from another, as is common at other times, since the Karimojong believe that anyone who has even a small surplus of possessions ought to show generosity in distributing it. The significance of these rules is clear; they are all designed to keep the peace among turbulent people. No one must raise any question which could lead to a quarrel, even by making a request that might be refused. No one must raise his voice in anger. There could be no clearer assertion of the ideal of order and peace among the fellow members of the political community.

There are also phrases used in common speech which express recognition of the common membership in one political community of all Karimojong: for example, when infringement of another's rights, disobedience to the elders, or refusal of assistance to another Karimojong is spoken of as 'wronging the country'.

*

Within this formal framework, which assigns to every man his appropriate rank and seniority, there is room for individuals to win for themselves positions of leadership. Whatever may be the formal rules conferring authority, the voice of men whose opinions command the support of many other voices carries extra weight in discussion. A man who owns a large herd is in this position. He can give cattle for many marriages, and through these marriages make many allies who will give him the support due to a kinsman in matters in which they themselves are neutral. He has more sons than other men because he has more wives, and it is an absolute duty of sons to stand behind their father. All

Karimojong make compacts of friendship with men outside their kin group by giving them cattle, and the more cattle a man has the more friends he can bind to himself in this way. Such a man, too, can win prestige by providing an ox for sacrifice when some ritual occasion calls for it, and at times when food is short he can provide meat to feast his neighbours. Moreover, his herds are scattered in different parts of the country, and so he has good grounds for claiming to be more knowledgeable than his fellows about what is going on.

Among such men, one sometimes becomes predominant in a neighbourhood and is known as its 'spokesman'; he is not deliberately chosen, but rather is found to be in this position when it is taken for granted that people look to his lead in any activity that needs concerted action. Essentially a 'spokesman' is a persuasive talker whose views have been proved wise by experience. When he is recognized as such, however, he can speak with authority. He proposes a course of action, and if this is opposed he tells the opposition to leave the gathering. But discussions of this kind are matters of policy, on which there is room for two opinions, and not of law and order, on which there should be only one, and the spokesman cannot call on physical force to carry his point. If the opposition is too strong he may cease to be spokesman, or the neighbourhood may be divided into followers of two spokesmen.

What is interesting here is the explicit recognition that a programme cannot emerge from the collective consciousness of a meeting, even a small one; it must have taken form in someone's mind. People look to their spokesman's lead when planning ceremonies and when planning raids: but where there is a recognized spokesman, it falls to him also to announce the elders' decision in a dispute which has been submitted to public discussion.

Some elders are also prophets: that is, they are believed to receive communications from God warning them of impending calamities which can be averted by sacrifices.

Occasionally such a prophet is recognized by the whole of Karimojong, and sacrifices are organized at his bidding (though not directed by him) at all the ceremonial places.

*

The agricultural Kikuyu, with the group of smaller peoples associated with them, also had once a system of government based on age, with the division of the population into warriors and elders, and the periodic handing over to the next generation, as its salient characteristics. Curiously enough, we know more about the military organization of the Kikuyu than we do about that of peoples who are much more famous for their fighting achievement.

It is very clear from the accounts which we have of the Kikuyu system that the ceremonial handing over did not represent an actual transfer of all functions into new hands. It is nearly sixty years since such a ceremony was held, but the process by which individuals work their way through different grades with different functions still goes on.

The Kikuyu consider that different public activities are appropriate to persons at different stages of life, but these are not measured simply in years from a man's birth or even his initiation. His advance through life is marked by his marriage and the birth and maturing of his children. These events qualify him to enter groups of increasingly senior status. The word 'council' is used of these groups in most of the accounts which have been written of them, but the descriptions of their activities which we have do not indicate that they are often expected to meet and deliberate; membership itself appears to be what is significant.

There is a two-way relationship between the events of a man's family life and his passage through these different stages. Each major event is the qualification for a higher stage, and at the same time the advance has to have the sanction of the men of superior grade, which is obtained by making payments to them. Payment was traditionally made in goats to provide feasts for these superiors. The first payment is made as part of a man's wedding ceremonies; this is regarded from one point of view as payment for the right to marry, while from another it is the fee for entry to the lowest grade of elders. Membership of this grade does not confer any exalted status, but those who have entered it are allowed to be present at the deliberations of their seniors. Their name is interpreted by some authorities to mean 'those who sit at one side' and by others to mean 'those who still carry spears'. Before the elders were organized into formal tribunals by the Kenya government, the junior elders acted as attendants upon their seniors when they met to hear cases, taking messages for them and cooking the goats which were brought as their payment.

Men go on paying further goats until the requisite number have been paid for full membership of the body of elders. To enter this body a man should have a child old enough to be initiated; but he cannot enter unless he has made the requisite payments, and if he has not made the payments he cannot have his child initiated either. This is the kind of circumstance which may lead to the postponement of initiation, and so place a man in an age-set most of whom are young than he is.

Some men are unfortunate and have no children, or their children do not live to grow up. These men are not condemned to remain forever in a grade junior to all their contemporaries, but are allowed to move up with the latest members of their own age-set to do so.

Full elders are entitled to hear cases, and this is their principal share in the government of their country. They carry a staff which indicates their status, and a bundle of the leaves of a special tree, which they use to wipe the sweat from their faces. But there is a still higher grade, that of the elders with ritual functions. It was they who organized the age-grade ceremonies of initiation and handing over, and performed the rites of purification which were frequently required among the Kikuyu, since they believed that a large number of circumstances might place a person in a condition of ritual impurity which was very dangerous; they also were held to have special powers which enabled them to curse wrong-doers.

According to some accounts the ritual elders must be men whose wives are past child-bearing or who are themselves past sexual activity, but it is also stated that sometimes relatively young men become ritual elders. The explanation may be that here the hereditary principle plays a part – not in the sense that the status of ritual elder is reserved for a particular lineage, but in the sense that every lineage has to have a ritual elder. This would be easy to understand in a society where the spirits of the ancestors bulk so large in religious belief, since such spirits are always believed to be concerned only with their own descendants and approachable only by them. It may be that in some lineages more than one old man attains this status, but it seems possible that the senior man of any lineage, who is also its secular head, has to be a ritual elder even if through some accidental circumstance he is a relatively young man.

The whole Kikuyu people never together took any collective action. Even the handing-over ceremony, when it was held, was organized separately, and at different times, in different parts of the country. On the last occasion when this happened, what was regarded as a single process of handing over responsibility to the next generation took about a dozen years to complete (c. 1890–1903). Yet the areas which co-operated for this purpose were much wider than those which did so for any other.

The elders' councils, then, when the system was functioning without interference, would consist of all men who had attained to elder status in a limited district. Even within these districts it is not certain that they were ever formally required all to meet together; if they did not, the junior elders must have had a position something like fags, liable to be called on if they were within earshot of any gathering of their seniors. Any elder was competent to hear a case in dispute, and men who had a quarrel could collect such elders as they wished to hear it. But if a number were gathered together, the ritual elders would give the final decision after retiring to discuss the case in private.

In the organization of raids the warriors were divided into four sections: the scouts who went ahead to spy out the land, the main body who attacked the enemy's cattle (and his men if they were on the spot), another which lay in wait to ambush pursuing enemy forces, and a fourth which was responsible for driving off the captured stock. The disposition of forces was in the hands of the senior warriors as a body, a grade into which men bought their way by a series of payments, just as they did into the grade of elders, over a period of about six years. The senior warriors were responsible for discipline generally among the members of the warrior grade.

*

The accounts which we have of the Kikuyu do not mention any person with a position comparable to that of the Masai *laibon* or Nandi *orkoiyot*. But it has recently been found that the different sections of their neighbours the Meru had each a prophet of a somewhat similar kind called the *mugwe*.* The very existence of these men is not known to Meru boys now in schools, yet as late as 1955 several of them were still alive, and in the remoter parts of the country were still accorded the respect which was their right by tradition.

Every *mugwe* had to be a descendant of the original leader of the Meru, who is believed to have brought them to their present home, parting the waters of the sea like Moses so that they could cross. Only a descendant of the original leader was able to intercede with the High God in whom the peoples of the Kenya Highlands believe. But any of his descendants could not do this. The mystical quality called *ugwe* was conferred on the *mugwe* alone. There was no automatic rule of succession to the office. A future

* B. Bernardi, *The Mugwe, a Failing Prophet* (1959).

mugwe was chosen while he was young by the *mugwe* in office, who consulted the elders of the lineage and the elders of the age-set to which he himself belonged. After the young man was chosen, he spent much of his time listening to the elders in council judging cases, discussing matters of public interest and recalling tribal traditions. He did not go through the ceremonies and ordeals of initiation, for it was held to be mystically necessary that his body should be without a blemish or wound.

The *mugwe* was expected to represent in his own life the highest ideals of his people, and to command their respect by his personality as well as for his ritual powers. He was thought of as the guardian of the whole people and their intercessor with God, but, like the *laibon* and *orkoiyot*, he had a special responsibility for the warriors, who could not go out on a raid without his blessing.

The *mugwe* was not, any more than the *laibon*, a chief or ruler. He did not usually join with the other elders in judging the disputes that were brought to them. But in the rare cases when they decided that a man must be put to death, they could not carry out the sentence unless he agreed. When matters concerning the warriors had to be decided, however, he consulted with the elders, and here he was not just one of a body of elders but was recognized to have a special position, 'like the queen bee', as the honey-eating Meru put it.

The *mugwe* then was a man whose position depended essentially upon religious beliefs about his special relationship with God, but who, in virtue of this position, had a considerable voice in the government of the Meru. He received a material return for the spiritual benefits which he brought them. Not only, like the *laibon*, did he receive his share of the cattle captured on a raid, but his people worked for him in the same way that the Anuak sometimes did for a popular village headman, building his house, mending his fences, and hoeing his fields. This is the kind of service that chiefs expect and enforce. The Meru say, however, that they gave it of their free will because the *mugwe* 'must not be let to suffer'. In the remote area of Tigania the people a few years ago were still contributing to pay his tax for him.

*

A function of government which we have not met with in any of the cases discussed so far is the proclamation of rules or orders which people can be punished for breaking. Sometimes these proclamations have been made at handing-over ceremonies, in which case it seems likely that they asserted generally recognized rules of conduct rather than made new ones, particularly as these ceremonies were held so rarely. The Kikuyu sometimes summoned meetings for the purpose; the call was blown on a special ceremonial trumpet made from a kudu horn. A gathering of crowds for a dance could be made the occasion for a proclamation. We have no clear picture of the way in which a decision was taken to make such announcements; nor do we know whose business it was to proclaim them. In Meru, according to Lambert,* it was the privilege and responsibility of the younger elders and the younger warriors to issue such orders and enforce them. Examples given by some Kikuyu elders were the prohibition of witchcraft; the announcement that habitual thieves should be executed; orders to protect supplies of food in times of famine, and declaring that people from the neighbouring Kamba might be allowed peaceful entry to seek for food; orders regulating the use of land, for example that certain tracts of forest should be left standing as a defence against enemies, or that a salt-lick should be open for general use. It is doubtful whether this activity would entitle one to say that the government of the Kikuyu included organs of legislation. If legislation means making rules of general application which change or extend the existing body of rules, none of these examples really fits the definition. Some are reassertions of recognized rules, others are orders dealing with specific situations. They do demon-

* H. E. Lambert, *Kikuyu Social and Political Institutions* (1956).

strate, however, that collective decisions could be taken in such emergencies as famine. We do not know how wide an area was covered by any of these orders, though it is fairly safe to say that it is not likely to have been the whole Kikuyu country.

We see, in fact, in all the examples in this and the last chapter, that there are some societies of which it is difficult to say that there is one 'political community' for all purposes. To Evans-Pritchard the important unit was that which accepts a common rule of law. By the rule of law is meant, not that people settle their differences without fighting, but that, although they are expected to fight, and above all to avenge a homicide, yet they can, and should, eventually agree to accept compensation and be reconciled with their enemies. Members of one tribe accept this as their common rule, and so form a political community. The Nuer people, although they regard themselves as in some sense an entity distinct from their neighbours, comprise a number of tribes which do not mutually accept this rule and so form a political community.

If, however, we are looking for a political community in the sense of a group for which decisions are taken in common, we have more difficulty. Perhaps the village is a political community, since in everyday life the people of one village do sometimes follow the lead of one man, and they would not look to anyone outside the village for such a lead. Somewhere between the village and the tribe comes that group of people who look to a common ritual leader, particularly for the ceremonies of initiation. The Nuer perform these ceremonies with the absolute minimum of organization and cooperation; yet there is an area a good deal wider than the village within which all look to one 'man of the cattle' to keep the formation of age-sets in line.

The whole Shilluk people can be called a political community in the sense that they recognize a single man – the Reth – as in some sense supreme over them all, and that when the Reth is installed different sections of them are responsible each for its particular duties. But in all other matters Shilluk settlements manage their own affairs.

With the western Anuak, the only political unit is the village, and yet the ties of kinship and affinity that link the people of different villages create a much wider community within which peaceful intercourse is possible, and in which people away from home may be 'guests' but are hardly 'aliens'. In eastern Anuakland, though all the villages competed for the sacred emblems, they managed their affairs independently until the time when those who were in contact with the Ethiopians got fire-arms and were able to attack their neighbours.

When we come to the peoples who base their political systems on organization by age, we find again that there seem to be different 'political communities' for different purposes. The community which arranges and takes part in the age-ceremonies embraces many more people than ever take joint decisions for any other purpose. Moreover, among the Nandi and Masai the ceremony of handing over the country was a national affair, but the initiation of warriors was organized independently by different sections. Of course in every large political community such as a modern nation there are local divisions which manage local affairs, but they are never completely autonomous; they are always in some way subordinate to the government of the whole country. The difference between such a system and those of the Nilotes and Nilo-Hamites is that the smaller units are *completely* autonomous in the matters that they manage for themselves. Yet both Masai and Nandi did recognize a single individual who alone was able to ensure that their raids would be successful, and this fact united them in the same sense that the Shilluk were united by recognizing the Reth.

With the Kikuyu we find that even the handing-over ceremony did not unite the whole nation, and the war-magician, though he existed, was of such little account that it was not necessary to mention him when describing their system. Yet it is recorded of them, and of them alone among the peoples we have examined, that rules of conduct and orders for action were proclaimed to public assemblies by persons with authority to do so. We do not really know how such assemblies were composed, or whether they consisted of people who combined for other purposes of government.

So we are forced to the conclusion that there are peoples among whom one cannot find a single clearly defined political community. Between the close-knit hunting band and the organization of state type there is a form of polity characteristic of populations which are a good deal larger than the hunting band, though not necessarily smaller than those which are governed as states. I am not prepared to offer a name for this phenomenon. To describe it as briefly as possible one could say that some populations regard themselves, and are regarded by others, as distinct entities, but yet do not recognize any person or body of persons as having general authority to take decisions in matters affecting them all. In different contexts, different subdivisions of the whole take collective action for the purposes for which they are autonomous; so that if such action is the criterion of a political community, there are series of overlapping political communities. Sometimes, but not always, such populations are linked by the recognition of a unique position the occupant of which has the same relationship to all of them, but often the occupant of this position has little or no right to command the actions of others.

CHAPTER 4

The Expansion of Government

IT is sometimes assumed that the form of government which we know as the state came into being as the result of wars of conquest. One people conquered another and then had to devise a system of administration which would keep the vanquished in subjection. It is certainly true that, where there is a state system, the population governed by it often consists of people of different ethnic origins among whom one group are dominant. But it is not necessary to assume that the dominant group have attained their position through armed conquest. There are other methods by which political control can be extended, and some of these can be illustrated by examples from the peoples of East Africa.

None of the peoples that have been discussed so far have a state form of government. In the context of East Africa we can say that we see a state where a hereditary monarch is at the head of a people who recognize that he has temporal as well as spiritual authority. The various other forms of state that have come into existence in the past two centuries have no counterpart in this region.

Earlier anthropologists made it their aim to reconstruct the development of institutions in an evolutionary series, from 'germs' which were to be found in the simplest forms of society, and some of their conjectures have come to appear rather ludicrous in the light of knowledge gained later. I shall try not to repeat their mistakes, and if I say that, in the minimal governments which have been described, we can see some of the prerequisites for the establishment of a hereditary monarchy, I do not assert that those peoples which now have hereditary monarchs must once have had a political organization like that of the Nuer. Nevertheless, it is reasonable to suppose that they have not had a state form of government ever since the dawn of their existence as human beings.

What I suggest is that, among all the Nilotic peoples, we can see one or both of the elements which are essential for the development of kingship, and so of government which is controlled from a single source. Of these two elements one is sacred and the other secular. The sacred element is the belief that ritual powers are hereditary. We have seen how this belief designates a limited number of persons to be peace-makers in those societies where it is left to each member to seek his own redress for wrongs: some of these also have the function, which some might say was hardly political, of making such sacrifices as are deemed appropriate to ensure that rain shall fall at the right time and in sufficient quantity but not in excess. This function is also performed by the Masai and Nandi war-prophets. I call attention to it because there are cases where hereditary rulers are sometimes also expected to be able to control the weather, and if they do not seem to be successful in this, they may be regarded as unfit for their position.

The secular element in kingship is ability to attract and keep a following. Of course every leader has a following; it is tautology to say so. But what matters is the kind of following. We saw how the men who became leaders among the Luhya did so because they could count on the support in debates about village affairs of a certain number of people who were under obligations to them. This could hardly be thought of as a first step towards monarchical rule. But this first step has been taken when we find a leader who can keep permanently associated with him a body of retainers whom he can call on to enforce his wishes, and who identify themselves more closely with him than with any of the divisions of the population. This is the first essential of state power, in however rudimentary a form. We could see the young men who attach themselves to the court of a successful Anuak village headman as such a body of retainers, although in the case of the Anuak no headman manages to keep his retainers for long. The reason is not difficult to understand; people expect to get something in return for loyalty to their leader, and in Anuakland what they expect is feasts of meat. In the economy of the Anuak with their small herds of stock, the richest headman cannot go on giving such feasts for long. We begin to see already how important it is for the building up of kingship that the society should have some surplus of wealth which can be concentrated in the hands of the ruler and used for purposes of state – among which one of the most important is rewarding services. We do not know much about the court of the Shilluk Reth, but we do know that he was able to maintain a more permanent following.

I propose to give four examples of the spread of political power from the history of peoples in this region. In each case the story is different, but in no case is it a story of conquest and subjugation. The four peoples are the Gusii of western Kenya, the next-door neighbours of the Luhya, the Mandari, the eastern Anuak, and the Alur of western Uganda. From the Gusii we learn how, in favourable circumstances, one lineage in a society without chiefs can become dominant over the others. The eastern Anuak show how the area that recognizes the special privileges of a noble clan has gradually extended. It also shows how important in this process was the fact that some people were able to import guns. This is what could fairly be called a historical accident. The history of the Alur does not go back to a time when they did not recognize hereditary chiefs, but in their recent history there are remembered many occasions when neighbouring people who themselves had no chiefs asked the Alur to come and rule over them.

*

The Gusii* are among the peoples who manage to maintain enough order for their needs with very little government. Like the Anuak, they are one people with two political

* P. Mayer, *The Lineage Principle in Gusii Society* (1949).

systems in different parts of their country. The Gusii are an agricultural people, living in permanent homesteads, though they possess and value cattle. Their country is on the western slopes of the Kenya Highlands, and their neighbours to the north and south are Nilo-Hamitic peoples with their organization of warriors expected to spend a large part of their time raiding their neighbours – Nandi and Kipsigis to the north, Masai to the south. There are seven Gusii tribes, and each has its own section of the country. Each of the tribes is divided into a number of clans – people who believe that they had a common ancestor some time in the past. In each tribe there are one or two clans who say that their ancestors were the founders of the tribe, the first men to come to what are now the tribal lands, and there are also several other clans whose ancestors are supposed to have been adopted by members of the founding clans.

Thus the Gusii, like the Nuer, have the idea that certain parts of their country are specially associated with – one might almost say *belong to* – the descendants of particular persons. We saw how a Nuer is treated as an aristocrat if he is living in the country of his own lineage, and a commoner if he lives anywhere else. The Gusii idea is that nobody ought to live outside the land that belongs to the ancestors of his own clan. But, in fact, people often do. So the fact is made to square with the ideal by saying that immigrant groups are the descendants of people who were adopted by the founder's clan and so, as it were, naturalized. Each of the clans, original or adopted, has its own section of the tribal land, and each has its own elders to whom people go to get quarrels settled. Members of the founders' clans are not treated with special respect or regarded as aristocrats, and they are not entitled to tell people of other clans what to do. All the clans are equal and autonomous.

This is a description of six of the Gusii tribes. The seventh is different. It is called Getutu, and its lands are higher and rougher than the rest of Gusii country and so less exposed to enemy raids. The founder's clan here is called Nyakundi.

When the Masai or Nandi warriors attacked Gusii country, refugees from the other six tribes poured into Getutu, and boys or young men begged the leading Nyakundi men to take them in. No doubt they looked for men of some standing, who had cattle and stores of grain and could offer them food. But of course they made a return in services to their protectors – herding, building, or whatever might be called for. The refugee would call his protector 'father', and the protector would provide his 'child' with the cattle that he had to hand over to his bride's father before he could marry. But he was not adopted into his 'father's' lineage; he was spoken of as a 'bought person' (although this did not mean he was a slave), and he was said to have been bought by the cattle provided for his marriage. What was actually bought was his political loyalty to his protector.

There were also women refugees, and they were taken into their protector's houses as wives. Some leading Nyakundi men got fifteen wives or more, since these refugee women had no parents to demand cattle for them. As a result the numbers of the Nyakundi clan increased very fast indeed, and it was soon by far the largest clan in Getutu.

Sometimes groups of kinsmen came into Getutu country together. In this case they did not ask for personal protection, but simply for a place to build their houses and plant their crops. These groups were not 'naturalized' by adoption, as immigrants had to be if they were to remain among the other tribes. They were called 'dwellers', a name which implied that they were only in Getutu country temporarily, and perhaps on sufferance, though in practice they were safe as long as they stuck to their protectors. These immigrants were not treated as a lower class. They were not expected to look up to *all* Nyakundi.

But they and everyone else living in Getutu were expected to accept the judgements of certain elders who were, and could only be, Nyakundi. In the rest of the Gusii country there were a number of respected older men, who attained prestige by their personality and their wealth in the manner I have described among their neighbours, the Luhya. But in Getutu the only elders with the right to judge cases were the heads of Nyakundi lineages, and they were entitled to this right in virtue of their descent alone. Like the Kikuyu elders, these men carried staffs as signs of their position. If a man wished to demand payment of a debt from someone at a distance, he would first persuade the elder in his own part of the country that he had a good claim. Then the elder would send one of his sons, carrying his staff, to the debtor's home to order him to pay. It is said that the symbol of authority was usually enough to secure obedience. But if the elder was afraid that the debtor would defy the order, he would send a number of his 'bought persons' to enforce it. If they had to seize a cow from the debtor, and this led to fighting and perhaps killing, it would not be a fight between real 'sons of Nyakundi', who ought to remain at peace.

In Gusii eyes this was the principal reason for employing the 'bought persons' on this kind of police errand. But the detached observer can see this as another case of the importance of the neutral band of supporters, loyal only to the judge and without lineage ties to either side in a dispute. A peculiar feature of the Gusii story is that the Nyakundi clan have established their claim to hereditary positions without the backing of any of those myths about the supernatural adventures of the founding ancestor, and his special relationship with divine beings, on which such claims seem to rest everywhere else. It is interesting to speculate whether such myths might have become current if the Gusii had been left alone a little longer.

*

A similar building up of power on a small scale can be seen among the small Mandari chiefs in the Nile Valley region. Each of these was the head of the lineage which claimed to 'own' the land of his territory, and which had the privilege of providing ritual specialists with the power to pray for rain on behalf of all the inhabitants. As among the Gusii (all the Gusii except Getutu) other lineages in each chiefdom are believed to be related to the land-owning lineage through some genealogical link in the remote past. Yet others, however, are descended from individuals who came to the chiefdom from distant countries and sought the protection of the chief. These were, essentially, men without kin. They might have committed some offence which led their kinsmen to disown them; some are said to have been guilty of the murder of a brother; one, famous in folklore, left home because his father had accidentally caused the death of his mother. Or they might have survived some famine or epidemic, or enemy attack, in which all their close kin perished. In times of famine people sometimes brought a child to a Mandari homestead owner and left it with them, receiving some grain in return. (It is easy to interpret such a proceeding as selfish cruelty to children, and indeed this interpretation is widely current in other parts of the world where this happens. But it is worth remembering that one of its effects is to save the lives of children who would otherwise die.) Some refugees, again, might be men who had been defeated in a struggle for the headmanship of their own tribe. Others, it is said, had had a reputation at home as sorcerers or incorrigible thieves, and so been driven out. (Note that these last are the kind of people who are said to have been 'lynched' among some Kenya tribes. It may be that the Kenya tribes were more severe towards offenders, but it is possible that they too drove away more people than they actually killed.)

Solitary strangers cannot survive in the African bush, so it was essential for such men to find protection. It was also to the advantage of their protectors to have dependents who had loyalty to them alone, and some of the stories of the founding of these dependent, or *client*, lineages tell how the stranger was found wandering in the bush and invited to come and settle. There were also ways of formally indicating that one wished to become the client of a chief.

One was to sit at the edge of his meeting place and wait for a summons. Another was to appear at the season when the ground was being cleared for sowing, and do some weeding after the villagers had finished for the day. These stories and these procedures emphasize the idea that the relationship was one for mutual benefit; though the client was inevitably at a disadvantage since he had no kinsmen to turn to for support.

The descendants of clients inherit the relationship entered into by their ancestor. They are not treated differently in any conspicuous manner from the family of the protector, with whom they work in the fields and in building houses and grainstores. A client is not expected to be at the disposal of his protector at all times; when he is married he has his own house, fields, and goats to look after. But he has certain personal duties of a kind required only of persons of his status. When his protector is on a journey he acts as a bodyguard, carries loads for him and takes messages for him. If meat has to be cooked in the bush, as it may after a hunt or a meat sacrifice at a distance from home, the client must cook it. At home he attends on his protector during the meetings under the council tree, fetching charcoal to light his pipe, and handing round tobacco to the assembled elders. He is also expected to act as a spy on behalf of his protector, reporting hostile conversations, and in the days when the chiefs fought one another, their clients spied out the enemy's country.

Of course every chief has a number of clients. They build their homes around their protector's, and so form a buffer between the chief and his enemies, and were a defence in the days when raiding was commoner than it is now.

The protector is not regarded as having earned unlimited rights to his client's services by the one act of extending his protection. He is expected to act as a benefactor. In the days when wrongs were redressed by self-help, the protector avenged those done to his clients as well as those done to his own family, and today a protector will help his client in litigation in the courts which the Sudan government has set up, and pay fines imposed on him. The client is addressed as though he were his protector's kinsman, and his inferior status is not referred to in public. Those clients who were highly favoured by their protectors could become important people, looked up to because of their influence with the chief; some married their daughters to neighbouring chiefs. The best safeguard for the client was the fact that every chief wanted to maintain and increase his following. Those of whom too many services were asked and to whom too little return was made could transfer their allegiance to another chief. This was not regarded as an offence; on the other hand, chiefs would prevent it if they could, even by killing the client, because of the obvious dangers of having a former retainer in an enemy court.

Although we know less about what happened among the Shilluk, it is of interest that the bodyguard of the Reth is supposed to have been originally built up of people who came to him because for some reason they were detached from their own kin or village. Some were war captives, some homicides, some just poor men; some had been possessed by the spirit of Nyikang and so should become servants of the Reth, the incarnation of Nyikang. These are the stories which account for the ancestry of the present class of 'Reth's people', now treated as a single hereditary client lineage.

*

Of the two stories that there are to tell about the eastern Anuak, we must begin with the one that explains how the contest to hold the sacred emblems has gradually spread to take in more and more villages. This turns on the fact that a man who sought to hold them had to have supporters. In the early period these were men who were willing to fight for him; later they only needed to be willing to raise the payment for him to be invested. These contests were different in a significant way from the contests for the headmanship of a village. Rivals for the position of headman were competing for the support of the same body of people, the inhabitants of the village. The villagers were choosing between two personalities, according to which they expected to get most from. In the contest for the emblems it was the emblems themselves that mattered. There was no issue to divide the village of the holder; all were united in valuing the prestige that came to their village through having the emblem-holder there. So a new claimant could not hope for any support in the holder's village; he had to seek it elsewhere, and he sought it in the village from which his mother came or in some village where a number of her agnates lived. Since a claimant had to be the son of a previous holder, all the claimants had the same agnatic kin, and full brothers also had the same maternal kin. But if two half brothers wished to contend for the emblems they could find different maternal kin to support them. They built up this support by going to live as guests in villages where a body of these kinsmen formed the dominant lineage. In the days of armed contest, the emblems were seized and taken back to the village from which the contender had come, and there the necklace was formally put over his head by the headman, his maternal kinsman. Later, when men gained noble rank by being invested with the emblems without actually taking possession of them, an aspirant to this honour was accompanied to the king's village by the maternal kinsmen who supported his candidature, and there formally invested by the senior of these kinsmen.

In the era when it was no longer necessary to kill the holder in order to be invested with the emblems, the number of persons entitled to investiture constantly increased. Former holders who had lost them continued to maintain the state in their own villages to which their possession of the emblems had entitled them, so that there was now a clan of nobles, who attained this rank by holding the emblems and retained it when the emblems had passed to

distributing guns that nobles succeeded in wresting the
leadership of villages from their maternal kinsmen. It appears to have been understood that in return the people so
armed would pay tribute in ivory and valuable skins, as well
as sending a share of all the game they killed to the noble's
household.

Here we can certainly see the prototype of the state system
of government, in which a number of territorial subordinates act as agents of a superior ruler and collect tribute on
his behalf.

*

Our last case, the Alur of western Uganda, illustrates ways
in which government by chiefs can be extended without
any act of conquest. The Alur are a people of Nilotic origin
who settled in the highlands west of Lake Albert some ten
generations ago. As far back as we know anything of their
traditions they recognized hereditary chief , and since they
arrived in their present homeland members of chiefly
lineages have extended their authority over the neighbouring Bantu peoples, the Lendu and Okebu, who had no chiefs
of their own. What happened was not the expansion of a
single Alur kingdom by the absorption of foreign peoples,
but the spread of a ruling clan, members of which have
often made themselves independent of the political unit
from which they originated. This process was still going on
at the time of the establishment of colonial rule, British and
Belgian, over Alur territory, and there are, or were until
quite recently, men still living who had been sent by their
fathers, reigning Alur chiefs, to govern new territories.

The total population of the country now under Alur
chiefs is about 200,000. It has been divided by the British
and Belgian authorities into twenty-one chiefdoms, but
there are thirty-six groups which were traditionally subject
to separate chiefly lineages. The present population of these
groups varies from 500 to 60,000.

One can see a comparison with the spread of the Anuak

noble clan, in that the prestige which the mere fact of having a chief is held to confer upon his subjects is like the prestige which an Anuak village derives from having a noble living in it. But Alur chiefs had ritual and political functions which Anuak nobles did not, and the value of these functions was explicitly recognized by the chiefless peoples. It is worth noting that these peoples did not regard Alur political institutions as something to be *imitated*. Rather, they saw chiefliness as a quality possessed by the Alur chiefly lineages. Indeed there was a word for this quality (*ker*); it could be possessed by different individuals in greater or lesser degree, but it could not be possessed at all by one who was not the son of a chief. Here we see the link between the hereditary principle and the sacred or mystical aspect of chiefship, though there is no belief here that a chief incarnates a divine ancestor. For the Alur and their neighbours, the mystical power which comes to chiefs from their ancestors is that of controlling the rain.

The secular function of Alur chiefs was the maintenance of order by the settlement of disputes which had led to fighting. Populations which did not have chiefs, or were some distance from the court of the chief who claimed authority over them, would go to a ruling chief and ask him to give them one of his sons to rule over them. The legends that are told describe these petitioners as having kidnapped a chief's son and carried him home bodily. There is no doubt about their having wished to obtain chiefs; sections of their subjects vie in claiming for their ancestors the honour of having 'bought the chief'. No doubt some of a new chief's new subjects had not wanted to accept this new authority; in that case they moved out of reach of it.

Sometimes the chief who was selected by his father for this position was one who was in disgrace or in disfavour at court, and the opportunity of what might be called a distant posting provided a convenient means of removing him; sometimes he had actually fled from his father's court, and on his wanderings he came to people who asked him to settle among them and be their chief. When he was first installed he was still subordinate to his father; he passed on to his father a share of the tribute which he received, and when it was time for the rain ceremonies he would go to his father to ask for rain. The ways of asserting independence were to neglect to pay tribute and to perform one's own rain ceremonies.

As long as any chief recognized the superiority of another, it was open to his subjects, if they were dissatisfied with him, to go to the superior chief and ask for another of his sons instead. Ten years ago, when Southall was working among the Alur, many old men told him of such incidents in their own or their fathers' lifetime. Here is one such story. The chief Nziri was asked to send one of his sons to a Lendu clan who said their people 'were scattering because of all the fighting'. Nziri said to his son Amatho, 'You go and break that land, you guard the subjects there.' Amatho went off with three followers, and later his father sent some more men to join him. Then Nziri died and was succeeded by an elder brother of Amatho. Some of Amatho's subjects went to the new chief to complain that Amatho was taking their cattle from him, and he gave another, younger brother to this disaffected section. He did not take any action directly against Amatho, but presently other subjects of Amatho transferred their allegiance to his younger brother. Later, Amatho with his followers raided and despoiled a section of his subjects who had offended him, and they too went to his elder brother and complained. Thus three sons of Nziri were planted out side by side. The populations over which they ruled must have been tiny. Eighty years or so afterwards they totalled 6,000.

*

We can see certain common features in these examples. One is the importance of a lineage which has secured, as a group, recognition by the population in general of its privileged status. Once the privileged status is accepted, lineages of high rank grow at a great rate in a polygamous society, where they can secure many wives and hence many children. This makes it possible for them to expand the area over which they claim superiority, and indeed also makes this necessary for men who have ambitions but cannot hope to succeed their own fathers.

But members of ruling lineages compete among themselves and so must seek support elsewhere than among their own kin. This may come from any of their own subjects, but an important element in it is formed by the 'stranger', refugee clients, people detached from the societies where their kinsmen would help them to stand up for their rights and so wholly dependent upon their lord's protection.

The Alur and Anuak illustrate a fluid situation, in which people who are dissatisfied with a ruler can transfer their allegiance. All these characteristics will be found in the larger political units in this region which are governed as states.

PART TWO

African States

CHAPTER 5

The Immigrant Rulers

THE other peoples of this region all have governments that can be readily identified as states. These differ greatly in extent and population, but all have the characteristics which entitle them to this description. Each has a chief or king who is recognized by all the population as supreme among them. Other men exercise authority in the name of the chief or king over divisions of the country. Every person is subject to some superior authority, and those in authority are able to punish disobedience against themselves, they try cases in dispute between persons subject to them, they collect taxes, and they organize public activities, of which the most conspicuous is warfare.

In the last chapter we noted some instances of populations among whom government was extended by other means than conquest and subjugation. These cases prove that armed conquest is not the only means by which one set of people can extend their authority over another, and they may suggest that it was not in fact the first step towards the development of the kind of government that we call the state. One might draw from them the conclusion that where no government of state type exists, such a government will not appear unless some set of people who regard themselves as forming a distinct group have an interest *of some kind* in establishing and maintaining superiority over others among whom they are living. In the case of the Gusii the Nyakundi clan formed such a group, as did the land-owning lineage in each of the tiny Mandari chiefdoms. Among the Anuak it was the nobles. Among the Alur, the chiefly lineages who were already pre-eminent in the Alur population sent out sons to rule as chiefs over neighbouring peoples, and these chiefs did not go alone, but with bands of retainers who became the founders of a ruling class. This could possibly be called colonization without conquest.

We need not, then, assume that whenever a state form of government exists, it must have been imposed after a war of conquest. The examples of the expansion of government that have been quoted all show how one group of people who are united by common descent have established some kind of superiority over others who do not belong to their group. One of these descent groups, the Nyakundi clan of the Gusii, did not expand territorially; they simply established domination over members of other clans living among them. The Anuak nobles and the Alur chiefs were continually extending the area within which their claims to superiority were recognized. There is no record of an increase in the power of Mandari chiefs, simply of an increase in the numbers of their subjects.

Now that we have these clues, it is perhaps easier to picture this process going on elsewhere than it is to conjecture just how a ruling class would come to the top *after* an armed conquest to meet the situation which the conquest had created.

When we come to consider the Interlacustrine Bantu states, we are confronted with peoples at a stage in the development of government when this hypothetical process, if it did take place at some time in their history, is irretrievably lost in the past. They were established long before literate travellers began to come to their country and record what they saw there, and we can do no more than conjecture how they came into being. In several of these states the population is divided into a cattle-owning people who are regarded as the aristocracy and an agricultural people who are often described as serfs, and these divisions are known by different names (the aristocracy are called Hima, Huma, or Tusi, the lower class Iru or Hutu). The picture of past history that the writers of thirty years ago took for granted was a picture of a sort of Norman conquest in which, at a given moment, the armies of the pastoralists invaded a territory and established an organization for governing it. The trouble about seeing the history of the Interlacustrine Bantu like this is that the counterparts of William the Conqueror seem to have arrived some time after the main body of the invaders. Some writers – though not many – suggest that the armies came from one direction and the rulers from another.

The question that has attracted the attention of most scholars is who the conquerors were. This is not really of great significance to a student of government, who would rather know, if he was able to find out, how they established their control and built up the organization that confronted Arab and European travellers in the nineteenth century. But conjectures about the origin of the rulers and the dominant classes may lead to conjectures about the way in which they came to be where and what they are.

These conjectures are not pure guesses. They rest on two kinds of evidence – that of language and that of traditional history. Of these, the evidence of language is the more conclusive. People may fake their history, consciously or unconsciously, but they cannot do much about their language. When many people who are politically distinct and geographically divided are found to speak languages with a great deal in common, it is certain that they have a common past of some kind.

By itself the similarity of language does not tell us much about what the common past may have been. The languages of France, Spain, and Italy have much in common because all these countries were part of the Roman Empire and learnt writing from the Romans. The English-speaking nations of today, and a number of others who use English as an official language, were all at one time or another governed from London. But obviously it is not this kind of reason that explains why peoples speaking Nilotic languages are to be found far apart in East Africa – the Alur in the extreme west of Uganda, the Luo on the eastern shores of Lake Victoria, and even possibly the Barabaig in northern Tanganyika, a long way from the great lake.

The only plausible explanation is that at some time their ancestors must have migrated from the country where Nilotic-speaking peoples form a solid block. But where they started, how they came – if we want to answer these questions we have to turn to our second source, the legends which the different peoples tell of their past. And there are some difficulties about relying on these legends. One is a characteristic which is common to all peoples, literate or not. Every people has a popularly accepted version of its own past, and this is always a flattering one. Where there are written records to check the story against, it often turns out that the truth is very different from what is popularly imagined. On the other hand, the popular version is not wholly imaginary; it is, as they say, founded in fact. The problem in handling oral tradition is to decide what one can safely take as the factual basis.

The second difficulty arises from the way in which non-literate peoples use their legends, what these legends mean to them. Such peoples do not usually think of their social order as the result of an unfolding sequence of events. They think of it as fixed and immemorial, and their legends, like the Genesis story of the creation, are assertions that it came into existence by divine authority and so should continue as it is. They may enshrine memories of past events, but the memory, if it is there, may have become submerged in the meaning of the story as a justification for what exists in the present. Some stories lead to conclusions like that of the one told among the Nuer which ends, 'And that is why we have always lived by war.'

This has been well shown by a study of the myths of the Shilluk, and the Shilluk are not as remote from the present topic as might be thought, for one interpretation of traditional history would include them among the ancestors of the contemporary rulers of the Interlacustrine Bantu. For the Shilluk, history begins with a time when all people were together; then the neighbouring peoples split off from the Shilluk and went away to their own countries, following leaders who were kinsmen of the leader of the Shilluk. Does this enable us to plot the course of migration of the Nilotic peoples, or does it just give the Shilluk a picture of the world that accounts for the existence of other peoples like themselves but politically distinct? Other peoples have similar tales of their relations with their neighbours, and out of them one scholar, Father Crazzolara,* has constructed a complete history of the migration of a single people, whom he calls the Lwoo, all the way from a homeland in Nuer country through that of the Shilluk and Anuak and then south into what is now Uganda.

An example of a particular Shilluk tale which can be interpreted either as cosmology or as history is the story of the Shilluk hero Nyikang, who fought the sun-god at the crossing of a river. Father Crazzolara locates this event in the chronology of the wanderings of the Lwoo. The anthropologist Lienhardt† notes that in the dry season, when the sun is at its hottest, the Shilluk herdsmen have to take their cattle across the Nile to find grazing, and that this is a hazardous business because there are crocodiles in the river. Nyikang, they recall, brought his followers safely across, and Nyikang defeats the sun-god in the end by bringing the rain.

The peoples of western Uganda – Nyoro, Toro, and Nkole – preserve a legend of a wonderful dynasty of kings called the Chwezi, supermen to whom they owe all the useful arts, including that of government. The stories usually say that when the Chwezi arrived, they found the country inhabited by savages who ate their food raw, and even sometimes had no meat except the fish from the rivers. These wonderful people are also said to have been lighter-skinned than the populations they conquered. They are said to have given their countries two or three generations of rulers and then miraculously disappeared. There are various versions of this event. One is that they deliberately plunged

* *The Lwoo, Part I*, 'Lwoo Migrations' (1950).
† 'The Shilluk of the Upper Nile' in *African Worlds*, ed. D. Forde, (1954).

into Lake Albert. But whatever tale is told of their dis-appearance, the sequel is always either that *one* was left behind or that one had begotten a son who appeared in due course to claim the throne, and founded the dynasty which has continued to this day.

One can see how well this story would be received when it was sung or recited by the court minstrels. One can even think of parallels to it in the popular history of later rulers of Africa.

The generally accepted view that the aristocratic classes and the ruling dynasties came from the north does seem to be supported by the many traditions to that effect, since there is nothing about having come from the north that is particularly flattering to anyone's vanity. Indeed the really gratifying thing is to have been 'always there', and to be able to say that your remotest ancestors dropped from heaven into the country in which they now are. This is the belief of the Ruanda rulers, and also of those of some very small states in Busoga, to the east of the Nile.

The story of the miraculous Chwezi is told among the Nyoro, Toro, and Nkole. But the rulers of many more have a tradition of common descent from the hero who followed the Chwezi. He is said to have been the ancestor of a group of clans called the Bito, which has for its totem or emblem the bushbuck. Rulers who either still call themselves Bito or claim to be descended from Bito are found today in Busoga, Toro, Nkole, and Bunyoro in Uganda; and in Tanganyika among the Haya and Zinza in Bukoba District on the southern shore of Lake Tanganyika. The kings of Ruanda preserve no such tradition, but say that their first ancestor fell from heaven into the country that they now rule. All scholars agree that they too are descended from northern migrant pastoralists, but some believe that their ancestors may have belonged to a distinct wave of migrants.

Whoever the miraculous Chwezi may have been, it seems pretty certain that the Bito were Nilotes, and we can get some idea of the nature of their migrations from Evans-

Pritchard's account of the Nuer methods in their warfare with the Dinka. In the early part of the nineteenth century, sections of the Nuer were seeking new grazing grounds for their cattle. They may have been pushed from behind by other Nuer, since it is recorded that tribes would fight for grazing grounds and the winner would drive out the loser. At some point in their expansion they came in contact with Dinka tribes. Sometimes they drove these tribes out of their grazing grounds, but sometimes they just captured their cattle; and the method of campaign was the same in either case. The Nuer warriors invaded the Dinka country, captured a cattle kraal, and used it as a base for attacks on any herds within reach. They usually stayed there several weeks, but sometimes for the whole of a dry season. But sometimes they did not go home at all. Their perpetual raids compelled the Dinka to keep their cattle out of reach. Thus in the course of time, almost imperceptibly, what was once Dinka country became Nuer country.

It is an open question whether the southward migration of the Lwoo followed this kind of plan or was more like the conquering marches of the Ngoni army. Perhaps it had both characters at different times. But whatever was the actual course of events, it is clear that some Lwoo settled down in countries from which they could not drive out the people they found there. And these countries are the present Interlacustrine Bantu states.

*

We cannot tell how the rulers of these states established political authority, a position where they could issue orders and be confident that they would be obeyed. But if we look at the records of the last century in Uganda we can see many interesting differences in the organization of these states – differences in the size of territory which recognized a single ruler and in the effectiveness of this person's rule. The records I refer to are those of explorers such as Speke, who discovered the source of the Nile; of soldiers such as Lugard;

and of anthropologists who have lived among the various peoples and been able to analyse the differences in political organization which can still be seen today.

The traditions of common descent which link the rulers of the Interlacustrine Bantu states within Uganda may be their peoples' way of projecting into the past the struggles for power that were being fought out in the nineteenth century. Persons who are linked by common descent are expected to recognize one of their number as senior; refusing to recognize the common head is one way in which a section of a clan can split off from the rest and establish itself as a new clan. In the political field the claim to seniority may be expressed in a claim to some kind of overlordship, and it seems to be well established that the recent history of the Bito rulers is full on the one hand of rulers seeking to extend their authority by planting out clansmen on their borders, and on the other of princes rejecting superior authority when they were far enough away from the centre of power to be able to disregard it.

All the peoples whose rulers claim to belong to the Bito clan, and not to an off-shoot with another name, seem at one time to have been linked with Bunyoro, and the Nyoro themselves believe that their country was once the centre of a great empire stretching eastwards as far as the inland part of Busoga. It seems unlikely that the distant parts of this empire were in any serious sense 'governed' from Bunyoro, but it is more possible that the rulers of these outlying areas were expected to pay tribute to the Nyoro kings. Since they claim to be of the same clan as the kings of Bunyoro, it is possible that their ancestors were princes sent out by their fathers to rule new lands, spreading ever further and further until the furthest off were out of reach of any control from the ultimate source of their authority. This would be the same story, on a larger scale, that we have already followed among the Alur.

Moreover, there is at any rate one historic instance of such a breakaway in the founding in the nineteenth century of the kingdom of Toro by secession from Bunyoro; Toro was not a distant colony but actually part of Bunyoro. South-west of Lake Victoria there are kingdoms which claim to have been founded by a single hero of the past, a descendant of the Bito who has been given another family name, Hinda. At the time just before Speke passed through this country one of these, Karagwe, had held sway over a wide area, which has been estimated to be comparable with that of Bunyoro (but we do not know how wide the sway of Bunyoro really was). Today Karagwe is one subdivision of an admin-istrative district, whereas Bunyoro, even shorn as it is of possessions which it held as late as 1862, is still one of four districts in a province.

Although Nyoro traditions tell how their first Bito king allotted Buganda to one of his sons, the Ganda kings do not claim to be Bito, nor do the Ganda cherish tales of the Chwezi. Is this because the Ganda were the nineteenth-century rivals of the Nyoro, and at the time when British occupation froze their boundaries (to the considerable ad-vantage of Buganda) were on the way to attaining domin-ance in the area of the great lakes? Before they came under colonial rule they had developed an organization of govern-ment more complex than that of any of their neighbours, and their Kabaka had more subjects under his direct con-trol that had any of his neighbour kings. Even if the Ganda population did not reach the three million with which they were credited fifty years ago, they were twice as many as the Nkole, the next most populous kingdom (and it is doubtful whether what is now Ankole was ever in fact organized under one man's effective rule). The Kabaka indubitably did send his emissaries to collect tribute from neighbouring countries, and doubtless punished those who refused by attacking them with his armies. Some twenty years ago an old Ganda chief, the famous Ham Mukasa, told me how as a young man he crossed Lake Victoria by canoe to collect the tribute due from the Zinza of the southern shore – and of his dismay at finding a German official in control. At the time when Lugard arrived in Uganda, it was the Ganda who were collecting tribute from the Soga rulers.

What we see, then, around the shores of Lake Victoria, is a multitude of political units, some expanding at the expense of their neighbours, others asserting autonomy by the refusal of tribute or retaining internal autonomy at the cost of paying tribute. There are three peoples who at the time of European occupation were still divided into a number of autonomous units – the Haya, the Zinza, and the Soga. A rough idea of the relative size of these units is given from the fact that the contemporary populations of the areas which they covered varies from 4,000 to 50,000.

*

In a number of these kingdoms there was a recognized division into a ruling and a subject class. Of course, everywhere those persons who have the right to give orders can be seen as a class in opposition to those who just have to obey. But what is meant here is that one whole section of the population – the section believed to be descended from the immigrant cattle people – is regarded as superior to the rest, the descendants of the cultivators. The line is drawn more rigidly in some places than in others, and in some of the Interlacustrine Bantu states no line is drawn at all.

This kind of organization of a society is sometimes called a caste structure. The word caste comes from India, where it describes the divisions recognized in Hindu society. Every Hindu is born a member of a caste, to which a particular occupation is appropriate. The priests form the highest caste, then come the soldiers, and then a great number of castes each specializing in a different activity – brewers, barbers, and so on. Members of different castes do not intermarry. The castes are ranked in order, and members of higher castes are held to be polluted, in a ritual sense, by contact with members of lower ones. Most students of India think the Indian caste system is so peculiar that the word should not be used to describe any social system in other parts of the world.

But some students of Africa think the essentials of the caste system are found among the Interlacustrine Bantu. The divisions among these peoples are nothing like as complicated as those found in India; usually there are only two, or at most three. The elaborate ideas about ritual pollution that are characteristic of India are not found in Africa.

But a strong case is made by Maquet* in his description of the kingdom of Ruanda in the Belgian Trust Territory for treating this as a caste system. The three levels of Ruanda society are formed by the pastoral Tusi, the agricultural Hutu, and the Twa, a people of pygmy type who live by hunting and also by making pots. Theoretically, members of these three divisions do not intermarry, but there are exceptions. Thus, they are not 'racial' divisions which depend on biological stock, and although each is supposed to have a characteristic physical type, a person's allocation to the appropriate division does not depend upon his appearance but on his line of descent. It was possible, though this did not often happen, for a Hutu to marry a Tusi woman with the approval of her family; in such a case their children could be, as it were, grafted on a Tusi line.

Each of the three divisions has its characteristic activities. The Tusi are cattle-owners and warriors. More significant, perhaps, they despise agriculture and will not practise it; their women have more leisure than any others in Africa. Practically all positions of authority in the traditional system were held by Tusi. The Hutu are the cultivators, but they often herd cattle for Tusi owners and are sometimes able to acquire small herds of their own; this blurring of the line of division based on occupation is perhaps contrary to the principles of a strict caste system. The Twa pygmies, in addition to being the only potters, are sometimes employed to amuse their Tusi superiors by singing, dancing, and clowning.

* *Le Système des relations sociales dans le Ruanda ancien* (1954).

Maquet argues that in the days when the kingdom was independent not only chiefs but *all* Tusi were able to exercise power over *all* Hutu and Twa, and that Hutu and Twa had to behave towards *all* Tusi as their superiors. But he does not show that a similar relationship of superiority and inferiority exists between Hutu and Twa, as it would if this system conformed to the Indian model of a caste structure. In fact the Twa lived in the forests isolated from the Hutu so that rules regulating relationship between them were not necessary.

The Nkole came closest to the Ruanda in the strictness of their division between the pastoral aristocracy (Hima) and the agricultural commoners (Iru). In Bunyoro the aristocracy (there called Huma) as a body are of less political significance than the large Bito clan to which the ruler belongs. The same is true of Toro, which was once part of Bunyoro. According to figures collected in Toro, six per cent of the population were members of the Bito clan and a further five per cent were Hima. The Rundi, the southern neighbours of the Ruanda, recognize a division of the pastoralists into Tusi and Hima, the latter forming a lower class. Similarly in the small Tanganyika kingdoms of the Haya and Zinza, pastoralists ranked higher than cultivators and the royal clan had the highest status. But it is important to remember that a clan *cannot* be a caste, since people who belong to the same clan must take their wives from outside the clan. Therefore, if we are to use the analogy with a caste system, we must say that Bito and Huma (or Hima) *together* constituted the higher caste among these peoples. Among the Zinza, however, those Huma who did not belong to the royal dynasty were not treated with especial respect by the Iru, and indeed were sometimes employed by them as herdsmen. But Huma would not allow their women to marry Iru men. In Buha political authority is exercised by Tusi, who will not intermarry with the rest of the population, but Tusi do not follow a distinctive way of life; everyone in Buha is both a cultivator and a cattle owner. In Buganda and in

Busoga there is no division of the population into sections claiming different descent.

This summary may appear confusing, but it is given here as a preliminary to discussion of the way in which these states, large and small, are actually governed. The term 'caste' will not in fact be used in this discussion. It will be clear from this short summary that there are great differences in the rigidity with which divisions are maintained among the different peoples, and that among some there is little distinction except that the section which thinks itself superior will not allow its women to take husbands from the other. This is characteristic of the people in any society who consider themselves to belong to a high class, and it hardly seems enough to constitute a caste system. Even in Ruanda, where the analogy has been pursued furthest, we find a significant contrast with the Indian caste system in that people who do not belong to the hereditary pastoral section of the community can both herd and own cattle.

A list of the divisions among the different peoples may be useful for reference:

Ha	Tusi, Ha
Haya	Huma, Iru
Nkole	Huma, Iru
Nyoro	Bito, Huma, Iru
Toro	Bito, Hima, Iru
Ruanda	Tusi, Hutu, Twa
Rundi	Tusi, Hima, Hutu, Twa
Zinza	Huma, Iru

CHAPTER 6

The Personnel and Functions of Government

IN the kind of government that we call the state a single supreme authority is recognized, and public affairs are regulated, decisions taken, and obedience claimed by persons acting in his name (or its name in some modern states). This is true of all the Interlacustrine Bantu peoples. Among each of these the supreme authority is a person who can appropriately be called a king, though some of them are very petty kings. In a tiny kingdom with a few thousand subjects the ruler obviously needs fewer subordinate officials than does his neighbour who has hundreds of thousands of subjects (or even millions if early estimates of the Ganda population are to be believed). It certainly seems to be true that as a state extends the area it controls it is obliged to develop a more complex organization of government, even though the germ of the organization can be recognized in places where there is no history of conquest to account for it.

If we were to try to put in a single sentence the essence of the state system, we might say that it consists in the delegation of power by the ruler who holds final authority, in such a way that he can expect his orders or decisions to be carried out throughout the land which he claims to rule. The effectiveness of such a system in securing obedience to the ruler may of course differ greatly in different cases. The important question is not how much obedience the ruler claims, but how much he actually secures. *1066 and All That* reminded us how school histories label kings as Strong and Weak. A good deal of more sophisticated discussion is carried on as if power was simply a matter of the personal character of rulers, or as if it was the same thing to claim absolute authority and actually to be able to make a whole population obey commands. Of course the extent to which an individual ruler wishes to make his authority effective is an important factor in the situation, but it is by no means the only one.

The impression that Speke derived from his stay in the Ganda capital was that its ruler was almost omnipotent. Certainly the Ganda in the nineteenth century had the most efficient organization of government of any people in this region, and the ostensible purpose of this government was to carry out the wishes of the Kabaka, as their king was called. But before we take it for granted that this means he actually held the fate of all his million or so subjects in his own hands, we might consider a comment that is of general application, though it was made with reference to the Ganda's neighbours in Bunyoro. This comment, by John Beattie, the anthropologist who has most recently worked among the Nyoro, is:

A ruler — at least in the conditions of a tribal African kingdom — cannot keep all his power to himself, but must give some of it away; this is one of the major limitations on political authority.*

Personally, I would even dispense with Beattie's qualification and say there is no such thing anywhere as absolute rule by a monarch. The nearest approach to it is the monopoly by the monarch and a small number of his associates of the right to make decisions in matters of public concern. Ostensibly and formally the monarch may always get his way, but yet the decisions may be very different from what he would have wished to do — if, for example, his associates have let him see that they will not (they more probably say 'cannot') put his wishes into effect. Then comes the further question whether the generality of subjects can be made to do whatever the monarch wishes. The answer, as we have seen even among the most totalitarian of modern states, is no. If one asks whether the Kabaka of Buganda was feared, that is another question, and the answer is yes. But this does not make a man omnipotent; it simply secures the subservience of those who are near enough to him to be within

* *Bunyoro, an African Kingdom* (1960), p. 28.

reach of his anger and of the punishments that he can inflict.

*

If the facts were available, it would be interesting to try to place the governments of the Interlacustrine Bantu states in an ascending order of complexity and show just where and how an increase in the scale of operations – that is the area and population to be treated as a political unit – had led to a new division of authority or some particular administrative device. Unfortunately the information that is recorded is very patchy. It all consists in what old men have said they remember about the past, since it did not begin to be collected until European rule had made great changes, and the people who made the records were not all equally interested in the problems of government. Where the most illuminating questions have not yet been asked, it is already too late to ask them.

We can say, however, that all these states, great and small, had certain features in common. The ruler had his palace, which in the smaller kingdoms was a homestead of the same type as ordinary men's, but better built and much larger, to accommodate his numerous wives and servants. He was surrounded with etiquette and ritual, more or less elaborate, which emphasized the uniqueness of his position and the difference between him and all his subjects. Special acts in this ritual, or the custody of objects used in it, were the responsibility of hereditary officials. The kings of Ruanda and Ankole, who kept to the purely pastoral way of life longer than any of their neighbours, were constantly moving about with their cattle and their followers, and the early kings of Bunyoro are also said to have done so.

From among the followers at his court, the ruler chose persons to administer different parts of his country. At the head both of these and of the court officials was almost always a 'prime minister'; only in the accounts of the little Zinza kingdoms is such an official not mentioned.

The functions of the territorial chiefs were in general the same. They were responsible for the organization of manpower for war and for public works, for the collection of tribute, and for keeping the peace within the areas under their control; to this end they held courts and settled disputes. In most of the kingdoms important chiefs were placed on the frontiers and made responsible for their defence. All chiefs were expected to call their men to arms, but only those who were particularly trusted were allowed to maintain standing armies. The labour that they were required to organize was called upon for the upkeep of the royal palace; in Buganda they were expected to build and maintain an elaborate network of roads, and in Ruanda the herding of the royal cattle was provided for in this way.

The most conspicuous difference between the small and the large states lay in the balance of power between the ruler and his lieutenants, expressed in the degree of their dependence on him for the offices which they held. In the smaller kingdoms the territorial chiefs were sometimes able to establish the claim that their sons should succeed them in office, and sometimes to extend the area under their control by fighting their neighbour barons. In the little Ha kingdoms a territorial chief, once appointed, remained responsible for the same area all his life and so had good grounds for claiming it as a family possession. Elsewhere the kings transferred their chiefs from one part of the country to another.

The prime minister, who in the smaller states was little more than the major-domo of the palace and close bodyguard of the king, was a more important person the larger the kingdom and the more complex the government. In Buganda and Busoga this official had the title of Katikiro, and under the British Protectorate the title has come to be widely used among other peoples, since in the early days the British appointed Ganda chiefs to administer other parts of Uganda which had not developed state systems of government for themselves. The position of the Katikiro has been described as it was in the small Soga kingdoms, in Ankole and in Buganda, and by comparing these descriptions we can see how the functions of government expand as the size of the state increases.

The Katikiro of a Soga kingdom* was essentially a palace official. He was in authority over the multitude of servants that are necessary to keep up the dignity of even a small court in a society with no labour-saving devices – cooks, slaughterers of cattle, brewers of beer, hewers of wood and drawers of water, these last being literal descriptions of offices and not mere metaphors for unskilled labour (when I lived in a Ganda village in 1931 I employed a 'wood and water man'). He also, and this was politically more important, controlled access to the presence of the king. It is an essential part of the dignity of a monarch that he should be in some way set apart from the people among whom he occupies a unique position, and in most monarchies one way of doing this is to make it difficult for ordinary people to approach him. In the Soga kingdoms, as in the larger ones, those who wished for an audience had first to see the Katikiro and state their business. Further, the monarch's person must be guarded from the risk of attack by rival claimants to his throne, and it was the Katikiro's business to prevent this. Visitors to the court might have many kinds of business – to offer a gift, to solicit a favour, to report some strange happening in their part of the country. The Katikiro learnt it all, and so had his finger on everything that was going on. He was probably not expected to exclude anyone whose business was legitimate, but he could always keep people waiting, and perhaps make them wait so long that they finally went away. So, although the king was 'the fountain of honours' (as we say of our own sovereign), the ultimate source of justice, the 'owner' of land and people; although he at will could raise up his subjects and cast them down, make them rich by his gifts or despoil them of their possessions; it rested largely with the Katikiro to determine

* L. A. Fallers, *Bantu Bureaucracy* (1956).

who should have the opportunity of attracting the royal notice. In the little Soga kingdoms this did not amount to very much; in Buganda it made the Katikiro a very important person indeed.

The word Katikiro is used in several of the Interlacustrine Bantu languages; in Zinza it is used of territorial chiefs. As far as I am aware, it does not have any connotations that would suggest what kind of qualities people associated with the holder of this office. But Oberg recorded* among the Nkole a great number of descriptions that are supposed to characterize the corresponding official there. He has the title 'Nganzi', which means the 'beloved' or 'favoured one', and his function as the king's chief counsellor is indicated by the metaphor which describes king and minister as 'power and wisdom'. A similar name is given to his counterpart in Ruanda. Maquet remarks of the Ruanda 'favourite chief' that he acts as a sort of lightning-conductor for dissatisfaction with the acts and decisions of the king. It would be generally true of many societies that kings are expected to epitomize the qualities that their subjects admire, justice in particular. If hereditary rule is believed to be part of a divinely appointed order of things, people must be able on occasion to reconcile this principle with their discontent at particular actions of particular kings. One way of doing so is to argue that the king, who 'can do no wrong', has been badly advised by a counsellor to whom none of the divine aura of royalty attaches, and this way is taken in very many African states.

The Ruanda chief minister is not described by Maquet as having any specific administrative functions. Of the Nkole Nganzi we read that he advised the king on the appointment of army leaders, he decided how the booty (particularly cattle) that was captured in war should be distributed, and he was responsible for organizing the collection of tribute.

* 'The Kingdom of Ankole in Uganda' in *African Political Systems* (1940).

Such titles as 'the favoured one' emphasize a special feature of the relationship between king and prime minister, at any rate in Buganda and Ankole. A king chose his own prime minister as soon as he was established on the throne. The prime minister could not be a member of the royal clan; otherwise the choice was free. In making it the king was supposed to consult his mother and his sisters, persons whose position in the Interlacustrine Bantu states must be considered later; but nobody outside his small family council had any say. That there should be a prime minister in office was almost as important for these states as it was that there should be a king, for when a king died it was the duty of the prime minister to install his successor on the throne. In none of these kingdoms was there an automatic rule of succession such as makes possible in the United Kingdom the traditional proclamation 'The king is dead, long live the king.' The new king had to be chosen from a number of sons who had an equal claim, and sometimes the issue was decided by fighting.

In Ankole the prime minister seems to have been responsible only for the formal installation of the new king after he had fought out the issue with his brothers. But in Buganda he had, with one or two other important chiefs, a considerable say in the choice of the successor. He was expected to be with the Kabaka when he died and to hear his last wishes, but he did not necessarily follow them.

A very detailed account of the duties of the Katikiro and the organization of the court was taken down by the missionary John Roscoe* from the recollections of old men who had lived under the last independent Ganda kings. Chief among these was Sir Apolo Kagwa, who was himself Katikiro to Kabaka Mwanga, and, when Mwanga was exiled after rebelling against the British, was appointed one of three regents to rule Buganda on behalf of Mwanga's infant son; hence his attainment of a British knighthood.

* *The Baganda* (1911).

He may, of course, have exaggerated the importance of his position at some points.

The first writer to describe the Ganda capital, however, was Speke, the explorer, on whom it made a great impression when he arrived there in 1862. 'The palace surprised me', he wrote, 'by its extraordinary dimensions and the neatness with which it was kept. The whole brow and sides of a hill were covered with gigantic grass huts thatched as neatly as so many heads dressed by a London barber and fenced all round with tall yellow reeds.'* These large dwellings – called huts only because the walls were made of reeds and the roofs of grass instead of the walls being of brick and the roofs of tile – housed the king, his many wives and servants, and his courtiers. Each ruler built a new capital on a different one of the innumerable small hills near Lake Victoria, but the pattern was always the same. The royal palace was in an oval enclosure on the top of the hill facing away from the lake. It could only be approached from in front; behind it were the banana plantations of the king's wives. Along the broad road which led up to it were disposed the houses of the most important chiefs, the highest in rank being nearest to the palace enclosure. Each separate household consisted in fact of a complex of dwellings enclosed by one of the reed fences which so delighted the eyes of Speke, as they have those of many others who have seen them since his day.

In front of the royal palace was an open space on which stood shrines, one containing the king's umbilical cord and a number of magical objects which were supposed to protect his health and good fortune. Here also there stood a sacred fire which was always kept burning. Immediately on the other side of this open space was the residence of the Katikiro, which, though it was much smaller than the royal palace, was much bigger than anyone else's. This siting clearly symbolizes his precedence over all other subjects.

* *Journal of the Discovery of the Source of the Nile* (1864).

The Ganda Katikiro was very definitely an administrative official; he took the lead in the organization of public works and the collection of taxes and also in the planning of wars. When a war was going on it was his duty to protect the Kabaka, whose safety was far too important to the country for him to go to war himself. The Katikiro also had judicial duties; he tried cases in a court-house which stood in the open space between his residence and the palace. Sometimes he left these to one of his followers, and simply decided what the sentence should be after this man had given him a report. He was expected to inform the Kabaka of the decisions that he had given, but he was not trying cases on behalf of the Kabaka; the latter had a court of his own. The Katikiro was ultimately responsible for the upkeep of the royal palace and also for the roads of access to it, which, like the palace itself, earned the admiration of early travellers, and were certainly unique in Africa before European governments organized the making of roads.

*

These activities were organized through a hierarchy of territorial officials. At the head were the great chiefs. Up to the time when British rule was extended over Buganda, there were ten of these men. Each was responsible for a named district, and had a title indicating what his office was; thus Kago was the chief over the district nearest the capital, Pokino of Buddu, the latest area to be annexed to Buganda. The name given by the Ganda to such a large district was *saza*.* The name is still in use today, since the British administration has used it for the twenty 'counties' into which it has divided Buganda. The administrative heads of these counties are nowadays commonly spoken of as 'saza chiefs', and this English term is the most convenient

* According to the orthography now in use in Buganda, this and many other words should begin with a double consonant. But non-specialist readers will probably prefer a spelling which simply indicates how the word should sound in an English sentence.

way of referring to them in a book that is not intended for specialists.

The ten original saza chiefs were ranked in order of importance, the rank depending on the office – Kago first after the Katikiro, Pokino last. Their houses, along the main street of the capital, were arranged in this order, the Kago's being nearest the Katikiro's. Probably their order of precedence was publicly marked in other ways – for example, in the place where they sat when the Kabaka summoned his chiefs to council, in the order in which they were served at meals, perhaps in the order in which they spoke when they were gathered together in the royal presence.

The striking feature of the Ganda system was that the saza was not a hereditary fief. The saza chiefs did not hold office because at some time in the past a Kabaka had conferred the same office on an ancestor, but because each had been appointed to it in his own lifetime. A man whose father had been a chief – particularly the son of an important chief – had a good expectation of getting an appointment of some kind, but he had no claim to the position which his father had held. We might liken this organization to a civil service with entry and promotion on merit. Merit, of course, was judged by the selectors, who in this case were the Kabaka and Katikiro and the other saza chiefs. As happens with most civil services, there might be different opinions about who was meritorious and where merit was likely to be found. Under British administration the Kabaka retained the right to nominate saza chiefs subject to the Protectorate government's approval, but they came to be chosen for very different qualities.

Nevertheless, the fact remains that the saza chiefs, like their counterparts in the other Interlacustrine kingdoms, were not hereditary barons. A conspicuous difference between Buganda and its neighbours to the west and southwest was the absence of a distinct upper class which claimed a monopoly of political office.

The ten large divisions of Buganda were themselves too

large for a single man to assume responsibility for the administration of each, and within each saza there was an
indefinite number of chiefs of lower grade. Some of these
were directly subordinate to the saza chiefs and exercised
authority delegated to them by him. He chose them from
his own relatives or other supporters, and their fortunes
were closely allied with his: if he fell from grace his successor
would appoint his own subordinates. Others owed their
position directly to the king, who rewarded individual services by the grant of what can be best described as 'fiefs'. A
favoured subject was given authority over an area of land
with the perquisites that went with this, and was expected
to maintain order among the population living there. But
whereas the saza chiefs and their subordinates were first
and foremost administrators who were rewarded for their
work by the tribute and services they took from their territories, these fief-holders were primarily beneficiaries who
incidentally maintained order within their domains. The
relation of both kinds of chief to the general population
was the same, but their position in the political structure
was different.

The territorial chiefs and their subordinates formed a
centralized government service that was unified by their
common allegiance to the king and dependence upon him
for their appointment to authority and their continuance
in it. This government was organized to arrange for the
maintenance of law and order, which was recognized as a
benefit by the people at large, and the allocation of the
resources of the country for public purposes, which directly
benefited the king and chiefs more than it did the rest of
the community.

Every chief, great or small – and some were very small –
held a court to which the persons under his authority were
expected to bring disputes that they could not settle amic-
ably. If commoners took the law into their own hands, they
were liable to be punished, though whether they were
actually punished must have depended on the force that

the chief could command – that is the members of his immediate following. The subordination of one chief to another was expressed in the relationship between their courts. Those who were dissatisfied with a decision by one chief could take a case to his superior.

We noted that those neighbours of the Alur who invited the sons of Alur chiefs to come and live among them explicitly recognized the value of a means of settling disputed claims without fighting. The Ganda did so too. Evidence of this is the kind of story that used to be told to demonstrate that anyone who had the right qualities could rise to the highest office. Such a story begins with a herdboy who finds the solution of a legal puzzle that has baffled the chief and his retainers, and is thereupon commended by his immediately superior chief to a yet higher one, and in the course of time to the Kabaka himself. The kind of knotty case is this: 'A man who was looking after another man's goats tied a goat to the post of a house. In pulling at the rope the goat dislodged a heavy object from the rafters, and it fell on a third man's head and killed him. Who should compensate the dead man's relatives – the owner of the goat, the man who tied it to the post, or whoever stored heavy objects in the rafters where they were liable to fall down?' (Note that there is no question of an accident for which nobody could be held responsible.)

But the duties of the Ganda chiefs were very much more extensive than this. In effect they were responsible for mobilizing the resources of the country for public purposes. The range of these public purposes was defined by custom. People knew what kind of services and contributions would be required of them; we are not told of any Kabaka that he suddenly devised some new activity on which to employ his subjects.

The collection of taxes was organized by messengers sent out from the capital to the headquarters of every saza. Then the saza chief added his own messenger to their company, and together they visited the chiefs of the next grade, and at the headquarters of each in turn awaited the actual collections of the required goods by this man's subordinates.

The other main responsibility of the territorial chiefs was to organize the supply of manpower required for the purposes of the state. These purposes were three – warfare, the maintenance of the capital, and the maintenance of communications. The last of these was peculiar to Buganda. The headquarters of every saza chief was linked to the capital by a road which he was required to keep in good repair, that is free from the grass that grows up everywhere in Buganda. Every chief of lower rank was similarly expected to make and keep open a road from his residence to that of the chief senior to him. For this purpose the chiefs called on the labour of all men under their authority. Some of these roads crossed swamps through which earthen causeways had to be built, with bridges over the deep water channels. Those which led to the capital were much wider than was necessary for people who had no wheeled transport. They certainly enhanced the dignity of the capital, and made a great impression on the first Europeans who saw them. Even the narrower roads were wider than the paths over which people walked in single file in most of the rest of Africa. This system of communication is said to have made it easy to muster the army for war. For the maintenance of the roads within the capital, levies were summoned by the Katikiro, as also for the maintenance of the buildings in the royal palace.

During the reign of Kabaka Mutesa (1854–84) there was created what might be called a corps of army officers; that is to say, chiefs were appointed who had no other duties but those of organizing the army and leading it in time of war. It is possible that they maintained bands of fighting men living near them, particularly on the borders of the kingdom, as we know was done in Ankole and Ruanda.

Buganda, with its long coast line, also had its navy. The chief responsible for it had authority over those islands in Lake Victoria which acknowledged the rule of the Kabaka, and it was his business to muster from among them a fleet of their big canoes, hollowed out of a single tree-trunk, to transport the army to attack the hostile islands. He was also required to provide canoes when important people wanted to travel by water to distant parts of the mainland.

*

We know more about the military organization of Ruanda than we do of any other aspect of its government. This has been reconstructed by the Belgian anthropologist Maquet from the recollections of old men given some forty years after it had ceased to exist.

This organization embraced the whole male population, though only a small number of them were actual fighters. There were a number of named armies, and every man belonged to the army of his father. Thus each army consisted of the men of fighting age of a number of lineages. The military duties of Hutu and Twa consisted merely in carrying food supplies and generally performing menial services for the Tusi.

The latter were divided into a small *élite* minority of fighters and a larger number of herdsmen. A company of about 200 fighters would be formed every few years from the sons of Tusi clients of the king. These companies, like the age-sets in Kenya, consisted of boys of roughly the same age, and they stayed in the same companies all through their fighting life. They did not go through any initiation ceremony, but they lived at the royal court and were taught to use the bow and arrow, sword, stabbing spear and throwing spear, to dance war dances and to recite poems recounting the exploits of earlier warriors. They were also taught to behave with the dignity and self-control which was thought fitting in an aristocrat.

These companies of young men were sent to live in encampments on the borders of the country. Possibly each new company remained permanently under arms until its successor was trained; the information about this is not clear. But it seems certain that it was these specially trained warriors who did the fighting in the frequent offensive wars.

The rest of the Tusi and a few Hutu were employed as herdsmen, and this really seems to imply national service of a civilian rather than a military kind.

Each army was responsible for the care of a number of herds of cattle, and it is possible that all the cattle in the country were allotted by means of this organization to the 'armies' of those herdsmen who were not warriors. In any case, each army had to supply herdsmen to tend a proportion of the royal cattle, and also the herds of the army chief and the members of the fighting division. Since Tusi had no other occupation than herding, they must have been herding their own cattle either independently or as part of the army. What seems most probable is that each army was required to provide a quota of herdsmen for the cattle of the king, great chiefs, and warriors. As each army consisted of a number of lineages, the lineage heads were made responsible for providing the number required. The army chief gave his orders to the lineage head and not directly to the herdsmen.

For fiscal purposes, however, all the cattle in the country *were* divided into armies along with their owners. From time to time all the cattle of an army were mustered and counted, and a proportion of those which belonged to the herdsman section of the army were transferred to the ownership of the king. Each army was also responsible for providing a number of milking cows to keep the court supplied with fresh milk; it had also to deliver at the court a fixed number of pots of the sour milk which is the staple food of the Tusi. The army also provided the labour for public works, which were less extensive than in Buganda since there was no road-making. It fell to them, however, to keep the royal residence in repair; when work on this needed to be done orders were sent to one or other army to supply the men.

Although it might seem that the allocation to armies in

itself answered most of the purposes of government, the kings of Ruanda employed a number of officials who were not chiefs of the army. Like the kings of Buganda and the other rulers in Uganda, they had a small number of superior chiefs who had general responsibility over large areas, and who assembled at the capital from time to time to advise them on affairs of state. Some at least of these men were also army chiefs, and one or two were allowed to raise and train their own armies.

Each of them had his subordinates, and it is a peculiar feature of the Ruanda system that the next grade of subordinates were paired. In each subsection of a larger chiefdom there were a 'chief of the land' and a 'chief of the cattle'. These officials were primarily fiscal authorities, responsible for collecting tribute in produce and in cattle respectively (so that owners of cattle were taxed in more than one way). Since the Tusi cattle owners did not practise agriculture, this meant in effect that there was one set of officials for the upper-class Tusi and another for the lower-class Hutu – rather as, in South Africa, the Native Commissioners are a distinct branch of the civil service responsible only for administrative dealings with Africans. The chiefs of the land also dealt with disputes about land rights.

These chiefs were bureaucrats in the sense that they did not claim their position by right of inheritance or by virtue of any prior connexion with the area to which they were appointed. The next rank of officials were responsible for one or more hillside settlements. They were chosen from among the people living there, and were likely to be heads of large lineages, since this position would give them authority; but they again were not hereditary, and no lineage had any claim to an office of this kind.

The highest chiefs of all – how chosen we do not know – were called 'chiefs of the stool', because they met in council, seated on stools, to advise the king when he wished to consult them.

In Ankole, as in Ruanda, military organization was important, and the chiefs who had highest status were those responsible for the defence of the country against raiders. They lived on the borders, each with a band of warriors and their cattle living near him. Perhaps these warriors were recruited and trained in somewhat the same way as those of Ruanda. The ruler himself gathered bands of Hima youths at his court, who accompanied him first in hunting and later in war, but there is no record of any elaborate training such as is remembered of the Ruanda armies. The king's bodyguard, who lived close to him wherever he was, were picked men from the frontier armies.

Other officials had the special responsibility of keeping up the strength of the ruler's herds by making a levy when necessary on those of all his subjects, particularly at times when he had lost many cattle, perhaps as a result of an epidemic or an enemy raid. Tribute in grain and beer was collected continuously; when the king was feasting his warriors, as he did before and after a raid, more was required than at other times.

This account has deliberately isolated the 'civil service' chiefs from other persons who also had the privileges and some of the functions of chiefs.

*

It is difficult to say much about the way in which the functions of government were actually performed, because there was nobody there much interested in observing and describing them at the time when they had not been modified by European rule. We know particularly little about the way in which justice was meted out.

Although in the larger kingdoms the kings and the most important chiefs employed their retainers to punish disobedient subjects, they did not apparently use them as a police force to execute judgements given in quarrels between subjects. The king of Ankole did not allow his subjects to seek redress by force before they had brought their disputes before him, but when his decision had been given it was left to the side adjudged to be in the right to seek the compensation due to it. This arose particularly in cases of homicide calling for blood revenge; in other disputes the party adjudged liable to pay compensation usually did so, knowing that if they refused they would be disobeying the chief.

Roscoe's account of the Ganda describes the right of revenge for homicide, the pollution attaching to the act of killing, the separation of lineages and their formal reconciliation after compensation had been paid, in a manner that takes one back to the Nuer. He implies that cases of homicide were discussed between the lineages involved, and the killer was handed over by his kin if they admitted his guilt.

From other sources we can gather that there was a good deal of what might be called diplomatic settlement of disputes by agreement between heads of lineages on the payment of compensation. The Haya recall the settlement of cases by the village elders, who might be called together for the purpose by anyone with a complaint against a neighbour. The Nyoro still do this, and today, when all formal justice is in the hands of courts responsible to the Uganda government, they think people should not take their quarrels to the courts without first trying to settle them by discussion among neighbours; moreover the chiefs who have government recognition also think that this method of settlement should be tried first. The elders have no right to impose penalties; indeed, in the eyes of the government they have no rights at all. What they do is to discuss the subject of complaint and decide who is in the wrong. This person then provides the meat and beer required for a feast of reconciliation. Of course there are many cases where more is at stake than can be put right by a feast; these must go to the formal courts.

But when we come to the larger states we do find a mode of action that is not common among peoples not governed under a state system, namely, punishment. This consists frequently in the infliction of pain, or even the taking of life: it can also consist in the imposition of a fine – that is to say that the offender has to hand over property, not to the person wronged but to the judge.

Are we to find in this the beginning of the conception of criminal law? This subject was discussed by Radcliffe-Brown, who remarked that primitive societies had very little idea of offences against the collectivity which cannot be made good by restitution but must be dealt with by the infliction of punishment. The present account has been concerned up to now almost entirely with redress for wrongs conceived in terms of the payment of compensation. The principal exception was the Kamba *kingolle*, the execution by a combined act of the whole community of a person who has become obnoxious to it. It is significant that there are no minor penalties; people who commit acts for which no redress is admitted are removed from the community, either by death or banishment.

Radcliffe-Brown made use of the Kamba example in a discussion of the types of offence that are thought of as crimes in the simplest societies. He also enumerated offences which other simple societies consider can only be dealt with by the death or banishment of the offender. He classed these together as types of action which are held to have wronged society as a whole, so that society as a whole takes action against them. This interpretation is not based on the views expressed by people belonging to the societies under discussion. It is a logical deduction from the premise that persons who are members of a society that recognizes certain rules of conduct must take action to reaffirm these rules when they are broken; otherwise they will cease to be obeyed.

But there is a sense in which all members of a society react against a wrong-doer even if they leave it to the wronged party to seek redress. People in general are interested in the rights and wrongs of every quarrel, and many instances of the public discussion of quarrels have been cited in this book. Moreover, as far as the records go – which is not nearly far enough – there is no sign of the existence of people with the function that western societies allot to police and public prosecutors, the function of bringing to justice offenders who have not done any injury to them personally. All accusations are made by the individuals who consider themselves injured.

The records also show that some injuries can be made good by the payment of compensation and others cannot. But does this imply the conscious recognition of classes of offence such as we make in the distinction between civil and criminal law? And does that distinction as we make it actually reflect the relative magnitude of offences? Many of our crimes are acts of disobedience to the government but are not in themselves very heinous. Such actions do not wrong any particular individual, and so nobody can be compensated for them: but it is not because they arouse particular moral indignation, and the whole community considers itself injured, that they are classed as criminal. If they are held to be 'wrongs against society as a whole' this is only in the sense that it is bad for society as a whole for the authority of the government to be disobeyed.

If we look at the offences that have been recorded as meriting punishment, and as not capable of being expunged by the payment of compensation, we find that they are a curiously mixed collection. One is witchcraft, that is the possession of a quality which enables, or even drives, its possessor to injure his fellows by merely wanting to. One is incest – sexual relations between close kin. One is the act of conceiving a child without having passed through the rites that give a woman adult status and secure the blessing of supernatural beings on her motherhood. Now, two of these three actions are sins: that is, they are held to offend the spiritual beings who are thought of as the ultimate guardians of the community, and to endanger the community by bringing their anger down upon it. Witchcraft is not looked on in quite this light, but it stands in all African societies for the essence of evil; the African belief in witchcraft closely parallels the Christian belief in the Devil.

So all these actions are more than crimes: they offend more than the human members of society, and more careful inquiry might show that a person who is guilty of one of them is held to pollute the community by his presence. In other words, such people are certainly sinners and possibly also sources of spiritual danger. The difference between these acts and offences for which compensation is payable is not one of magnitude; the offences are of different kinds.

If these were the only actions to be penalized, one might say that primitive societies recognize only civil wrongs and sins, but no crimes. But it is also on record that people have been expelled from Kikuyu and Kamba communities for what Radcliffe-Brown calls 'the crime of being a bad lot'. Such people are habitual thieves.

What are we to say about this? That one theft is a tort and ten a crime? There is here no question of different kinds of offence, one more heinous than another, but of a quantitative difference. A habitual thief has annoyed a great many individuals; is that the same thing as saying he has offended society?

This is where the lack of information creates a real difficulty. We know from the existence of a named institution, the *kingolle* of the Kamba, that people were *sometimes* put to death by the combined action of all members of a community. We know from all kinds of sources that people were sometimes banished by their own kith and kin and reappeared to become the clients of leading men in neighbouring countries. And we know that when a man was banished it need not be for 'the crime of being a bad lot' but might be the result of trouble of different kinds.

What we do not know is whether there really is any society that lumps together all these kinds of action, treats them in the same way and conceptualizes them as belonging to one category, that of crimes as opposed to civil wrongs. My guess – which can never be more than a guess – is that the *kingolle* was reserved for offences of the type that were held to bring pollution on the offender's neighbours, and that those who simply made themselves unpopular were ostracized in a more informal way.

The purpose of this digression, however, is to point a contrast between the activities of government in the Interlacustrine Bantu states and among the peoples described earlier. Accounts of these states are full of references to punishment, both corporal and in the form of the infliction of fines.

Oberg tells us that in Ankole an important source of the ruler's revenue consisted in beasts which were either taken in fines or paid as fees for hearing cases. Maquet's account of Ruanda frequently refers to fines, though he gives no account of the judicial procedure and we have to guess how the fines were incurred. Roscoe's description of the Ganda is full of references to savage corporal punishments, and Speke recorded many which he witnessed. The offence which Roscoe discussed at greatest length is adultery. He describes a heavy 'fine' imposed on the adulterer, but it is clear from what he says that he is really talking about the compensation to be paid the wronged husband. He tells us that adultery with a peasant's wife was punished by a 'fine', but that in the case of a chief's wife the penalty was death, or the loss of a limb or an eye; even in this context, however, he admits that compensation could be accepted. Then he tells us that thieves were punished by having their hands cut off; but without any context, so that we do not know what thieves or from whom they stole.

Speke recounts many instances of punishments inflicted for acts of disrespect to the Kabaka, some apparently trivial, or for want of diligence in his service. One begins to wonder whether what we see here is the development of the idea that some acts are offences against the community as a whole, or the expression of a conception of the relation of ruler and subject which follows logically from the ruler's position. Once he is recognized as the unique, ultimate authority, entitled, at least in theory, to make such claims as he pleases on the property of his subjects, it is meaningless to speak of any compensation for offences against him. At the same time the recognition that he has the right to despoil his subjects and inflict upon them severe corporal punishments undoubtedly upholds his authority.

One can see a foretaste of the 'criminal justice' of the Interlacustrine Bantu kings among the Shilluk and Anuak. When the Reth of the Shilluk thought that the people of one settlement were unjustifiably attacking another, he went with his retainers and with fighting men from neutral settlements and plundered them, keeping the plunder for himself and to reward the members of his forces. Anuak nobles claim the right to seize the property of commoners in punishment for what we should consider small offences against themselves, such as injuring a pet animal. An Anuak noble also sometimes uses his bodyguard to plunder the possessions of somebody who has offended him by wronging another of his subjects, and in this case he keeps the plunder and does not pass any of it on in damages to the wronged subject. Can it be then that historically the idea that some offences are to be treated as crimes does not spring from a general feeling that certain actions wrong the whole of society, but rather from the specific claim of rulers to assert their power?

*

It has been a principal theme of this book that a man who wants to secure and maintain a following must be able to offer his followers some material advantage. If his following is very small, he can provide this from his own resources, as does the 'bull' of a Nuer village or a leading elder of the Luhya. His followers may of their own volition help to increase his resources, as the Anuak youths do when they clear additional fields for the headman's wives to plant the grain that will later be made into beer to feast them, and will enable the headman to maintain the dignity of the village by entertaining strangers in due style.

But the larger the following the more impossible it becomes for the leader to reward their services out of his own resources, and the more necessary it becomes to levy contributions from the people at large. Such contributions are of two kinds: the 'bread-and-butter' type goods of everyday use and consumption, and the class of specially valued objects which are reserved for people of high rank and enable them to make a display, in their clothing and ornaments and the furnishing of their houses, which common people cannot emulate.

Though only the first class, in which the ruler claims a share in the goods produced by his subjects, is commonly considered in discussions of taxation, both are equally significant in their different ways for the maintenance of the ruler's position and the prestige of his court.

Much the same kind of objects in both classes are claimed by rulers throughout East Africa, for the obvious reason that the prized natural products – the skins and horns of animals – are everywhere much the same, and at the technical level that East African societies had reached before they were invaded from outside, the man-made products were much the same too.

The Alur chiefs, although they did not rule wide realms, received in tribute quite a wide range of goods. They did not employ tax-gatherers, but expected the heads of the clans subject to them to bring to the court what was due to it. Since no subject lived more than a few miles from his chief, it must have been easy to deal with anyone who failed to do so. Grain was brought in after the harvest, and was represented as a thank-offering to the chief for the prosperity which his ritual activities had brought to his people. Obviously this was the appropriate time of year to pay tribute in grain; if it was left till later, when people had begun to wonder whether their supplies would last out, it would be much more difficult to collect. Southall thinks this, rather than any rule that tribute must be paid at regular intervals, explains such regularity as there was. Chiefs claimed the right hind leg of every large game animal that was caught, and the tusks of elephants and the skins of lions and leopards. These must have been sent to the court immediately after the hunt, but hunting had its regular season, immediately after the harvest. Craftsmen and people from parts of the country which had local specialities brought contributions of these – salt from an area with salt deposits, dried fish from the low land near the Nile and sesame from the higher ground, shea butter nuts (a delicacy claimed as the chiefs' monopoly in other parts of Africa), ironwork, animal horns perforated so as to be blown in hunting or war, woven baskets. Chiefs' sons who acknowledged the overlordship of their fathers received the tribute of game and ivory from their subjects and sent some of it on; to cease to do this was to assert autonomy. These minor chiefs received humbler kinds of tribute – the offal of every goat that was killed for eating, and a share of the winged termites that are caught when they swarm from the great red ant-hills, and considered a rare delicacy.

In addition, Alur subjects worked for their chiefs. They hoed the chief's fields and built his houses and grain bins. Sometimes people at a distance from the chief's place cultivated fields at their own villages, the produce of which was brought to him at the harvest. All this was done on such a small scale that there was no need for special officials to organize it.

A distinction commonly drawn between tribute and taxation is that the former is paid in kind and may be demanded at irregular intervals and the latter is paid in money at a fixed rate and is due at fixed times.

It is not clear where the Ganda stood in this matter. Ganda time-reckoning differed from that of Europe because countries near the equator do not have a clearly marked winter and summer. Their seasons follow a six-months' cycle, three wet months followed by three dry, and this is what they call a year; that is, it is the longest natural unit of time which they experience. Was there then a 'yearly' tax collection? Or were the tax messengers sent out when the Kabaka and Katikiro thought the palace resources were running low? The latter seems on the whole more likely. The goods collected were of various kinds – livestock, cowry-shells, iron hoe-blades, and the cloths made from the bark of a fig-tree beaten out thin, which provided the clothing and bedding of the lakeside peoples before cotton goods were within everybody's reach. Cattle were required of superior chiefs, goats and hoes of lesser ones, and the peasants contributed the cowry-shells and barkcloths. According to Roscoe's account, the tax-gatherers did not take a proportion of every herd but required a fixed number of cattle from each chief.

Of course the hoes and barkcloths had to be new, and they were not made and stored up in anticipation of the tax-collection. It took some little time to produce the required number, and the tax-gatherers had to wait for this and then supervise the transport of the goods and cattle, first to the saza headquarters and then to the capital. The amount due was calculated in consultation with the subordinates of the saza chiefs, who were supposed to know the exact number of men under their authority, and they were responsible for seeing that it was delivered.

In the two kingdoms which held most firmly to their pastoral traditions, Ankole and Ruanda, the most significant taxation took the form of levies on cattle to supplement the royal herds. The aristocracy of these two kingdoms still take the purely aesthetic interest in cattle that the Nilotes do, prizing them for characteristics that have no utilitarian value such as the length and shape of their horns, and singing songs in praise of them. In Ruanda all long-horned cattle were held to be the property of the king. Indeed, the whole political system of these two kingdoms was directed to the acquisition of cattle, and would have had little meaning apart from this. The military organization of both kingdoms existed to increase the number of cattle and protect them against counter-raids, and in the case of Ruanda this was combined with a herding organization designed to ensure that cattle and their products were available to the ruler as he required them. So important was this aspect of the system of government in Ruanda that the description already given of the functions of chiefs has covered the subject of taxation in that country.

Of Ankole, which has been much less well described, it remains to mention that all the vegetable food consumed at court was produced by the Iru, and that this was collected from them not once a year but all the time, by Iru collectors appointed by the prime minister. In one district it is recorded that there were two such officials who were responsible respectively during the waxing and waning of the moon. Extra quantities were required before and after a military expedition, when the ruler feasted his warriors.

The retinue of the rulers was partly recruited in ways which have something in common with the claims made on their material wealth. The recruiting of the warrior bands in Ruanda was compulsory, though we do not know quite how it was organized, and we know nothing at all about the way such bands were formed in the other kingdoms. Every Kabaka of Buganda is said soon after his succession to have 'made a levy on the country for girls who in due course became his wives, and for boys to be pages, and every chief was required to give at least one boy as a page to the king'.[*]

Alur chiefs demanded from any subject who was guilty of murder a boy and girl in compensation. Children who were sent to court in this way might do well out of it if they found royal favour when they grew up. At the same time this enabled the rulers to increase the number of their wives without making the bridewealth payments which were required for ordinary marriages.

* Roscoe, *The Baganda* (1911), p. 205.

The bringers of Christianity and colonial rule to Africa, and indeed some later writers, have interpreted the claims of rulers to tax or tribute from their subjects as mere rapacious exploitation. How far it can be said that the rulers' wealth served public purposes will be discussed in the next chapters.

CHAPTER 7

Kings, Chiefs, and Peasants

In the discussion of the expansion of government it was shown how significant in this process is the building up of a body of persons who depend upon their leader in such a way that their first loyalty is to him. This relationship of *clientage* may well be the germ from which state power springs. It is certainly of prime importance in the Interlacustrine Bantu states, where it can sometimes be seen to run through the whole society from top to bottom, everyone except the king being somebody's client and everyone except the lowliest peasant having clients of his own.

The process of entering into the client relationship with the ruler has been most clearly described in the form which it took among the Hima and Tusi states of Ankole, Ruanda, and Urundi. In these states, where the pastoral aristocracy formed a distinct class, it was essentially a relationship based on the transfer of rights in cattle. In Ankole it is remembered as having originated in a voluntary act of the client, who came with a gift of cattle to the Mugabe (the Nkole king) and offered to be his man. This meant that he undertook to fight in the Mugabe's wars when called upon, and to present to him a share of any cattle he might capture in a raid which he organized on his own account. He was expected to keep the relationship alive by further gifts of cattle from time to time; if he did not do this it would lapse, in the sense that he could not expect from the ruler the protection implied in the client relationship. This protection signified, above all, security from attack by cattle raiders; not that the Mugabe provided a police force, but he was in a position to punish anyone (including another client) who infringed the rights of one of his clients. It was not considered legitimate for a client of the Mugabe to seek redress against another without first bringing the case before the Mugabe. This applied to blood revenge as well as to minor matters. Oberg does not record what happened to people who took the law into their own hands. In Urundi fights between chiefs over whom the king claimed authority were going on well into this century. Sometimes such turbulent clients were punished by losing their official position. The king of Urundi sent trusted courtiers to arbitrate in disputes between his chiefs, whereas the impression given about Ankole is that the chiefs came to the Mugabe for judgement.

The Mugabe was expected to organize retaliatory raids against anyone who raided the cattle of his clients, and if one of them lost all his cattle, either through a raid or an epidemic, to give him some to start a new herd. Whereas, on the one hand, the client was expected to give the Mugabe a share of any cattle that he captured by private enterprise, on the other he could expect to receive a share of those taken in wars that were ordered by the Mugabe (in which, of course, he would himself fight).

As this picture is reconstructed by Oberg, it seems that some of the Nkole Hima were clients of the ruler and others were not; and that clientship could lapse, be repudiated, and be renewed. It is likely that this was so in the outlying parts of the country, for it seems that the boundaries of Ankole as delimited by the British government of Uganda included territory which the king of Ankole had never really controlled before. But where his authority was established it is hardly possible that people who accepted it were intermingled with people who did not. More probably every Hima formally entered into clientship, but some were more punctilious than others in the performance of their obligations and were rewarded accordingly with larger shares in the booty of war and perhaps with chiefships. The clients were the heads of lineages who owned and managed their herds in common. When one died, his successor was expected to present himself at court and renew the relationship, bringing with him a beast known as 'the cow of burial'.

Those of the Mugabe's clients who were appointed by him as chiefs were entitled to collect tribute on their own behalf from the Iru living in the territory for which they were responsible. They gathered their own following around them. Hima who were not chiefs attended on them to pay their respects. They stayed some time, and the chiefs fed them from the beer and grain which they took as tribute from the Iru. Hima who had not been accorded the status of chiefs were not authorized to demand these supplies and had to get them by barter. A chief's household had attached to it a number of Iru craftsmen, workers in iron and wood who made his spears and wooden bowls for milking.

It was permissible for Iru, as well as Hima, to visit the king with presents in attestation of their loyalty. They brought small stock, beer, or produce such as millet and beans. This action was described by the same word as the formal rendering of homage by the Hima, and an Iru who made and kept himself known to the king by such small offerings was well placed to beg for his help in times of difficulty. But there is no record that Iru entered into client relationships with the Hima who were in immediate authority over them.

In Ruanda, however, every Hutu sought to be the client of some Tusi, for the protection entailed in this relationship was highly significant; moreover, the status which the Ruanda scheme of values accorded to the Hutu was such that a Hutu who had no protector was at the mercy of any Tusi. The Tusi also sought the protection of other Tusi richer and more powerful than themselves. The greatest chiefs were clients of the king, and had their own clients who had their own clients who . . .

The traditional procedure for entering into this relationship contrasted with that in Ankole, in that the prospective client did not offer cattle, but received them from his lord. The client sought the relationship, but it was the lord who put him under the obligation to serve him by giving him cattle.

The client made only a token gift – a pot of beer or of the fermented honey which was much prized in Ruanda. He spoke a stereotyped formula : 'Give me milk; make me rich; keep me in mind; be my father; I will be your child.' The lord could refuse to accept the client. If he did accept the relationship he gave him a cow, or more than one, and the client was entitled to their milk, their bull calves, and the meat and hide of any which died. A Tusi client could also secure clients for himself by placing some of the offspring of these cattle in their care.

The client had the duty of personal service to his lord. He followed him on journeys, to court, or to war. He acted as his messenger, and was required to build and keep in repair a length of the reed fence around the lord's homestead. A Hutu client also had to cultivate fields for his lord and keep guard outside his house at night. A great man with many clients allotted different jobs among them, such as cooking or brewing. The Belgian authorities in Ruanda recognized this relationship as part of the customary law of the country, and sought to limit and specify the claims that might be enforced in virtue of it. But such precise specification is not characteristic of the relationships recognized in pre-literate societies. A client could have a number of lords, and send his sons to perform the services required of him.

A client who fulfilled his obligations expected to be able to count on his lord's protection in most kinds of trouble. If he was involved in a case at the king's court, his lord would take his part, and, if he was required to pay a fine or compensation for some offence, would pay it on his behalf; the fine would usually consist in cattle. If the client was killed, and his own lineage were not able to avenge him, the lord was expected to do so, and if he died leaving no close kin to look after his widow and children, the lord should take them under his care. He should help his client with any cattle products that he might need urgently – hides,

meat, or milk if his children were going short. A Hutu client
might be given a hoe.

Either party could break off this relationship, though
neither could do so unless he considered that the other was
failing in his obligations; indeed there would be no other
reason for breaking off an arrangement for mutual advantage. But it was expected to be hereditary, and to be formally
renewed on the death of either party to it. When a client
died, if the lord did not like his successor, he could transfer
the cattle on which the relationship rested to another member of the lineage or take them back altogether. Important
chiefs had a great number of clients, and would sometimes
organize a muster of the cattle placed with them and take
back a proportion.

Thus, most of the population were linked in client-lord
relationships which stretched far back into the past. Every
Tusi was the client of one lord at least and the lord of many
clients. Those who had positions of authority, as army or
territorial chiefs, accomplished their administrative duty to
the king or to their immediate superiors as their way of
fulfilling the obligations of clients. For persons as important
as this the lord's protection was expressed in a different kind
of patronage – in appointment to some position of authority
which carried with it material benefits as well as prestige.

Both the 'chiefs of the land' and their subordinate 'chiefs
of the hill' were entitled to keep a share of the produce which
they collected as royal tribute, and the latter, who were
responsible for turning out labour when this was not obtained through the army organization, were also allowed
to call on labour for their own purposes. We have seen how
the army chiefs were allowed to make a periodic levy on
the army cattle. Clearly the greater chiefs cannot have had
fewer privileges than their subordinates.

There is nothing in the accounts of the Nkole and
Ruanda, or indeed of most of the agricultural peoples, to
suggest that there was any but a purely secular relationship
between the kings and their client chiefs. But in Bunyoro

the appointment of a chief was accompanied by a ritual which did not merely symbolize the conferment of authority but was also held to convey to the chief some part of the spiritual power belonging to the king himself. In the past the central act of this ceremony was the drinking of milk from the cows of the royal herd. Nowadays there are hardly any cows in Bunyoro, though the Nyoro preserve the memory of their past by describing many situations in metaphors about cattle. Chiefs are still formally invested, even though today their posts are part of a fixed civil service establishment, but the act of investiture now consists in the presentation of coffee berries, which has long been the formal expression of hospitality in neighbouring Buganda. When the delegation of authority has thus been symbolically made the chief kisses the king's hand. The power which he is believed to have received enables him both to rule well and to dominate the persons subject to him. In the past the most important chiefs were presented with a beaded crown, which not only marked them out as the possessors of special dignity, but made them sharers in the ritual power of royalty to such a degree that they had to observe many of the ritual prohibitions of the king himself.

Mutesa of Buganda honoured the chiefs whom he favoured in a more secular manner, by authorizing them to dress in the cotton cloth imported by the Arabs instead of the locally made barkcloth. To this day the approved dress of persons of high status in Buganda is the Arab *kanzu*, a garment reaching from neck to ankles with a little embroidery round the neck opening. The best ones are now made of tussore silk, and their wearers look extremely dignified, even with the now usual addition of a western-style jacket over the robe.

*

In the primarily agricultural states clientship was the means of pursuing political ambitions for people who were minded to do so, rather than a necessity for survival as it was for at any rate the lowlier of the clients in Ruanda. For a Hutu in Ruanda the value of clientship was that it got him the use of cattle even if he did not actually own them, and protection against marauders who might seize them. It is necessary to have a personal protector in a society where there is no general impartial authority able to guarantee the security of all members, and this is particularly true of those societies whose main wealth is in cattle. There is no commodity so easily stolen as cattle, and this may be one reason why so many pastoral peoples have not developed the kind of government that claims impartially to guarantee the rights of all its subjects. Land, the precious possession of cultivators, cannot be seized and carried off, and the foodstuffs won from it cannot be stolen without actually entering people's homesteads (unless they are picked from the fields, which does sometimes happen); also they cannot be displayed as a pastoralist displays his herd.

So in the agricultural states clientship is not a relationship initiated by the client and entered into by a formal compact; it is rather the tie between a political superior and a man to whom he has delegated a part of his authority. It is a relationship by which rulers raise a small number of their subjects above the general level; it is sought by more people than can hope to attain it. The parallel with the procedure described in Ruanda is to be found in the process which initially brings the commoner to the notice of his chief. This is just what we have seen already at the court of Anuak headmen and nobles – certain persons voluntarily attach themselves to a leading man, wait on him, carry messages for him, entertain him, and share in the organization of his household. It is from these that in the course of time he selects the few who will assist him in the actual governance of the country. As the court comes to be more formally constituted, people living near it will send their sons, while they are still boys, to serve the king or chief; this is at the same time a compliment and an expression of loyalty, and a way of starting a boy on the only career that exists in a society of peasant cultivators. It may also, of course, pay dividends to the father and other relatives of the boy; the expression 'a friend at court' is full of meaning in this context. From these attendants a king or chief selects not only his Katikiro but those whom he will set over divisions of his country, and they become his clients in the active sense of the word.

Why should these 'client-chiefs', as Fallers has called them, do their master's bidding and place his interests above those of any particular section of his subjects? Not only because they are sensible of the honour done them, or even because of the solemn ritual which binds a Nyoro client-chief to his king, but because they gain a great deal from their position. They are entitled to make the same demands on the peasants under their authority as the ruler makes through them. They have their own courts, their own clients, and their own client-chiefs; sometimes they may have to secure the king's approval of the appointment of the latter by formally presenting them to him. Hardly any territorial chief is responsible for so small an area that he will not subdivide it among followers of his own. In Busoga chiefs place their clients at the head of villages or even subdivisions of villages, and in Bunyoro the lowest rank of chief might have only half a dozen homesteads under his authority.

The chief responsible for an area of land – and this means the chief of the smallest subdivision – also has the right, within limits, to say who shall live there. The limits that are set to his exercise of this right depend on the rules of inheritance and the effectiveness of the claims of lineages to particular stretches of land, matters which will have to be discussed later. But all the territorial chiefs in the agricultural states had the sole right to decide whether newcomers might take up land and where, and to re-allot the holdings of peasants who died without leaving an heir, often also of those who left the village. This put them in a position where they could bestow favours, and in a sense make clients by the grant of land as the Ruanda made clients by the grant of cattle. The analogy is not close, because the territorial chief does not undertake towards the newcomer any obligations other than those he has towards all persons under his authority; and he does not offer physical protection because these villages do not expect to be raided. But it is there, because every peasant who comes to a territorial chief to ask for land does so by offering to be 'his man' (there is a special verb expressing this relationship in Ganda and kindred languages), and because he can be expelled from the village for failing to give the services which are due from him. In the eyes of the Ganda the words which are commonly translated 'chief' and 'peasant' mean essentially a man who has independent control of land and one who has had to beg someone else for a holding.

Thus every minor chief is a replica in miniature of his superiors. In Buganda, according to the information obtained by Roscoe, it was not only a privilege but an obligation for the saza chiefs to keep up residences built on the same pattern and in the same style as the Kabaka's. All chiefs surrounded their homesteads with a high fence of elephant-grass canes, a work that would be far too much for the members of an ordinary commoner's household. Their right to call on labour has been mentioned. They were also entitled to receive their own tribute – a pot of beer whenever anyone in their territory brewed it, a share of fish or game caught, of pots made and so on. In Buganda the senior chiefs were entitled to a share of the taxes which they collected for the king, and the Katikiro was entitled to a proportion of the total.

In Buganda, and doubtless elsewhere, great importance was attached to the ranking of chiefs. This was indicated by a series of titles, which were the same for the chiefs dependent directly on the king, the chiefs who were subordinate to them, and any subordinates which these subordinates might attach to themselves. I even knew a minor chief who introduced his wives to me by these titles. But it does not seem likely that the peasants had to pay taxes several times over to chiefs at different levels of a hierarchy all operating in the same area. More likely every chief of whatever grade had an area from which he alone could claim dues and services, while the saza chiefs also transmitted orders from the Kabaka to those below them in rank, and tried cases which their lower chiefs had failed to settle.

Within the large and populous territory of Buganda, the kings from time to time created new fiefs – if we can use the feudal analogy – to reward individuals who had given them some special service. These were essentially authorizations to receive the tribute and services of a given population, defined by the boundaries within which they were living at the time of the grant. These grants were made for the recipient's lifetime only. Men who received them, and all other persons who were given territorial responsibilities, did homage by brandishing spears and proclaiming their loyalty. The grants which were made as rewards for personal services were not usually very large: they did not give the holder a status anywhere near that of a saza chief. But these fief-holders did not come under the authority of any other chief; if demands were made on them for payments or labour, they were made direct by the Kabaka. It is also recorded that certain persons, such as the craftsmen who supplied the royal palace – building experts, potters, and the like – were rewarded with 'estates' from the resources of which they did not have to pay tribute.

When Sir Harry Johnston was sent as Commissioner to Uganda, to establish the terms on which the Ganda and the other kingdoms should be brought under the Protectorate government, he had the idea of recognizing only chiefs of the highest rank, and giving them administrative responsibilities in return for which they should continue to hold estates and have the right to the services of the peasants living on them. Apart from this small number, all other Ganda would be treated alike in the matter of land rights; he was not concerned with their political or social status under the Kabaka. But since social status depended directly on the question whether or not one had the right to allocate land, this arrangement seemed intolerable to all the minor chiefs, and they succeeded in getting 'estates' – which were now held in freehold tenure – allotted to themselves. The first list of chiefs with such claims numbered 783; later this was brought up to the round figure of a thousand.*

None of these office-holders or fief-holders had any claim to pass on his position to his sons, and it seems that in Buganda the offices did not in fact become hereditary. As the situation was remembered by the men I talked to in 1932, there was much movement of chiefs from one office or fief to another, both in the way of promotion to better positions and relegation to inferior ones; but by that time memories of independent Buganda belonged to the distant past. However, Roscoe's informants also described the transfer of chiefs from one part of the country to another, taking with them those of their followers who hoped to share the benefits of the new appointment, and the same kind of procession is also remembered in Urundi. Here we see another of the advantages of successful clientship. A new senior chief would choose his subordinate officials not from people he found already living in the area under his authority, but from the courtiers he brought with him.

Chiefs had many sons because they had many wives, and they could not hope that all their sons would attain to high office. But they were well placed to offer their sons as pages to higher chiefs, or even to the Kabaka, and so put them in the way of advancement, and when an important chief died the Kabaka probably would not let his heir sink to the position of a mere peasant. Thus, although there was no clearly defined upper class, as there was in the pastoral kingdoms, there were 'great families' from whom it was likely that chiefs would be chosen. Nevertheless, it was believed that in principle office was open to the talents.

Some examples recorded by Fallers from the Soga show

*D. A. Low, *Buganda and British Over-Rule* (1960).

how the principle that every client-chief holds his position in virtue of a personal relationship with the ruler works out in practice. At the present day there are village headmen whose fathers were brought from other parts of the country and appointed to the villages that their sons now rule. In Busoga even a village headman has his Katikiro, which in this context means an assistant and stand-in. In the village of Gasemba the late chief, an appointee from outside, made the head of the largest lineage in the village his Katikiro. When he died his successor as lineage head became Katikiro to the son of the chief from outside who had installed his father.

The headmen of Soga villages, and even subdivisions of villages, describe themselves as 'owning' these places, as though the office of headman were family property. Today such claims are contested in the courts. The kind of case that arises is this: Several generations ago the ruler of one of the kingdoms 'gave' a village to a client, who was succeeded by his son and grandson. At the time of the grandson's death there was a famine, and his successor was away from the village wandering about the country looking for food. This was also the time when the Protectorate government had entrusted the administration of Busoga to the famous Ganda chief Semei Kakunguru. Kakunguru 'gave' the village to a client of his own, and refused to reinstate the previous headman's heir. On the death of Kakunguru's man, the ruler put in another client. But in 1949 the son of the man who was dispossessed by Kakunguru in 1900 was claiming that the headmanship was his by right. His rival, who was in office at the time, claimed, on the contrary, that he held the office in direct descent from his grandfather, to whom a different ruler had given it, and that his opponent's ancestor had merely come into the village to get land from his own ancestor.

In another case, a man claimed that his grandfather had been the fifth headman in one line of a sub-village. When the grandfather died some thirty years ago, there had only been two families in the sub-village, and the village head-man had joined it with a neighbouring section. The grand-son nevertheless insisted on his right to a headmanship. The present headman of the two sub-villages, however, asserted that the whole area had been transferred by the ruler at that time from the claimant's grandfather to his own.

These cases show both that the right of a ruler to transfer these offices was recognized and that it was rarely exercised.

Although nobody has gone into the question, and it is now too late to do so, it has always been assumed that the Katikiro of one of the large states was chosen without any reference to his descent, particularly as each ruler chose a new one soon after his accession, while his father's Katikiro was still alive. But Soga records show that in those small king-doms, where admittedly the office was less important politic-ally, even this position could come to descend in a family. Here is the story of Isumwa, the Katikiro of Busambira, a state consisting of only twelve villages. Isumwa was a famous warrior, who came from a neighbouring kingdom. The ruler of Busambira invited him to be headman of one of his sub-villages, and when the ruler died and a new one had to be chosen, Isumwa supported the successful candidate, who made him his Katikiro. Isumwa's brother attached himself to the service of the new ruler's son, and when this man succeeded he made *him* Katikiro. This Katikiro, by name Biwawana, remained in office under the next ruler. When Biwawana died a son of Isumwa was chosen to take his place.

Fallers has remarked that if these offices come to be regarded as hereditary, it is no longer necessary for the holders to show personal devotion to the ruler. At the same time, it was always recognized that they were held at the pleasure of the ruler, and that a subordinate chief who seriously displeased him could be deprived of his office. In Buganda the constant creation of new fiefs had the effect of taking from the territorial chiefs parts of the areas under their control, and this could be used as a way of diminishing the stature of those with whom the Kabaka was dissatisfied.

Of these states, then, it might be said that offices created in the past in recognition of the personal services of clients have become crystallized in the course of time, so that some people consider they have a claim to positions of authority that is quite independent of any services they themselves have rendered. Their personal loyalty to a ruler has become loyalty to a system – but what keeps this loyalty alive, in addition to very strong feelings of reverence for royalty as such, is still the recognized right of the ruler to deprive people of office and the privileges that go with it. In the larger states loyalty to the system, in the sense of cooperating in the pursuit of its aims, was also a means of rising higher and higher in power and prestige.

Moreover, when the state organization is as fully developed as it was in Buganda, the opposition between loyalty to the 'Establishment' and loyalty to one's own kin is less important than it is where the ruler's power is only beginning to be built up, among people who take it for granted that the only way to be sure of your rights is to be prepared at any time to join the rest of your lineage in fighting for them. At that stage it is a question of the greatest significance whether a chief commands a force which he can count on to be neutral between disputants and compel the submission of the side he judges to be in the wrong. But in a country such as Buganda, as we know it through recollections of the nineteenth century, many other influences must have been at work to secure the general acceptance of centralized government, the operation of which it is too late to trace out. One, quite clearly, is that preference for the peaceful settlement of disputes by a recognized authority which was expressly given by neighbouring tribes as their reason for seeking the rule of Alur chiefs. As has been suggested, this preference may well increase when the goods in which compensation is sought are of a kind which cannot be seized in a foray. It may be significant that revenge for murder was still left to the victim's kin to execute, even where courts of justice were as highly developed as they were in Buganda.

No doubt one reason for this is the idea of vengeance as the last duty owed by kinsmen, but another may be that it continues to be practicable when other means of self-help are less so – we are told of Buganda that the avengers would seek an ambush rather than a pitched battle, as indeed would their counterparts among the Nuer.

*

Every state has fiscal power; this is one of the essential attributes of the state. Its officials take a part of the possessions of every subject from him to be utilized for public purposes. One of these purposes is to reward the people who carry on the government, and what has been said of the collection of tribute and the claim of chiefs to labour services must have made it clear that in the Interlacustrine Bantu states a very large proportion of the work and tribute exacted went in this way. Indeed it had the effect of a concentration of wealth in the hands of persons with political authority which was not balanced by any of the other means of accumulating wealth that are available to private individuals in a money economy.

Maquet has argued that the effect of the political organization of the Ruanda was to enable the Tusi aristocracy to enjoy a large share of the total wealth of the country without doing any work for it. This could not be said in such an unqualified way of the chiefs in the agricultural states, whose wives grew their own food like anybody else. Yet the question has to be asked what the system provided for the people as a whole and whether it could be said to be worth what they paid for it.

The rulers themselves benefited the country by their mere existence. They personified it, and their state of health and fortune affected its welfare; the ritual prohibitions to which they were all subject were intended, by preserving their own persons, to protect the country as a whole. It is an essential part of the theory of hereditary kingship that only one individual, who must belong to the appropriate line of descent, can have this ritual relationship to spiritual beings on the one hand and to his people and their country on the other. This topic will be treated more fully in a later chapter.

It is certainly true of some peoples, and is probably true of all, that they took collective pride in the splendour of the royal capital and of the smaller courts of chiefs nearer to them. Even the cruel punishments, which are well attested, that were meted out by Ganda rulers to people who offended them were matter for pride in a power so relentless. I remember being told with some complacency how King Suna obliged people who came to do obeisance before him to kneel on iron spikes; whether this statement was true makes no difference to the attitude it reflects.

The near vicinity of the powerful was obviously dangerous, and the humble may well have preferred to keep out of their way except when the drafting of labour made this impossible. On the other hand, a reward for labour was expected, in the form of better food than the peasant would expect at home, particularly meat. This is no small thing to people who eat meat as rarely as most Africans. When the Ganda and Nyoro look back regretfully to the old days, one of the things they talk of is the generosity of the old-time chiefs to their people, partly in the form of personal help in trouble, but more often in meat feasts and beer parties for the people who worked in their fields or at building their houses. The surplus of grain and cattle to provide these feasts could never have been produced by the manpower of the chief's household; it came from tribute.

War service too was rewarded, though again it is likely that the officers got a bigger share of the booty than the other ranks. In Ankole the Iru were not allowed to go to war, so all they got out of the state organization for warfare was the general protection that it afforded. In Ruanda the Hutu belonged to the army, but only as non-combatant carriers, and so they had no opportunity for the kind of exploits that earned rewards.

Lastly, there was access to justice, certainly not given

without fear or favour, but at least preferable to having to fight for your rights, and perhaps sometimes giving redress to people who would not have been likely to get it by fighting.

Was the cost exorbitant? Were the common people simply exploited for the benefit of their betters? Was the clientage system, formal or informal, an arrangement which offered any advantage to the peasant, or just a means of fastening oppression more firmly on his neck?

In some African countries the labour that a peasant was expected to give to his chief was reckoned as a fixed number of days in the year. There is no such record for any of the peoples described here, except for the Haya, of whom it is now remembered that every man was expected to give a month's work.* Where labour is given in cultivation, it is always possible that at crucial times such as the planting season a peasant might have to neglect his own fields for the sake of work on his lord's. But building and road-making can be arranged at other times. In Buganda, moreover, men traditionally took no part in farming, not even in the clearing of the ground which is the man's share of the farm work in so many parts of Africa.

It is difficult to give a confident judgement of the value of clientage to the humbler clients. If we were dealing with records, we might be able to find out what exactions had been made and what proportion of a peasant's resources they represented. We might find out what kind of offences were punished, how often, and how severely. We might even be able, by piecing many names together, to find out something about the chances that a humble client had of advancement in life through pleasing his lord. Even then we should always have to remember that these personal relationships depend on personalities, and that different lords must have treated their clients very differently.

The nearest approach to such a record is a collection of three or four personal histories of clients in Urundi which

* *East African Chiefs*, ed. A. I. Richards (1960).

was recently made by the Dutch anthropologist Trouw-borst.* The tellers of these stories are identified only by initials, and I have given them imaginary names.

Segore, a Hutu, was the son of a maker of drums to the palace, who was also the client of a great chief. When Segore grew up his father presented him to this chief, who did not want his services but passed him on to a son of his own. The latter sent him to another brother, who was a subordinate chief of their father. Segore became this man's client and several times visited the royal court in attendance on him. He used to be sent to other chiefs to ask for cattle. Later he became head cook to his chief, who as his protector gave him the goods he needed as bridewealth, and even did this a second time when his first wife proved to be barren. Presently the chief quarrelled with one of his neighbours. They fought one another, and the king punished them by removing them both from office. Segore had fought on his chief's side and been wounded. He now went to the chief's brother, who had himself become a chief, and was given a house by him and set in authority over all the men who worked for him. When this second chief died, his heir kept Segore in the same position. Segore was given ten cows by his first chief and others by the others whom he served. This is not a pure success story, however, for the time came when all his cattle died, and, being now an old man, he tried in vain to get anyone to give him more.

Inasango, a Tusi of high rank, told how his grandfather had been principal herdsman to the chief of an army. His father was killed fighting in this army, and his mother married again and took her little son to the territory of another chief. When he grew up he found that his stepfather treated him 'like a slave'. So he went back to the court of his father's lord. When this chief saw him he said, 'Why, there is the son of my warrior who was killed fighting for me.' He treated Inasango like a son and gave him cattle. Inasango fought in

* 'La Mobilité de l'individu en fonction de l'organisation politique des Burundi' in *Zaïre* (1950).

his chief's army against another chief. He was sometimes sent to take messages to other chiefs, and on one occasion he found in attendance on one of these a subject of his own chief who had left his lord without asking leave. Inasango persuaded this chief to send his master's man home. Later on his father's brother died childless, and the chief gave his homestead to another man, but Inasango begged to be allowed to have it and pass on his own homestead to a brother. The chief agreed. Finally Inasango was appointed assistant to a subordinate chief.

Rusato, another Tusi, was the son of a man who had received cattle from the king himself. But as he had not enough land to pasture them he attached himself to a chief who could give him some. But the king, not wishing to lose a client, sent for him, and gave him a homestead which was vacant because the previous occupier had been turned out for stealing pumpkins from the king's fields. Rusato fought in many wars against chiefs who rebelled against the king, and was rewarded for his services with cattle. On one occasion he was part of a company sent to deal with a Hutu who was a minor chief, but had set himself up as a king and was receiving homage and offerings of cattle from large numbers of people. This man ran away on the arrival of the royal forces, and they plundered his possessions, which was the object of the expedition. Another commission which Rusato remembered was being sent to a Tusi who had been given cows to herd for the king and had neglected to send the king one of his own in sign of gratitude. Carrying a cock, the sign that he was a royal messenger, Rusato had to summon the delinquent before the king with orders to bring the cow that was due, a second as a fine, and a third as Rusato's reward for his services.

Another Tusi of high rank, Bukuru, was a royal client, and was often sent to convey messages from the king to his chiefs and also to collect tribute in cattle. Once he was required to seize the cattle of a Hutu who would not work for his lord. Once he went in the train of a chief who had been appointed by the king to settle a dispute between two other chiefs. Once he went with one of the king's sons to the festivities when a chief's wife gave birth to twins. He also was appointed as a sort of general overseer of all the other clients whom the king sent to arbitrate disputes.

These are all stories of fortunate clients, and three of the four heroes started as the sons of well-placed clients. The less fortunate would be less likely to remember their life-histories in detail. The stories illustrate a good many aspects of Rundi political life – how unauthorized persons could defy the ruler by receiving homage, how the disobedient were punished by having their property 'eaten up' (as the Zulu would have put it), what kind of offence led a chief to turn a man out of his village, what kind of occasion led the king to pay a visit of compliment, how warriors were in fact remembered and rewarded by their chiefs, and how the sign of royal authority was respected – this last a quite important point when one is estimating the efficacy of government.

*

In the kingdoms where the pastoral aristocracy form a distinct social class, the peasants are often described as serfs. Their position was not exactly like that of serfs in Russia or feudal Europe, since they were not 'tied to the soil' nor to a particular lord. But they were certainly second-class citizens and were subject to a number of disabilities. In Ankole the Iru were not allowed to own productive cattle, so that a peasant could never build up a herd. Occasionally a Hima might give a barren cow or a bull calf to an Iru who had done him some service. These animals were used in bride-wealth payments, but they had no other value except as meat. Iru could not take part in war, and they were not appointed to any but very minor chiefships – for obvious reasons, since otherwise they would be in positions where they had authority over Hima. They were not entitled to blood revenge if one of them was killed by a Hima, though they might be successful in begging the Mugabe to award them compensation. But if a Hima were killed by an Iru, his kin could take vengeance without waiting for the Mugabe's authorization as they had to do if the killer was another Hima. But if Iru were second-class citizens, they were still citizens. They were entitled to seek protection from the chiefs against exactions by Hima who were not chiefs.

The Hutu of Ruanda and Urundi were better off in the sense that they could get the use of cattle through clientage agreements, though their control of these was always conditional. The lord might take them back if he was dissatisfied with the client and wanted to break off the relationship, and he did take his share of the increase from time to time, and presumably used this to attach to himself other clients. Hutu had to follow the armies to war, though they did not fight and so had no chance of capturing booty. In Urundi all herding was expected to be done by Hutu, and those Tusi who did their own herding were members of clans believed to have come relatively recently from Ankole and described as Hima (which in Urundi is a derogatory term).

All these descriptions are built up from memories of the past. From what they tell us it would seem that the peasants were rather better placed in Ruanda than they were in Ankole. But in Ruanda there have been riots in recent years in protest against the domination of the Tusi, whereas nothing of the kind has happened in Ankole. One reason for the discontent in Ruanda seems to be that the Hutu are short of land for cultivation because so much is required for the grazing of Tusi cattle. It may be that the Tusi have suffered less than the peoples of Uganda from the epidemics of rinderpest which have decimated the herds from time to time. Also British policy has allowed Iru to attain posts in the modern administration of Ankole, whereas the Belgians until very recently showed much greater respect for the traditional political structure. So many extraneous factors have affected the recent history of both these peoples that one could not take this contrast as evidence of a similar contrast in the past.

The existence of slaves in the households of important people is remembered in several of these countries. They were war captives who were either brought home by their own captors or allotted by the ruler to favoured warriors. It fell to them to do the heaviest and most unpopular work, notably fetching wood and water. They were not chattels to be bought and sold, since in the economy of these countries there was no buying and selling, except perhaps in Buganda after the Arabs had introduced cowry shells as currency. What put them at a disadvantage was that they had no kin to defend or assist them and so were more completely dependent upon their masters than a client on his lord. According to Roscoe, the owner of a slave was entitled to kill him, and obviously there would be no one to seek vengeance for him. Chiefs gave one another slaves as presents, and, Roscoe says, in payment of debts. According to him people who could not pay debts were enslaved by their debtors or gave their children in pawn; these are customs familiar in West Africa but not recorded anywhere else in East Africa. It is also open to question whether 'thousands of slaves' were actually sold to the Arabs from Buganda.

There was definitely not a permanent hereditary slave class. A slave could marry a woman of his master's household or village; his master would probably pay the necessary bridewealth. His children's origin would gradually be forgotten, or at least not referred to. The Ganda like to remember the past as a time when any bright boy could go any distance, and they can support this view up to a point by the fact that the Ganda were not, like the Nkole and Ruanda, divided into two by a theoretically impassable barrier. Both in Ankole and Ruanda it was actually possible for members of the peasant class to be appointed to minor offices. The Iru tax collectors in Ankole have been mentioned. In Ruanda people told Maquet that Hutu were sometimes appointed as 'chiefs of the land' with responsibility for collecting tribute in produce and also for settling boundary disputes. But when he asked for names, the anthropologist's nearest equivalent to consulting records, the same two or three names were mentioned again and again, leading to the conclusion that the cases where this had happened were so rare that they had become famous.

When it is too late to observe the relationship of lord and client or of master and slave in operation, one's mental picture of it is bound to be influenced by one's personal estimate of the kind of thing that is likely to have happened. Such a judgement in its turn is influenced by each person's reading of history, his political attitude, the extent of his general sympathy with the under-dog, his inclination to view the past in a rosy light or desire to defend African institutions against hostile prejudice. One can say, 'Of course clients were sometimes ill-treated, but . . .' or 'Of course there was some limit to oppression, but . . .'

Maquet points out that the client-patron relationship in Ruanda was only voluntary in the sense that a client could choose his patron. In the general insecurity of the pastoral states no person of small substance was safe without a protector, and this applied particularly to the Hutu, who seem to have had no rights at all except as clients of a Tusi who would assert his own rights in protecting them. He also remarks that it was a serious matter for a client to break with his protector, since he was likely to lose all his cattle, including any that he might have acquired by barter or as a reward for labour as well as the herd which constituted the bond of clientage. He also remarks, however, that the right of the lord to take all his client's cattle appears only to have been formally recognized since native custom was codified by the Belgian authorities.

Maquet does, however, show that, even if the lord got more out of the relationship than the client, there were some checks on his exploitation of it. Granted that it was difficult for a client to break with his lord, it was not impossible.

More important, young men as they grew up entered into new clientships, and great men wished to have the kind of reputation that would attract new followers. The possibility for one man to be the client of several lords also enabled him to play one off against the other. There was also recourse to those superior chiefs who held courts, and of whom we know so little. Every man had his political superiors as well as his personal lord – his army chief, chief of the land, and chief of the cattle, whose support could be invoked against injustice.

The situation of the Ganda peasant was less complicated; he had one chief and one only, and was obliged to render tribute and labour to him as well as to the Kabaka. But there was a parallel in that the recourse against injustice was the transfer of allegiance, and that this might be difficult. The Ganda peasant, not having cattle, had less to lose, but it is said that if a chief knew that one of his men was planning to leave him, he would fall on him and seize his possessions. But Ganda chiefs too wanted followers, and indeed needed them if they were to produce the manpower expected of them for work at the capital, and keep up their own state in the manner thought to be fitting. These were the influences which kept the exactions of Ganda chiefs within bounds and even led them to approximate to the ideal of the just and generous chief.

CHAPTER 8

Kings, Courts, and Princes

EVERY leader who has a following also has a court, that is a place where his followers gather round to do honour to him, and which is made conspicuous and different from ordinary people's houses by its external appearance and its internal organization. This is as true of the Anuak village headman as it is of the Kabaka of Buganda. Both of them, and all the leaders and rulers in between, are distinguished from the rest of the political community by the right to wear special dress and ornaments, to use particular furnishings in their houses, to be addressed and referred to in ways that are appropriate for no one else. It is worth while considering these external symbols of the leader's position as we find them in these two examples, for in this respect there is no sharp distinction between those which are governed by states and those with less familiar kinds of government.

An Anuak headman's court is marked out from the rest of the village by the posts which his followers carve to put in its fence. He wears sandals because it is not consistent with his dignity for him to touch the earth with his feet, and everyone who walks past his court must either keep out of sight or bend double so as not to pass across his line of vision.

A noble's court is more conspicuous. It is quite differently planned from an ordinary homestead, which consists of one or two huts in a cleared space surrounded by a fence, with a hearth outside the entrance at which a fire is kindled in the evening for men to sit around and talk. The noble has his homestead consisting of the huts of his wives (more numerous than any commoner's), but his court is additional to it. It consists essentially of a large open space to which people can come to pay their respects. The noble sits on a big circular mound of beaten mud, either in the open or under a thatched roof. If the mound is in the open he still has a roofed hut to withdraw to if it rains or the sun is too hot. He also has a fenced-in dining enclosure where he entertains guests of equal rank. A grass fence may surround the court or these buildings may simply stand in the open near the noble's homestead. Near them is the place where dances are held, and there is a forked post to hang up the drums which accompany the dance, and others against which dancers lean their spears. The more important nobles provide shelters for their officials to sit in in the daytime; they all have their homes in the village.

Special words are used to describe all the parts of the royal household as well as objects used in it. These words must be used when speaking of the noble's court and his possessions and must never be used in any other context; this custom reminds people, even when they are not in his presence, of the difference between a noble and ordinary folk.

Every important noble has officials responsible for seeing that the court is adequately provided with ground grain and beer (which his wives prepare), for cooking and serving his food, accompanying and protecting him on journeys, and other duties. He also has a captain of his bodyguard. One of his sons organizes hunting and fishing expeditions for him, and could be sent on his behalf to other villages. One official is left in charge of the village if the noble himself goes away. Each has a title, a special form of greeting given to himself alone, and is supposed to build his house in a special position in relation to the court.

The youths of his following cook his food and fetch water for him to drink, in special pots, covered with fur, which they carry on their heads. These pots are treated with the respect due to the noble himself, and when they pass, anyone who meets them must get off the path and crouch down in the grass.

When nobles themselves travel they expect to be treated

with similar or even greater marks of respect, and sometimes they are accompanied by musicians whose strains both cheer their journey and give warning of their approach. The kings of Buganda once travelled with drummers and flute players too; but the present Kabaka traverses his realms by car.

These small-scale courts have all the essential elements of a court; a special recognizable lay-out of the buildings, with special furnishings not used by ordinary people (in this case the skins that floor the reception hut, lion and leopard skins of which the noble claims a monopoly); a special etiquette; a numerous body of servants with officials to organize their work.

The same elements can be seen in the courts of all the Interlacustrine Bantu chiefs. They were developed to the highest degree of elaboration in that of the Kabaka of Buganda, as it was when Speke saw it and as Sir Apolo Kagwa remembered it. The importance of a court when one is examining political and social relations lies in the gathering of persons all in some way dependent upon the king. The humblest of these are the court servants who actually work to maintain the splendour, formality, and hospitality of the court; these may be people who spend their whole life there – slaves taken by the king as his share in war spoils or presented to him by their masters – or they may be people who are supplied in relays by the chiefs of different parts of the country. These people hardly expect to rise above the performance of menial tasks, and one of the hazards of their life is the recognized right of the ruler to punish in the most painful ways any action which could be regarded as an offence against his person.

More important in the system of political relationships, even if they do not have any specific responsibilities in the government of the country, are the court officials, the men who are responsible for the smooth running of everyday life. Of course this was not expected to be as streamlined at a Bantu court as it must be at Buckingham Palace. Still, food had to be provided for larger numbers of people than ever ate together in any subject's household, the royal state had to be kept up in whatever manner tradition had laid down, and an African court had a ritual aspect which has never characterized the courts that we know of in European history, contemporaneous as they are with Christianity and the growth of a church with its own hierarchy of officials.

Beattie's description of the personnel of the Nyoro court as it is today gives a very good idea of what can be regarded as characteristic of Interlacustrine Bantu courts, with the inevitable proviso that that of Buganda in its heyday was more elaborate than any of the others. Beattie's list includes 'the custodian of the royal graves, men responsible for the more important of the royal drums, caretakers and "putters-on" of the royal crowns, custodians of spears, stools, and other regalia, cooks, bath attendants, herdsmen, potters, barkcloth makers, musicians, and many others'. In Speke's time in Buganda listening to music was a favourite royal pastime.

Beattie's list falls into two parts. It begins with the ritual officials – people who take care of the material objects which the king has to possess in order to be king, who repair them when necessary, and are responsible for producing them on the ceremonial occasions when they are needed – and goes on to those on whom the daily life of the court depends.

In a royal household as large as that of Buganda, this day-to-day organization and provisioning was in itself a major task of administration. It does not seem to have been the direct responsibility of the Katikiro, as apparently it was in small kingdoms like those of the Soga. If it had been possible for an anthropologist to live there in the days of its greatness – as some have at other African courts – an intensely interesting study might have been made of the distribution of authority within the palace. As it is, all we know is that there was one titled official who was the royal cook and another who had the special responsibility of seeing that the royal household was supplied with firewood. Speke saw 1,600 men engaged in moving bundles of firewood from one courtyard in the palace to another; he said this was done as a means of counting them, and found it very ridiculous.

The royal cook did not of course himself prepare the innumerable parcels of plantains, wrapped up in green leaves and boiled and then placed in shallow wicker baskets, which constituted the standard dish at a Ganda meal. This was the responsibility of the royal wives in turn. It was their business to know how much food was needed for any given meal and to see that it was cooked by women servants and slaves. The entire staff of the royal household was fed from the royal kitchens – serving-women, slaves, bodyguards, pages, the court musicians who played for the king at night or when he went on a journey, the gate-keepers who were stationed at the passages from one courtyard to another to make it harder for anyone to steal into the presence of the king or of one of his wives. Kauta, the official cook, was responsible largely for the provision of meat, a luxury in Africa and one that all persons of importance were expected to offer their guests. All the baskets of food were displayed in front of the Kabaka, and he allocated appropriate numbers to be distributed by the persons whom Roscoe tantalizingly calls 'the heads of each department' of his household.

In addition to the chief cook there were a chief brewer, a chief herdsman, an official responsible for the supply of firewood, another for the well from which the king's water was drawn, and another in charge of the pages – the swarms of little boys with their heads tied up in barkcloth turbans whom Speke saw constantly going to and fro with messages, and who suffered such frightful punishments for being late with a message or getting it wrong. An important official looked after the sacred fire at the entrance to the royal palace which had to be kept constantly burning and was extinguished only on the death of a Kabaka.

All these people can be thought of as personal servants of the king in a different sense from that in which he was served by the territorial chiefs. They were not responsible for the government of his realms but simply for the maintenance of his court. Nevertheless they have their place in a study of government, since the court was the centre of government and the maintenance of the royal dignity had its part to play in securing acceptance of the royal authority. Also, the king's control of foreign relations was maintained by the rule that strangers to the kingdom must come there before being allowed to proceed further, and for their reception too the dignity of the court was important.

But the king also had officials whose functions were purely ritual. The ritual of kingship is a subject that needs to be treated separately, but an enumeration of the Ganda court personnel would not be completed unless it included one very important ritual official who had the title of Kimbugwe. This man was in charge of the shrine which stood in the open space before the entrance to the palace, beside the sacred fire, and contained various magical objects that were believed to be necessary to the king's welfare, and also his umbilical cord. The cord was enclosed in a container decorated with cowry-shells. It was supposed to contain the spirit of the after-birth, which was thought of as the king's twin, and at each new moon it was brought out and presented to the king; then it was placed in the doorway of the temple for the moon to shine on it, and then rubbed with butter (the only oil known to the Ganda). When a king died a temple was built in which this and his jawbone were preserved, and the Kimbugwe who had looked after it during his lifetime continued to do so as an official of the temple.

Although the Kimbugwe had no governmental authority he had privileges shared by no one else except the Katikiro and the Kabaka's mother and sister. Areas of land were allotted to him in various parts of the country in which he had the services of the peasants but did not have to turn them out for work in the capital. Not only was he not required to collect tribute for the king from these areas, but he received a share of what was collected on the king's behalf, as did the Katikiro and the royal ladies; and each of these four dignitaries appointed messengers to go with those sent by the king and see that the due amount was collected.

Anyone who rendered a personal service to the king might be rewarded with authority over an area of land and the right to say who should live in it and to receive tribute and labour from these people. This authority implied the right and the duty to keep the peace and settle disputes between people living on the land, so that these fief-holders can appropriately be called chiefs. But they were not subordinate to the great territorial chiefs who were described in the last chapter; rather, they formed a counterpoise to them as 'king's men' with a more direct and personal loyalty to the Kabaka.

The Ganda court represented the extreme of elaboration in the Interlacustrine Bantu area. But that of Ruanda included a number of officials to whom there was no parallel in Buganda, or indeed anywhere within many hundreds of miles. These men, who numbered about a dozen, were the official guardians of the traditions of the royal ritual. Their office was hereditary, and each of them was responsible for passing on his knowledge to his successor. They were responsible for the correct performance of the national rites at harvest and in wartime, and those which needed to be done in case of disasters such as drought, untimely rain, or epidemics. Each had only a part of the necessary knowledge; that is, each had his part to play at one particular point in the ceremonies, and he jealously guarded this secret which made the king and indeed the kingdom dependent on him, while they all depended collectively on one another. A tradition had been established in Ruanda that certain lineages had the right in turn to provide the king's chief wife, and these officials were responsible for seeing that the right order was followed. In practice this may sometimes have meant deciding between competing claims, and it is easy to see what power their position gave them. Three of them had the right to know which of his sons the king had chosen to succeed him. Like the Ganda Kimbugwe they were rewarded with control over areas of land from which no tribute was collected.

*

Another characteristic which is shared by rulers, great and small, in East Africa is that they are, or have been when they were independent, privileged to inflict punishments on their subjects of a nature which would not be tolerated in the 'anarchic' societies, and for actions which would not be considered as offences in the relations between other people. They have been able to do so because they could employ their personal followers to enforce these punishments, which consisted in physical injuries or death or spoliation of possessions.

This privilege of the Anuak nobles was mentioned earlier. It is said that some of them keep pet birds or animals in the hope that some child will injure one, and the noble can then punish the offence by seizing the goods of the child's father. Anyone who smashed a pot belonging to a noble, or used the private path from his house to the river, would be punished in the same way.

There is an eye-witness record of the types of punishment inflicted in the Ganda court in the journal of the explorer Speke, who had to spend three or four months there before he could persuade the Kabaka to allow him to travel further; without such an authorization he could not have counted on safety from attack, and if he had gone on against the Kabaka's expressed wishes he would certainly have been attacked by Mutesa's warriors. To Speke, what he saw was evidence that the Kabaka was a bloodthirsty despot, and descriptions such as his helped to convince people in England that it must be for the advantage of the Ganda to be brought under British rule; and it has been the aim of all colonial rulers to put an end to this kind of physical violence. The fact that it was practised has also been one of the principal reasons why Europeans have regarded African peoples as 'savage' or 'barbarous' and requiring to be civilized by outside influences; and comparable facts are quoted in this sense by some writers today. They provide welcome arguments to people who wish to claim an inherent superiority for 'European civilization' – an entity which is not always very clearly defined.

Anthropologists try to see the societies they study through the eyes of the people who belong to them, and who take for granted that their social system as a whole is good despite its disadvantages (just as most members of European societies do). We have been accused of romanticizing ways of life that ought to be obsolete even if they are not (and in this case they are). We have certainly tended to minimize the physical cruelties practised and suffered in the simpler societies – or to evade the issue with *tu quoque* arguments about the cruelties of modern warfare.

Let us then conceal nothing from the reader but note what Speke actually saw. He got the impression that most people were really afraid of what would happen to them if they displeased the Kabaka. A little Indian boy in his own party, no doubt echoing his elders, told him he 'disliked Uganda, where people's lives are taken like those of fowls'.

Speke's first experience of the assertion of royal privilege was made before he entered Uganda. He was travelling with an uncle of the Kabaka, called Nyamugundi, whom he had met at the court of a neighbouring chief. A letter from Grant, who had been left behind ill, was brought by a young man wearing a leopard skin, which in Uganda is the privilege of persons descended from a Kabaka. Nyamugundi challenged the young man's right to wear a leopard skin, and first ordered two followers to tear it off him. When the young man resisted Nyamugundi called on him to prove his claim by tracing his ancestry, and when he failed said, ' "What could he do now to expiate his folly? If the matter was taken before Mutesa he would lose his head; was it not better he should pay one hundred cows?" All agreeing to this, the young man said he would do so.'

Speke saw the son of a high official 'led off for execution' for having failed to carry out the correct formalities of salutation to the Kabaka, but was able to beg him off, as he was later when, on a hunting party, one of the royal wives plucked a fruit of some kind and offered it to the king, apparently not knowing that it was regarded as impudence in a woman to offer him a gift. A small boy who misreported a message from Speke to the king had his ears cut off. One of Speke's own men strayed into forbidden quarters and was put in the stocks (but given food, and he managed to get out and run away). Speke also saw the Kabaka on his way out hunting shoot 'a woman tied by the hands to be punished for some offence' whom he happened to notice in passing. There seems no doubt that Mutesa enjoyed beating and shooting people, and that this was recognized as his prerogative.

When he had been living near the royal palace for about ten days Speke wrote that 'nearly every day' he had seen women led away to execution, and he records an occasion when 'some thirty women' were brought before the Kabaka for punishment. He also describes how, when the army came back from an invasion of Bunyoro, the men who were said to have fought badly were seized, bound, and 'led or rather tumbled away' to be executed. The penalty for them, according to Roscoe, was to be burnt to death on faggots kindled by a branch from the sacred fire that burned outside the palace gates. Speke tells of even more gruesome treatment, but does not say he witnessed it. On one occasion the king asked Speke to turn out his soldiers to plunder the household of a courtier who had offended him.

Speke several times saw warriors just back from raids coming to pay their respects to the king; he also once heard a courtier ordered to go out and seize those who had been too slow in coming. A few days later 'the whole country around the palace was in a state of commotion' and in this man's courtyard 'men, women, and children, with feet in stocks very like the old parish stocks in England, waited his pleasure, to see what demands he would make upon them as the price of their release.' Later he saw 'no less than 150 women, besides girls, goats, and various other things, seizures from refractory state officers, who, it was said, had been too proud to present themselves at court for a period exceeding propriety.'

All these are specific instances. In a general description of the Ganda court, however, Speke says that people who had been condemned could buy themselves off by making suitable presents to the king.

The people who denounced the cruelty of African rulers were not always in a position to throw stones. Their line was more apt to be, 'When I do it, it's different.' Here is a story that Speke tells with some complacency: He had in his household a girl who had been in high favour with King Suna, Mutesa's father, and on his death had become part of the retinue of the queen mother. She gave this girl to Speke, explaining that such a present was a normal part of the hospitality offered to distinguished guests. The girl seemed very unhappy and cried all the time, and eventually became ill – 'shamming ill', Speke called it. She would not take the medicine he prescribed and said a goat should be sacrificed to make her well. Speke then discovered that a 'magician' had given her this advice, or rather 'had put Meri up to this trick of extorting a goat from me in order that he might benefit by it himself'. 'I immediately ordered him to be seized and bound to the flagstaff,' says Speke. He then held an inquiry which established that the magician had been in his house without permission; this would not have been tolerated by a Ganda. Speke therefore 'sentenced him to fifty lashes'. The unhappy girl begged him rather to punish her. Speke saw that there was something in the situation that he did not understand. His method of dealing with it was to dismiss the girl from his service and have the sentence carried out. Then he lay awake all night worrying about his cruelty to the girl.

Two questions are prompted by these facts. First, do they

justify us in making the assumption that people living in primitive society are morally less developed than members of the kinds of society which, without closely defining them, we call civilized, and second, do they justify us in calling this kind of government despotic, a word very often used to describe it?

There is indeed plenty of evidence that at this and other African courts people who displeased the ruler suffered severely for it, and in ways that those of us who call ourselves humanitarians condemn as the infliction of suffering to no purpose. We are reminded of the association of the word 'cruel' with the word 'savage'. Speke also condemned Mutesa. He thought that the punishments Mutesa inflicted were out of all proportion to the offences committed, and that their infliction was arbitrary and capricious. He was particularly concerned at the execution of women. His descriptions were among the influences that led Christian missionaries to feel that they could improve the lot of many unfortunate people by teaching their religion to the Ganda, and they are part of the literature that led the nineteenth century to see the partition of Africa wholly as a civilized mission. It is also indubitable that no African wishes for the return of this particular aspect of the past.

Flogging is, admittedly, not a death sentence, and it is not reckoned as a form of torture, nor as one of the 'cruel and unusual punishments' which the American authors of the Bill of Rights considered it necessary to ban; indeed some respected members of our own society regret that it is no longer practised in our prisons. Speke would no doubt have argued, with these ladies, that it is necessary to be feared in order to be obeyed, or, more specifically, that certain actions can only be prevented by attaching extremely painful consequences to them. The Conservative ladies, to do them justice, only wish to inflict the painful consequences on persons who themselves inflict pain.

There are two separate questions here: whether and why people are callous about physical suffering, and whether and when the infliction of physical suffering is necessary for the maintenance of authority.

The answer to the first question is that a callous attitude towards human suffering, which is certainly characteristic of African society, has been characteristic of most of humanity throughout most of its history. If one is thinking of social values rather than of individual behaviour, one need only consider how often in European history nations which could claim great intellectual and aesthetic achievements have approved of all kinds of physical brutalities. (Nobody in Buganda was ever hanged in chains, as were traitors against Tudor kings, and African technical knowledge was not advanced enough for such instruments as the rack.) This callousness, I suggest, is the attitude of people who expect the ordinary course of life to bring them a good deal of physical pain that they must just put up with; and its opposite, great concern with the avoidance and prevention of pain, goes with the advances in medical knowledge that make this possible. But this latter attitude certainly does not characterize the action of political authorities in all the states which today call themselves civilized.

This brings us to the question of the place of corporal punishment in the maintenance of law and order. There was no such thing in the societies with minimal government described at the beginning of this book. Killing was permissible in revenge for killing, but all other wrongs were righted by the payment of compensation. Of course there was nobody who commanded enough force to inflict the kind of punishment described by Speke. Why, though, should rulers who do command force use it in this way? To make themselves feared and show their power, undoubtedly. Also, undoubtedly, they liked it – as did some of the 'hanging judges' of our own history.

Physical cruelties in general are much more revolting to people whose interests are not involved in the actions being punished than they are to people who identify themselves with the injured party; Speke is our example of this argu-

ment. The number of people who, even today, really believe
in the humane treatment of criminals is a small minority.
Then Speke's revulsion against the cruelties of the Ganda
court must have been due in part to the fact that he actually
had to witness them, and in part to his feelings that they
were capricious and out of proportion to the offence. Most
of us would have felt the same in his place. We certainly
could not have been persuaded that a breach of court etiquette deserved instant death, for we have long ceased to
believe in the sacredness of royal personages; yet it is not
unreasonable to think so if one rates this sacredness high
enough. But it might not have been so hard, on reflection,
to accept the argument that the majesty of the Kabaka must
be maintained by his right to punish whom he chose. The
acceptance of this principle maintained the political order
from which his followers benefited – as long as they avoided
offending him themselves. It may be that political power
needs to be more securely based before it can afford to
refrain from showing its teeth. In a modern highly organized state the citizen knows so well how little chance he has
against the guardians of the law that the latter do not need
to demonstrate their power by maltreating him. And yet
they very often do – so often that we may conclude that this
particular feature of Ganda society was not the best to
choose as an index of its savagery.

Was the Kabaka a despot? This depends what is meant
by a despot. Once it simply meant a ruler who was not
chosen by popular election. In this sense, of course, the
Kabaka and his brother kings were all of them despots. As
this word is popularly used, however, it implies a ruler whose
subjects gain nothing from his rule and lose much, and it
is also implied that, apart from the favoured few, all his
subjects suffer equally. It is certainly true that the tax-
gathering organization of the Ganda was so well organized
that few can have escaped it. It is on record that peasants
from the country were afraid of being summoned to work
at court because it was so easy to get into trouble. But people

outside the immediate range of the royal presence must have carried on their lives undisturbed by his caprices; after all, in order to incur his wrath it was necessary to have some personal relationship with him. In primitive conditions of transport and communications, the larger the realm the less despotic the ruler can be.

Another question which is raised by this discussion of the punishments inflicted by the Kabaka is that of the beginnings of criminal law. Modern states divide breaches of the law into civil offences which only injure the wronged individual, and crimes which are offences against the public peace. Civil wrongs can be put right by compensation. Crimes must be punished; either the guilty person is made to suffer or he has to make a payment to the representative of the state. In the political communities with minimal government there are no crimes; all wrongs are righted by revenge or compensation. Radcliffe-Brown thought the *kingolle* of the Kamba – the collective killing described in Chapter 2 – was the most rudimentary African example of punishment as opposed to damages. So, he argued, the actions which the Kamba thought were so injurious to the common weal that they could not be left to be settled between individuals were witchcraft and repeated theft.

But the offences described by Speke are of quite a different nature. Unfortunately he too often describes punishments and executions without saying what offences were being punished. But when he does tell us, the actions punished were offences against the dignity of the ruler. There is here no element at all of the idea that a wrong done by one subject to another is so serious a matter that it must be treated as an offence against the whole community. Only if we say that to the Ganda the Kabaka personifies the whole community can we argue that it is a crime in this sense to sneeze in his presence. What we seem rather to see here is the idea that the Kabaka is so high above his subjects that offences against *him* cannot be made good by compensation but must be punished – and also that actions which would not be offences if done to anyone else are so when done to him.

Speke's description leaves us with the impression of a rule which had no aims beyond the indulgence of a capricious pleasure in the infliction of pain. We cannot dispute the fact that he saw what he says he did unless there are grounds for regarding his statements as unreliable, and no such grounds have been advanced. Then must we say that the state in the form in which we find it here is no more than an engine of exploitation? Several answers can be made. One has been suggested already – that the Kabaka embodied to the Ganda their power as a nation, so that expressions of his power over people who failed in respect or obedience were matters for satisfaction to those who were not themselves the victims. Moreover, although it might appear from Speke's account that his powers were without limitation, there were checks upon it at least in theory. There was an ideal of a good ruler, and this was publicly expressed in the form of exhortations during the ceremonies of accession. Very little of these has been preserved for the Ganda, but an account of the Nyoro court written by the present king tells how he had to swear that 'he will never frighten his nation, he must rule his people peacefully, he must admit foreigners to settle in his country, he must equally love his subjects, however poor they may be, he must look after orphans, and he must justly cut cases' (i.e. decide disputes – the metaphor of cutting is used for this in several Bantu languages). Then, the Katikiro was expected to use his influence to restrain a tyrannous king. And finally there was the danger that a rebellious prince would readily secure support against a king who had provoked the resentment of too many of his subjects.

*

Hereditary rulers belong to royal houses, and in most African societies – all those discussed here – there is no rule that establishes unequivocally how the succession is to go.

Hence the sons of a king are competitors from the moment they are old enough to understand who they are. They may also be in competition with the king himself if he is unpopular; since the essence of the belief in hereditary rule is that only a son of the king can replace the king. A king's son, even if he does not actually seek to usurp his father's throne – and few have done this – may be able to establish the independence of a corner of the kingdom.

So relationships within royal lineages are uneasy. The duty of sons to obey their fathers, of brothers to stand by one another in defence of their common interests, is recognized. But the conflict between duty and self-interest is particularly acute when the prize is a crown, and in the larger kingdoms this was so clearly recognized that princes were not employed as court officials or as territorial chiefs, though of course they exercised authority over the estates allotted to them. It was mainly in the smaller ones that rulers entrusted their sons with a share of political power.

A little was said earlier about kinship systems based on lineage. The essence of such systems is that for the purpose of the transmission of rights and property people are organized into groups tracing descent through *one* parent – in East Africa the father. These groups are the lineages. Members of the same lineage cannot marry. Hence, everyone's father and mother belong to different lineages, and in addition to his lineage kin everyone has maternal kin – that is the members of his mother's lineage. The description of the rivalry for the emblems of nobility among the Anuak, and also for the headmanship of a village, shows how when members of the same lineage are in competition they draw support from their maternal kinsmen.

The account of the expansion of the Alur chiefly lineages shows how a chief could deal with unruly sons by planting them out at a distance, in places outside the domain which he actually claimed to rule. As the generations went on, the descendants of these unruly sons might become independent chiefs or be tribute-paying vassals of the line which inherited the original chiefship; they would be too far separated from it to be rivals for a single throne.

The little Soga kingdoms illustrate a practice which took no account of the danger of princely rivalry. A ruler would set over a part of his territory the favourite son whom he wished to succeed him. But he could not determine the succession by his own choice. Another son might be installed as his successor, and then this son would find his brother in possession of part of the kingdom. Brother probably would not fight against brother, but as the generations passed and the relationship grew more distant, these princes rebelled, sometimes successfully. The Soga fully recognize that the chiefs from commoner lineages who were the ruler's clients were his best protection against his own kinsmen, and one story told to Fallers ends 'from then on he ceased to trust the princes and relied instead upon his chiefs'.

Most of the peoples in this area who recognize any kind of kingship have various arrangements expressly designed to limit danger to the ruler from his kin. One such method is to keep the princes away from the court. A Shilluk prince is born at the home of his mother and is brought up among his maternal kin. A settlement chief, probably one of these maternal kinsmen (in-laws of the Reth), is put in charge of him; the Reth chooses for this duty a man whom he thinks he can trust. When he grows up he has his own village, near the kin among whom he has grown up. It is believed that the Reth ought to be killed when his strength is failing, since the welfare of people and country are bound up with his physical condition; and since only a son can succeed him, such a son might be entitled to kill him. Evans-Pritchard doubts whether princes actually killed their fathers, and thinks it more likely that, if some misfortune such as drought or sickness afflicted the people, feeling would turn against the Reth and some prince would rebel with the backing of his maternal kin. However, Shilluk kings were afraid their sons might murder them, and princes were not allowed to be in the capital at night.

The Ganda court officials included a chief, Kasuju, who had the sole function of taking charge of the royal princes. He allotted each of them to a guardian, and at the same time land was allotted to the prince, which when he grew up would be his estate. The precaution against rebellion here was that a prince was not allowed to attach himself to any of the great chiefs, or even to visit one as a guest. Ganda kings feared their brothers as well as their sons, and once a king had begotten enough sons to feel confident that the succession was secure, even in African conditions of high mortality, he had his own brothers put to death.

All these kingdoms have stories of rebellions led by princes, some of them successful, others not. But of course the moment when rivalry between them came to a head was the moment when a king died and his heir had to be chosen from among his sons. There is usually a recognized procedure for making the choice, yet at the same time it is never taken for granted that the accession will be peaceful. It may happen, for example, that the king-makers cannot agree.

The belief is common among these peoples that a time when there is no ruler is a time of lawlessness and anarchy, though this may only be a metaphorical way of expressing their conception of the king as the ultimate source of order and justice. But it is certainly possible that it will be a time of civil war.

Generally there are king-makers whose right to choose the successor is recognized. Ruanda has the three *abiru*, who are supposed to know the wishes of the dead king, though these are secret from all others, so that they may perhaps follow their own wishes. Soga kingdoms rely on the senior men of the royal lineage, just as commoners would in choosing an heir. For the Shilluk the choice was made by the most important settlement heads, and this does mean that more heed was paid to the views of the nation at large than in the Inter-lacustrine Bantu states. In the Ganda procedure, as described by Roscoe's informants, the princes were summoned to the capital by Kasuju, who, with the Katikiro, had attended the royal deathbed and knew the last king's wishes. The decision was actually taken by these two chiefs along with the ritual chief Kimbugwe, and then put before the ten saza chiefs for their approval. The princes were lined up in front of the palace and the Katikiro asked Kasuju to give the Ganda a king; Kasuju walked down the line as though making his choice, then took the chosen one by the hand and led him to the Katikiro. The Katikiro challenged anyone who was not satisfied with the choice to fight for his candidate, and, according to Roscoe, fighting would begin at once and go on till one of the rivals was killed. If this did happen, it must have followed on a period during which rival princes were mustering support, and both must have taken care to have their supporters on the spot. It is easier to imagine them gathering their forces in different parts of the country for a later confrontation.

Of Ankole Oberg tells us that the succession was expected to be decided by a war to the death between the king's sons, a test which satisfied the people that their new ruler was the strongest among the eligible competitors. To secure political control of the kingdom it was necessary to have physical possession of the sacred emblem of the nation, the royal drum; we are reminded of the contest for the Anuak emblems, and in fact some sacred object of this kind figures in all rituals of kingship. The princes, then, did not begin by attacking one another; they fought if their armies met on the way to seize the drum. There does not seem to be any story of an attempt to wrest the drum from the possession of the prince who had it. Sometimes princes killed one another by assassination or poison, avoiding a pitched battle. During this period of uncertainty the great chiefs on the borders of the country were expected to keep out of the struggle and protect the country against invasion by enemies. The victorious prince did not necessarily have to kill all his rivals; some might flee the country. But there was expected to be a duel between the two last remaining contestants. Then the new ruler could consider himself safe from attack by rivals, and he further ensured this by substituting followers of his own for his father's chiefs. Many of these would be members of his mother's lineage, on whom he would have relied for his main support. His own mother's brothers would be made leaders of warrior bands, and their sons would form the nucleus of his court attendants. In Ankole the king's mother's brothers had the right to collect tribute on their own account as the king himself did.

The contestants also had recourse to sorcery against their rivals. This was a sphere in which women could help them, and the mothers of rival princes, and sometimes their sisters too, employed sorcerers for this purpose, and in Ankole were also expected to perform rites that would protect them from the angry spirits of their slain rivals. In Buganda the princes' mothers were kept under strict surveillance during an interregnum in the hope of preventing such activities. The rewards of victory were almost as great for the mother and one sister of the winner as they were for himself, for reasons that will be given shortly.

Unfortunately no traveller with the observant if censorious eye of a Speke or Baker passed through any of these countries at the moment between two reigns, and there is no record that would give any idea how many competitors for the succession there were likely to be. Kings had many sons, but not many, probably, could gain a following strong enough to make it worth while embarking on a civil war, and although Oberg's description does sometimes make us think of a tournament with a series of heats, it is more likely that there were not more than two contestants on most occasions.

Although the death of a ruler was followed by a period of uncertainty even when there was not actual war, and although the time when there was no ruler was popularly thought of as a time of lawlessness, the whole political structure did not collapse and have to be built afresh for every new reign. Everybody knew that once the succession was decided government would be carried on by the new ruler and his new chiefs on the same basis as before; new men would fill old offices. One would be justified in speaking of a constitution. In Ankole there was a guarantee of continuity in the position of the great frontier chiefs, who kept out of the struggle and protected the country against invasion by enemies.

*

In all the large kingdoms two female relatives of the king had a special position. These were his mother and one of his sisters, who had gone through the rites of accession by his side. Queens have no place in these polities; kings have many wives, and the one who is to attain pre-eminence as the mother of the heir cannot be known until he has been chosen, after her husband's death. It is customary in Buganda for a commoner too to be accompanied by his sister when he goes through rites of succession; this may signify in some way that the women members of a lineage as well as the men have an interest in its affairs. But among commoners the position of the woman co-heir has no significance outside the ceremony of installation itself. Among commoners, on the other hand, no widow has any particular status.

With the royal family it is different. The king's mother and his chosen sister have many of the privileges of important chiefs. In Buganda they had their own estates, over which they had the same authority as other private fief-holders, and they had the same privilege as the Katikiro and Kimbugwe of sending their own messengers out with the tax-collecting parties dispatched from the capital. Each had her subordinate chiefs with the same titles ranked in the same order as the Kabaka's. They were entitled to have people put to death, a statement which suggests that this was a royal prerogative, and confirms the view put forward earlier that the hazards of life for the general population of Buganda were only great in the immediate neighbourhood of royalty. They were called 'kings', and at the capital each had a residence separated from the Kabaka's by a valley with a stream in it, since it was said that 'two kings cannot live on one hill'. Speke got on much better with Mutesa's mother than with Mutesa himself, and she promised to provide food for his forty-five men from her own gardens, though actually she never did so.

The royal ladies of Ankole had a similar honoured position, having each her own cattle with herdsmen and warriors to protect them, receiving their share of cattle captured in war, and having, like the king's mother's brothers, the right to demand cattle from whomsoever they pleased. Here the king's mother sat with him when he judged cases, and her consent was required if he wanted to have anyone put to death. She received foreign envoys before they went to the king, and could forbid them to see him. Both she and his sisters performed rites on his behalf, of the kind which male household and lineage heads do among commoners. In Bunyoro also the king's sister has a special position; she holds authority over all women of the royal clan, and is responsible for dealing with disputes arising among them over inheritance or precedence.

The kings of Bunyoro are also said at one time to have had to fight their way to the throne over the bodies of their brothers. One was exempt from the competition: the eldest son of the late king, who was debarred from the succession but made responsible for domestic matters within the royal clan.

Beattie argues that the existence of these two offices of king's brother and king's sister with responsibility for looking after the interests of the royal clan – who are a very numerous body of people because it is a royal privilege to have many wives – makes it unnecessary for the king to concern himself with them and frees him to be the impartial ruler of all Nyoro. There are other ways in which the ties of kinship, with the special obligations that they create, may be limited in the case of rulers. We have noted that most rulers look to their mother's kin for their support against rivals. In doing so they are following a line of conduct which is not peculiar to royalty. Within every lineage there is rivalry, and all men, while recognizing the duty of standing by their lineage kin against outsiders, look to their mother's kin for the disinterested help that can only be given by someone who is not a rival. In many African societies a man is entitled to make demands on his mother's kin which they may not resist. Kings may be in difficulties if they are exposed to such demands, and some societies have rules which protect them. Among the Shilluk, for example, daughters of a Reth are not allowed to marry – so that no Reth has sisters' sons who can make inconvenient claims on him. The Kabaka of Buganda is isolated from lineage claims also, in another way; every Kabaka is affiliated to the clan of his mother, so that although the common descent of princes is recognized, the one who is chosen to rule is set apart from the rest.

CHAPTER 9

Kings and Ritual

IT was suggested earlier that there are two requisites for the establishment of kingship: the support of a following whose first loyalty is to their leader, and some claim to a specially close relationship with supernatural beings. This claim may rest on a belief that the king is actually descended from a god. Or people may believe that certain rites which are essential for the well-being of all can be performed only by a member of the royal lineage, and this only when he has been installed as king with the correct ritual. The king, once chosen and installed, may be held to embody in his person the welfare of the nation, and so be obliged to observe ritual precautions the neglect of which would endanger his whole people.

There are ritual officials among peoples who have no kings, and they are always members of lineages with an exclusive claim to contact with the supernatural world. The Nuer leopard-skin chief, the Dinka master of the fishing spear, and the Nandi *orkoiyot* are examples that have been mentioned earlier. All of these have ritual authority without political power. They are indispensable for certain of the purposes of the political community, but they do not directly command the actions of others.

There are commonly a number of such ritual specialists within a political community, and sometimes one is regarded as pre-eminent, though this never means that the others are treated as subordinate to him. The Nuer do not regard any particular leopard-skin chief as having superior powers to others, for the good reason that they do not look to these men to control forces which are beyond the control of ordinary mortals. The ceremony which a leopard-skin chief performs does not bless a risky venture or cause the forces of nature to behave as they ought; it simply ratifies a situation that already exists, the willingness of enemies to make peace. In some parts of Nuerland the leopard-skin chiefs do not even belong to the aristocratic (or 'dominant') lineages of the divisions of the country where they live.

The Dinka believe that every subdivision of a tribe should have its own spearmaster, a man pre-eminent among many who have ritual powers of the same kind. A new division cannot establish its independence unless it has its own spearmaster, and the move to break away is often initiated by such a man. However, the Dinka ideal is that all of these should recognize the pre-eminence of one, to whom people would look to protect them by his prayers in crises affecting the whole tribe. But in practice there is no such universally recognized hierarchy and the status of individual spear-masters depends upon their reputation for the success of their prayers.

The Nandi *orkoiyot* is also a member of a lineage all of whom are credited with supernatural powers, including the power to harm others by supernatural means. With them, however, only the one 'great *orkoiyot*' is looked to for blessing and magical aid in activities affecting the people as a whole – war and the initiation of the warriors, and the planting of the crops. He is not the only man who claims to be able to control the weather, though people turn to him when others have failed, and if he, the last resort, fails them too they must indeed despair. But his position is inherited; he has not to compete for reputation against other members of his lineage as the Dinka spearmaster has. There is no myth accounting for the magical powers of the *orkoiyot*'s lineage; on the contrary, there is a very matter-of-fact tradition that they came to Nandi country from the Masai about a century ago.

With the Mugwe of the Meru we come for the first time to a person who, without being treated as a king, has the essential spiritual aspect of kingship, that he stands to his people as the symbol of their existence as a people, a unique entity differentiated from their neighbours. What is interesting in this case is that there is not in fact *one* Mugwe: there is one for each of the Meru tribes. Yet all these men are believed to be in some sense one; the supernatural power which they hold is one, though it is embodied in different objects. All are believed to be descended from the first Mugwe, and the first Mugwe, as tradition has it now, was one for all the Meru. Also, it is believed that the Mugwe's lineage is in some way connected with power to control the weather; an early Kenya official recorded that it was supposed to be descended from the rain.

*

It is characteristic of the peoples recognizing kingship that they cherish myths which link its origin with some crucial event in their past history. The first king is not always thought of as contemporaneous with creation; indeed, perhaps more often he is conceived as having come into a world in which there were already people. But his appearance is somehow linked with the establishment of the political order under which his subjects live. The myths of the first Mugwe tell how the Meru escaped from enemies who were persecuting them. Remarkably enough, he saved his people by striking the waters of a lake with his staff to that they parted and left a passage across; and, according to some stories, it was after this crossing that the Meru became a distinct people separated from their neighbours.

The myths of the Shilluk are among the most elaborate that have been recorded; this does not prove necessarily that the Shilluk have an exceptionally rich mythology, but rather that many people have taken pains to collect and write down their myths.

All these myths look back to the events which are supposed to have established the Shilluk polity in its traditional form. The ceremonial with which a Reth is installed on his throne recalls the most important events of this mythical past, and reaffirms the rightness of the order which, as

Shilluk in general see it, has lasted unchanged from the time
when it was first set up. The myths tell how the Shilluk were
led to the present country by Nyikang, a hero of partly
divine ancestry, who brought with him the emblems of kingship. Nyikang made the Shilluk a separate people; their ancestors followed him from a country where they were living
together with the ancestors of the neighbouring peoples. He
travelled with them through the present Shilluk country,
founding as he went the villages that are still recognized and
placing in them the ancestors of their present inhabitants.
He divided the whole kingdom into two parts, one called by
his name. When a Reth is chosen the leaders of these two
divisions must agree on the choice, but an important part of
the ceremonial of accession consists in a mock fight between
them.

The Shilluk believe that Nyikang did not die but simply
disappeared; thus he need never be thought of as suffering
old age or sickness. Moreover, the continued existence of the
Shilluk people is held to be in some way bound up with the
continuance of Nyikang as a living being: 'If Nyikang
should die the whole Shilluk race would perish,' they say.
The Reth is the living representative of Nyikang, and at the
time of his installation the spirit of Nyikang is believed to
enter into him; when this happens he trembles in the
manner that indicates possession by a spirit, and this is the
moment at which he becomes king. Thereafter he partici-
pates in some way in the supernatural qualities of Nyikang.

The Interlacustrine Bantu kings are not considered actually to incarnate the spirit of a divine ancestor. But their
kingship too has its spiritual aspects, linked with the descent
which gives them their claim to the throne. Though a king
may be spoken of as 'owning' his country, it is not simply
inherited as a property. He inherits a total relationship with
land and people (and cattle) for which only one of his line
of descent is held to be fitted, and in virtue of this relationship he symbolizes the total polity so that its health reflects
his health, and his least action may affect his whole king-

dom. Thus it is said that the king of Ruanda must not bend his knee because if he did the extent of the kingdom would become smaller.

What gives the rulers these special powers is their descent from ancestors who, though they are not believed like Nyikang to have actually shared in divinity, are like him in being thought to have originated the traditional order. The rulers who belong to the Bito clan trace their ancestry to the marvellous Chwezi, who, though not gods, are thought of as supermen and as having brought all useful inventions to the countries where their descendants now rule. The ancestor who links them to the Chwezi is remembered as the *only* one left when the Chwezi disappeared, and thus as having founded the only line which could perpetuate their greatness.

Those who do not believe this myth, notably the kings of Ruanda and Buganda, look back to the first appearance of the founder of their line in the kingdom which his descendant now rules. Whereas Nilotic kings take their origin from rivers, the most conspicuous natural features of their flat country, the legends of mountainous Ruanda and hilly Buganda depict the first kings as falling from heaven on a hill-top. For the people of Ruanda it was a later king who 'discovered' cattle and brought to their country the bovine ancestors of the present herds; and yet another gave them their principal types of grain. Kintu, the first of the dynasty of the Ganda, is also believed to have alighted on a hill-top, and, like Nyikang, to have disappeared so that nobody saw him die. Some stories say that he had a 'white' face. Too much has been built on the use of this word. Whiteness symbolizes good things to many peoples, ourselves included; indeed this may be why we flatter ourselves with the adjective 'white'. Its normal associations are with white birds, white animals, and, in some African languages, with the brightness in the sky in daytime. If Kintu's face was white, it was like that of the Chwezi, to look at whom, the people of Ankole say, was 'like looking at the sun'.

When these kings are censured for behaving in a despotic manner it should at least be remembered that the dogma of their more than human origin and powers was not invented by themselves. However it may have come into existence, at the time when we know of their rule it had become an essential part of the world view of their subjects. The man who was invested with royalty played a part which had been written for him generations before, though no doubt he had some freedom in interpreting it. It was a part which authorized and perhaps even required him to act in a way that would not be permitted between two ordinary mortals.

Some peoples have a word for the supernatural power that goes with kingship, and some have ideas about ways of maintaining and reinforcing it, and, occasionally, of distributing it. The Meru call this *kiragu*, and some of them think of it, not exactly as a substance, but as an entity distinct from the person of the Mugwe, given to him by God, possessed and protected by him, and still existing even where there is no Mugwe to hold it, as is the case now in much of Meru country. The Mugwe is thought to hold this substance in his left hand, and for that reason must never at ordinary times let his left hand be seen. This is the hand which he raises in blessing, and it used to be thought that by merely raising it he could halt an enemy.

For the Alur the power of chiefs is called *ker*, but this is not conceived as a power that can be given or taken through any performance of ritual. It is simply known by its fruits. If a chief prospers, and rain falls when he prays for it, this shows that he has *ker*; if he does not have *ker* he ought not to be a chief, and in the old days this would be a reason for neighbouring peoples who had recently accepted an Alur chief to go to his father and request another of his sons in his place.

In Bunyoro chiefly power is associated with a kind of ritual potency called *mahano. Mahano* not only implies power, it also involves danger to its possessor and to others who may come into contact with him, and in order to avert this he has to observe many ritual prohibitions. Many of these prohibitions – for example, that a king must not be seen eating – are observed by other rulers, and are associated with a general notion that they are essential to maintain the well-being of the king and so of the nation; indeed it may be that some of the apparently arbitrary punishments which so impressed Speke at the Ganda court were inflicted for breaches of these taboos. The peculiar feature of the Nyoro conception of *mahano* is that when the king confers high office he confers *mahano* with it, so that his great chiefs are required to observe some of the same taboos as himself.

*

The ritual duties of East African kings are essentially of two kinds. They are responsible for such approaches to spiritual beings as it is considered necessary to make in the interests of the welfare of their people. Kings are not always priests as the Reth of the Shilluk is; their responsibility may be limited to providing sacrifices to be offered at temples by the priests in charge of them. In addition to this responsibility for what may be called national ceremonials, kings have to maintain their own persons in an appropriate ritual state for the sake of the land and people whose well-being is held to be bound up with their own physical condition. The complicated ritual which every king goes through on his accession has two essential meanings; it asserts the permanency and rightness of the order which he symbolizes, and it gives him the power of a non-material kind that he requires in order successfully to play his royal part. Much royal ritual involves the taking of life, and this is regarded as proper and necessary to maintain the potency of the kingship and so the strength of the nation. It is worth noting that there is little connexion between the rituals of kingship and the qualities of justice and generosity that are ascribed to the ideal ruler. At a king's accession he may be admonished to rule his people justly, but the rites are not directed to ensure this end. They are concerned with making him strong and victorious.

It has been remarked already that the most important duties of the Reth of the Shilluk were probably ritual in the days before Turkish and British overlords sought to make him into a subordinate agent of administration, and he still has these duties. It is his responsibility to make sacrifices on behalf of all his people at the time when rain should fall, and when they are embarking on war with their neighbours. He is responsible also for the upkeep of some of the shrines of Nyikang, though others are in the charge of the dominant lineages of the parts of the country where they are. The Reth has to supply cattle to maintain two herds which are sacred to Nyikang, and also a canoe for a river-side shrine.

In the field of public ritual, the Ganda king appears almost as a secular monarch responsible for the upkeep of an established church. The Ganda recognized a number of divinities, each with one or more temples in different parts of the kingdom, the service of which was the privilege or duty of the lineage claiming to be descended from the first priest. State labour was provided for the building of these temples, organized in the same way as the labour for building the royal palace, and offerings were made by the king, which consisted partly in animals for sacrifice and partly in men and women to be temple servants, cattle for the temple herds, and barkcloths and cowry shells for the temple treasure. Each of these divinities spoke through oracles, and advised those who consulted him on problems concerning that aspect of life over which the god presided; thus there was a god of plague, a god of hunting, a god of women's fertility.

The most important gods, however, were those concerned with the welfare of the nation as a whole rather than the personal problems of individual members. These were two: Mukasa, the giver of general welfare, and Kibuka, the giver of victory. According to Roscoe's account there was an

annual festival at the temple of Mukasa which lasted for
twenty days. This was the occasion when 'the king sent his
presents to the god to secure a blessing on the crops and on
the people for the year.' In addition, the king consulted
these gods at times of anxiety, and sent them offerings on
occasions calling for thanksgiving and at other times as well.

The king of Ruanda presided over two national ceremonies
a year. One of these recalls the tradition that ancestors of
his brought cattle and grain to the land. This was the first-
fruits ceremony, at which the king ate the first mouthfuls
of the new crop of grain, from a field expressly cultivated
for this purpose by a member of a particular clan. The other
was a commemoration of the royal dynasty; every year there
was a period of mourning for all dead kings, closing with a
feast to end the mourning such as characterizes all African
mortuary ceremonies. At both these national festivals the
royal relics, each associated with a particular king and
his exploits, were publicly displayed. Another feature of
national ceremonies was the display of the royal herds,
whose herdsmen danced before the king and the assembled
multitude.

The councillors who were responsible for the conduct of
these ceremonies have been mentioned already. What made
them indispensable to the ritual welfare of the Ruanda kingdom was the fact that the esoteric knowledge was divided
between them; each knew only his own part, which he
taught in the deepest secrecy to the son who would succeed
him. The description of each ceremony takes the form of a
long poem.

In 1945 the king, an educated Christian who had abandoned all the traditional ceremonies, persuaded these old
men to let some of their secrets be recorded by another
educated Ruandese, Father Alexis Kagame. This was the
first time the king himself had heard them; and the
guardians of the secrets were willing to describe only in
broad outline rites which will soon be forgotten and beyond
recall.

It is clear from what Father Kagame was able to record that Ruanda kings were responsible for the performance of rites on behalf of their people in a great many circumstances: in time of drought or of excessive rain, when bees swarmed repeatedly instead of making honey, when cattle were attacked by sickness. There was a special ceremony when the king went hunting, and a large number of ceremonies connected with war (including one when seven enemy kings had been killed in succession).

A particularly interesting feature of Ruanda ritual is that certain rites, which were performed only at long intervals, appear to have had the express purpose of reaffirming and in a sense renewing the traditional order. The kings of Ruanda bore, in addition to their personal names, a series of four royal names which came round always in the same order. Two of these names were associated with the performance of rites of renewal; thus every king knew at his accession (or the guardians of the secrets knew) which ceremony he was due to perform. One of these focused on the renewal of the sacred fire which symbolized the continuity of the line of kings (but in Buganda was renewed at the beginning of each reign). The second was a national sacrifice for long life to the king, victory over enemies, peace at home and plenty of grain and milk. It closed with a formal dismissal of the spirits of all the Ruanda who had died since the death of the king who last performed the ceremony; sacrifices in their honour came to an end, and no more rites of ancestor worship were performed until new deaths peopled the country with new spirits. This ritual renewal of the world of spirits along with that of men and cattle is most unusual.

The very elaborate and prolonged rituals which used to accompany the accession of Ganda and Nyoro kings have been described by Roscoe, and it is likely that other monarchs in this region performed equally elaborate ceremonies which have been forgotten. Rituals of this kind have two aspects. From one point of view they 'make statements about the social structure'. The king himself and the as-

sembled multitudes are reminded of what is meant by
kingship and why it is valued. In Nyoro rites of accession
the new king imitates at one time the actions of a just judge,
at another those of a victorious war-leader. Weapons are
handed to him. He is addressed in formulae which combine admonitions such as 'Rule justly' with good wishes
such as 'Vanquish your enemies'. In most royal rituals important parts are allotted to persons representing major
divisions of country and people. Such actions represent a
public assertion of the rightness of the existing political
order and desire that it should continue.

The other aspect of accession ritual is that which imparts
to the ruler the mystically conceived power that does not
come from the command of physical force. The participants
in these rites would doubtless not make such an analysis.
For them the *whole* complex of rites would be necessary to
make a king. But the outsider can distinguish the acts that
are more directly concerned with the attainment of kingly
power. At the accession of a king of Bunyoro most of these
preceded his presentation to the people and the mimed
enactment of his kingly functions. Sacrifices were made to
the high God, and the person of the king was subjected to a
series of treatments which may be thought of as freeing him
from impurities and magical dangers and then enduing him
with the mystic qualities of kingship. He was washed and
shaved, anointed with oil and smeared with white clay, his
nails pared, the crowns that are the Nyoro emblems placed
on his head, and he drank milk from the nine cows specially
set aside for his use, thus inaugurating an action that he
would have to repeat every morning of his reign.

Much of the public ritual is still performed, and is repeated at a ceremony held every two years to remind the
Nyoro and their king of the relationship which ought to
exist between them. In the past an important part of the
strengthening and protective ritual consisted in the taking
of human life. The blood of the victims was smeared over
the Nyoro royal regalia, and in Buganda the most sacred of

the royal drums was supposed to be made with the skin of a man. During the Nyoro accession ceremonies a 'mock king' was placed on the throne for a few days and was then killed, in the belief that he would take with him any malign influences that might have been seeking to harm the real king. The prolonged ritual which Roscoe records for the Ganda, of visits some time after the accession to sacred spots in different parts of the country, involved the killing of men at various points. Both Ganda and Nyoro believed that at intervals during a king's reign more persons should be killed in order to augment his strength; in Buganda, according to Roscoe, travellers were seized at random for this purpose when the oracles of the gods announced that it was necessary for the welfare of king and people. It is impossible now to form any idea of the frequency or extent of these killings.

The personal ritual of kings is largely a matter of preserving their bodies from defiling substances and maintaining their physical health, the state of which was believed to be mirrored in the prosperity of the nation. The pastoral kings also performed rites specifically associated with cattle. Thus the Nyoro king had to be present every morning at the milking of the nine cattle specially dedicated to him, and then to drink some of the new milk. Each morning two bullocks were brought to him, and he laid his head against one and said, 'May all evil be taken away from me.'

The preservation of ritual purity was largely a matter of rules concerning food. Certain foods were taboo to a Nyoro king, and people concerned in the cooking and serving of his food also had to be in a state of ritual purity. The girls who churned the royal milk had to be virgins, the boy who herded his nine cattle had to be below the age of puberty, the men who cooked his food had to abstain from sexual intercourse. Like many other African kings he ate alone.

His physical health was protected by keeping sickness from him; sick persons and even sick cattle were not allowed to be within the bounds of the royal residence. He could not

P.G. – 8

attend funeral ceremonies, for he had to avoid any contact with death. If he himself suffered any physical mutilation it was held to make him unfit to be king and he was supposed to take poison. From the conception of this close association between the king's physical health and the well-being of land, people, and cattle it follows logically that the fatal illness and death of a king should bring every kind of disaster on his country. And it is often said of the Inter-lacustrine Bantu kings, and indeed also of the Reth of the Shilluk, that they were not allowed to grow old and die but were secretly put to death when their strength was observed to be failing.

Doubt has been cast on this tradition, notably by Evans-Pritchard in the case of the Shilluk. According to the records many Shilluk kings met a violent death; that is they were assassinated by enemies, not secretly stifled by their wives. There is an alternative Shilluk tradition that any prince could challenge the king to single combat, and, if he proved himself the stronger by killing the king, could claim the throne. Evans-Pritchard suggests that sometimes, if a national disaster was attributed to the failure of the king's physical powers, a prince may have raised enough support to rebel against him, but he does not believe in the literal truth of the tradition of single combat. It has also been remarked that the last two or three Reths have died in hospital, so that if it was ever thought necessary for the welfare of the Shilluk that the Reth be secretly strangled, it appears to be so no longer.

If it be argued, however, that the tradition that kings should not die naturally is nowhere more than a symbolic statement of the importance to the nation of the king's life, there is evidence against this view from an African people outside the area covered in this book. The Nyakyusa of southern Tanganyika have a tradition of a ritual king who could not be allowed to die naturally. They no longer have such a king, for nobody can be found to accept the burdens and taboos associated with the office. But only twenty-five years ago old men gave a detailed account of the process of ritual killing to anticipate the natural death of the king which is so circumstantial that one can hardly suppose it refers to a purely imaginary happening. This proves nothing about the death of kings in the region under discussion; it simply suggests that the ritual killing of kings is not impossible.

*

Objects associated with royal ritual may sometimes have political significance. The association of kingship with the possession of emblems has been repeatedly referred to, and is not characteristic only of primitive monarchies; the crown of the remaining European kings is not an abstraction, it is a solid object. The Interlacustrine Bantu kings, like the Anuak kings, established their claims to a throne in dispute by securing control of the national emblems, in their case sacred drums (the emblem of the Anuak village headman too, it will be remembered).

A drum is a fitting symbol of rule, for among people without writing it is a way of conveying information and orders at a distance. Travellers' tales about talking drums have often been very much exaggerated, but the fact is that the beat of a drum carries very far, and that a limited number of situations can be represented by characteristic rhythms in drumming. In Buganda every clan claims its own drum-beat, and important men have it beaten on such occasions as births or weddings in their families. This tells the world that X have something to celebrate – not the exact nature of the occasion. There was a recognized drum-beat in the old days to summon the people to war. The royal drums were beaten when a new king entered into his realm, when a king entered a new house, to announce the death of a prince, and to announce preparations for war. Temples and saza chiefs each had their own drum-beat. In the old days, when a man was appointed to a chiefship, the drum-beat appropriate to it was beaten during his progress there.

Sometimes the most important of the drums was treated as if it were itself a royal personage. In Ruanda it travelled when the king died, carried in a hammock and with the other drums beaten in its honour. The Nkole drum had a wider significance; it was an object of worship in its own right. Just as the king was king for all the people of Ankole, the Iru peasants as well as the aristocratic Hima, so was Bagyendanwa a recourse for all alike. He (for the drum was personified in Nkole speech) was believed to have come into the country with the marvellous Chwezi, and to be greater than the king himself. He was thought to embody the life of the country, so that as long as he remained there the people would be sure to prosper. The drum was kept in the same shrine as the sacred fire, and had old men, its priests, in constant attendance upon it, who must never show disrespect for it by raising their voices. It was ritually protected from harm, and was fed or strengthened by offerings of cattle, milk, meat, millet, and beer. Bagyendanwa was not held to love all his children equally; such a belief would have been too strongly in contradiction with the dogma of Hima superiority. The Hima were said to be the cattle of Bagyendanwa and the Iru his goats.

Offerings made to him were in some sense made also to the Chwezi, who had power over matters outside human control, including the state of mind of the king; so that people who proposed to ask him for a favour would sometimes go first to Bagyendanwa with an offering. The Hima sought his help in enterprises such as cattle raids or the digging of a new water-hole; the Iru if they were moving to a new part of the country or going hunting. He could also be asked for help in disaster such as the failure of crops or the death of children; he could give protection against supernatural dangers and make women fertile. Most important of all, he could be appealed to to punish wrongdoers against whom human justice was of no avail, and it was thought that for the Iru Bagyendanwa was a surer recourse than the king, who was not over-solicitous about injuries done to them. Of

So one cannot find any East African ruler who conforms
at all points to Frazer's picture of the divine king, although
the close connexion believed to exist between the king's
state of ritual purity and bodily health and the welfare of his
kingdom does correspond to one part of it.

CHAPTER 10

Kings and Descent Groups

ACCORDING to Sir Henry Maine, who was quoted in the first chapter, the history of political ideas begins with the assumption that kinship in blood is the sole possible ground of community in political functions. I disputed that statement as being too sweeping. Nevertheless, it points to a fact that has become very obvious in the foregoing pages, that in the simplest forms of government, groups of kin play a very important part. The groups which hold property in common – the lineages – combine to defend their rights. They maintain their own internal discipline. The senior men deal with troubles within the lineage, and among some peoples they can be appealed to when one of their juniors has injured an outsider; but in such discussions they are expected to make as good a case for their kinsman as they can.

Nuer and Dinka lineages are equal in political status: the 'aristocrats' who claim to be owners of, or first comers to, different parts of these two countries do not base on this assertion any claim to give orders to others. Shilluk and eastern Anuak recognize one pre-eminent lineage, and Shilluk a pre-eminent individual, the Reth. But these individuals do not exercise authority in matters which concern the lineage heads. Neither the Reth nor the Anuak noble is in any sense an organizer of public affairs or a maker of community decisions. But among the Shilluk the heads of dominant lineages have a relationship with the Reth that foreshadows the place of lineages in the Bantu states. In each of the Shilluk settlements the lineage which claims to have first settled there supplies a headman who is acknowledged by the whole settlement and has certain public functions, notably the reconciliation of feuds. He is said to have been expected to execute orders of the Reth, though we know little about the kind of orders that the Reth may have given before he was made the agent of colonial rulers. He was responsible for looking after any shrine of Nyikang which might be in his settlement. But he was not the territorial agent of the Reth. He was the man whom the lineage heads of the settlement had chosen, but when the choice was made he went to the Reth to have it ceremonially confirmed by the tying of a skin cloak on his shoulder.

Indeed it seems to be inherent in the recognition of a single individual as supreme in any sense of the word, ritual or secular, that every one of his subjects who succeeds to a position of authority must seek his formal recognition, and this is expressed in some symbolic act. But it is rare, if not unknown, for chiefs or kings to intervene in the choice of the head of a lineage; though Southall says that an Alur chief would refuse to recognize one who claimed the headship in defiance of the recognized rules of succession.

So there is a type of polity in which all authority below that of the chief or king is in the hands of heads of lineages.

It is an essential characteristic of the state form of government that the ruler relies on territorial agents of his own choice for the execution of his orders. Where government is organized in this way the political importance of lineages is clearly less. Yet it might be truer to say that new kinds of governmental activity have been devised and entrusted to new kinds of agents than to speak of lineages losing power. The state systems organize the activities of wider groups of people than any lineage can control, but lineages do not cease to be of account in the process of government. They are still organizations for mutual aid and protection, for seeking the redress of wrongs suffered by their members, and sometimes even for prosecuting vengeance. Even the Ganda state did not forbid this altogether, and when the king of Ankole dispensed justice it consisted in deciding whether or not he should allow the party complaining of a wrong done him to seek his own redress.

Often the lowest level in the hierarchy of chiefs who carried out the royal orders consisted of heads of lineages. Not every lineage head would hold political authority in the sense of responsibility to the king for the government of a part of his kingdom. Those who did were the heads of lineages with a claim to superiority in a given area. This might be based on a tradition that their ancestor was the first settler. But it did also happen, as was mentioned in relation to Busoga, that the descendants of a man who had once been appointed by a king to administer a village or a group of villages established a claim to 'own' the area; that is to say, to provide a hereditary headman. In Ruanda the lowest rank of chiefs were kinship heads, of whom we know very little. It was also mentioned earlier that in Ruanda the elaborate arrangements for 'national service' in the herding of the 'cattle armies' were made by requiring lineage heads to find the number of herdsmen required. Of course this is not a quaint custom, but a thoroughly common-sense arrangement in a society where numbers of kinsmen do recognize a single head. It is the system by means of which taxes were collected in Nigeria through fifty years of British rule. Lord Lugard believed that the best way to get a fair distribution of the burden of taxation was to assess each 'compound' at a lump sum and have the head decide how much each member should pay.

But as the organization of the state develops, with its ruler appointing his agents to carry out his decisions, the autonomy that is characteristic of lineages among the Nilotes comes to be more and more circumscribed. Lineages can no longer decide for themselves whether they will or will not prosecute vengeance, for superior authority can intervene to check them. A man's lineage-mates, though they are still important in helping him to get his rights, are not his only resource. He can attach himself to a patron outside the lineage, a rich man or a chief superior in authority to its head. If the clients of the Shilluk Reth and the Mandari chiefs were men who had lost the support of their kin, this is not true of the clients of chiefs in the Bantu states; these were men who saw greater opportunities outside the sphere of operations of the lineage. Hima in Ruanda who belonged to the armies, and this means all Hima of fighting age, were entitled to expect their army chief to support them in presenting claims for compensation. Thus the dependence of lineage members on one another grew less, and at the same time new obligations were imposed upon all citizens by authorities external to the lineage, so that a considerable part of their lives were spent in activities outside the range of family or lineage control. What happened was not a revolutionary recognition that the inhabitants of a common territory should recognize a common authority, but a very gradual building up of relationships outside the sphere of kinship.

❊

In the kind of society with which most readers of this book are familiar, kinship ties outside the immediate family have almost ceased to have any significance; and when it is found, as it was in relation to the Bank Rate incident, that what Victorians called 'cousinage' still operates as a network of communications, this is held to be matter for great indignation. The modern theory is that ties of kinship have no rational basis; they provide means of advancement to persons who would not get far on their merits; it may not be wrong that people should want to help their kinsmen, but it is wrong that they should be able to.

Such an attitude is characteristic of a society which is not in fact atomized, so that every individual competes on his merits as judged by impartial authority, but is so organized that most people can ally themselves with others having common aims through an immense variety of associations which exist to further particular interests.

The societies we are considering in East Africa have not developed this multiplicity of organizations each directed to a specific end. In contrast, they know two significant types of relationship, that of kinsman to kinsman and that of client to patron; out of the latter grows the specifically political relationship of ruler to subject, and this is extended to cover persons who have not entered into individual relations of clientship.

It has been argued that a society which recognizes two, and only two, principles of association must be politically unstable, because every man in it is at some time caught in a conflict between loyalty to his kinsmen and loyalty to his political superior.* This characterization of the Lacustrine Bantu, which could be applied to many other states with a simple technology, is unduly gloomy; at any rate the conflict has never reduced any of them to chaos.

But there is one field in which these two principles of association have in fact proved to be incompatible and their existence side by side has been a source of conflict; this is the field of rights to land. Little has been said up to now about this subject, because so many of our examples have been peoples for whom cattle are the most important form of property and the land rights that matter are rights to water and grazing.

What the family herds are to the Nilotes and Nilo-Hamites, the family lands are to the agricultural Bantu. For those of them who have not been organized into states, rights to the control of land use derive wholly from descent. A man is entitled to land for cultivation in the area that is owned by his descent group. There he has an indefeasible claim; but if he wants to go elsewhere he must have the permission of another land-holding group. The ideal of such societies is that lineage members should live together, and they do their best to realize this ideal unless the lineage is too numerous for the land that is available.

The state organization introduces a new principle in the control of land use: the principle that chiefs whom the king appoints and may transfer – and the chiefs whom they appoint – have the right not only to take a share of the

* L. A. Fallers, *Bantu Bureaucracy* (1956).

resources of the land but also to say who shall live on it. This principle is of course the counterpart of the principle of clientship: the client in a pastoral society receives cattle from his patron, the client in an agricultural society, land.

As far as one can reconstruct in imagination what went on in Buganda when it was an independent kingdom, people chose what chief they would 'serve' or 'follow' on personal grounds, and the consequence of this choice was that they lived on land which he allotted to them. In spite of the large population with which the country is credited in those days, there seems to have been no difficulty in finding land to grow the bananas and millet and groundnuts which were the food of the Ganda. Nevertheless, if a man did leave his father's village because there was not room for him to cultivate alongside his brothers, he would go to a chief and not to another commoner to find him some. Virgin land was thought of as being at the disposal not of kin groups but of political authorities.

But alongside this principle went the older one that land belongs to the descendants of the first settlers.* I call this older not only because it is logical to suppose that the absence of a state organization is older than its presence, but because the Ganda themselves believe that the claims of descent groups over land are older than the rights of chiefs, and indeed go back before the first Kabaka.

If either of these claims is pushed too far, it must come into conflict with the other, and both chiefs and descent groups have sought to make the most of their claims. A chief's claim to the right to dispose of land is established along with his general claim to authority, by the equivalent of 'royal letters patent'; that is, the king appoints him, receives his homage, and sends a messenger with him to install him in office. The claim of a descent group is that they were there before he came, and that the land they occupy is not his to dispose of; they make this claim good

* M. Southwold, *Community and State in Buganda* (unpublished thesis).

by showing the graves of members of the lineage who have died and been buried on the land.

The most venerable of such claims are the claims to the burial grounds of the thirty clans into which the Ganda people are divided. These are descent groups in the sense that all members of one clan believe that they are descended in the male line from a common ancestor somewhere in the remote past. There are far too many members of one clan to be able to trace their actual relationship. But people take the clan membership of their fathers, each clan has a number of distinctive personal names, each clan has its distinctive ritual avoidances (foods which they must not eat and so on), and members of the same clan may not marry. Each clan, or sometimes a subdivision of a clan, claims an inalienable right to a village somewhere in Buganda that is thought to have been either settled by their founding ancestor or granted to him by the Kabaka. At the beginning of this century an agreement made with the British Government allocated all the land in occupation in Buganda in freehold to individual owners. The allocation was made only to chiefs exercising political authority; the clan heads said later that they did not know what was going on. However, as they remember the past, the rights of the clans to these lands (known as Butaka from the word *etaka*, earth) were respected by all authorities including the king himself. The original members of the clan were buried in the Butaka, and their graves were the evidence for their descendants' claim; moreover, it was believed that the ghosts of these ancestors guarded the graves and would afflict with illness or misfortune anyone who sought to possess himself of the land. The head of the clan was the chief of the Butaka village. Old-fashioned Ganda still believe that a man ought to live in his clan village, although it would be quite impossible for everyone to do so.

But even if it had ever been possible, nobody would live in the clan village if he thought it was more important to seek his fortune by becoming the follower of a chief; or if the clan head, who need not necessarily have had a more admirable character than any of the king's chiefs, treated his villagers in a way that made them prefer to leave him. Both clan heads and the king's chiefs sought to attract people to live under their authority, but the clan heads had an ideological argument to support them which the chiefs had not; indeed, it is interesting that Ganda speak of the duty, rather than the right, of people to live on their clan lands.

New Butaka were sometimes created. The king might recognize a village as Butaka when it was pointed out to him that several members of a clan or of one of its divisions had been buried there, or he might expressly grant an area to a clan.

In the old days the king's chiefs seem to have been anxious to prevent, if they could, the establishment of any new claims to Butaka in the areas under their authority. Of course the Butaka heads received orders from them like everybody else, but the creation of a Butaka reduced the area within which they could decide who should live on the land and so attach clients to themselves.

But the possibility of establishing a Butaka by gathering kinsmen around him was open to every chief, and it seems that chiefs who thought they had little chance of further advancement from the Kabaka sometimes chose this as a way of attaining another kind of prestige, and one that could not be taken from them.

Since the land settlement and the political changes under British administration, the position of the chiefs has greatly altered. A much smaller number are officially recognized as agents of government and are subject to promotion and transfer. Many whose grandfathers held land at the Kabaka's will have become freehold landlords with no officially recognized place in the organization of government. Some heads of clans have managed to make themselves very important people, but this is not in virtue of their rights to clan lands, which, as has been remarked, were disregarded in

the land settlement. Claims for the return of the Butaka
to the clan heads have been made from time to time, and
in recent years the wrongs of the Butaka holders have
been made to stand for every kind of complaint that the
Ganda have against the Kabaka or the Protectorate government.

But what is more interesting for the present subject is the
persistence through all the changes of this century of the
ideal of the Butaka village, in which the men of a descent
group live clustered around the senior member, and respect
him as the head and 'owner' not so much of the land as of
the corporate group.

The existing land laws of Buganda do not recognize the
joint ownership of land by a kin group, and the present
policy of the governments in both Kenya and Uganda is to
follow Buganda's example in this respect. They believe that
this will stimulate dealings in land and that as a result it
will be put to the most economic possible uses. If these
policies are successful, the descent group will lose as much
economic importance among other peoples as it has already
among the Ganda.

But long before the Africans began to grow cash crops,
when questions of the best economic use of land had not
been thought of, the existence of a state with territorial
authorities responsible to the ruler had curtailed the rights
of lineages over the distribution of land. A comparison of
the Kikuyu with the Interlacustrine Bantu should make
this clear. The Kikuyu have recently themselves adopted
with enthusiasm considerable changes in their land-holding
system, but we are concerned here with their traditional
rules. According to these all the country of the Kikuyu was
divided between lineages, and the heads of every lineage
administered the lineage land. What this meant in practice
was that every family of the lineage had its own fields and
managed them as it pleased; but if a family had surplus
land and wanted to admit an outsider to it, the lineage
heads must give their approval, and if a family died out, the

lineage heads decided who should use the land left vacant. No authority outside the lineage had any say in this.

In the Interlacustrine Bantu states, in contrast, it is for the village headman to say who shall cultivate abandoned land; and even if he is the head of the dominant lineage in the village, he is an outsider to the other lineages. In other words, the lineage in a Bantu state cannot claim to control the use of a fixed area of land whether or not it is occupied by lineage members. It still has the right to nominate from among its members the heir to land which is actually in occupation, but nothing more. Here again we can see how the lineage has become less necessary to its members as they have opportunities of pursuing their interests outside it. When there is as much to be gained by becoming the follower of a chief as by asserting one's claim to a share of lineage land, it is no longer essential for the lineage to assert its rights over as much land as possible. Writers who have reconstructed the history of Buganda say that the kings deliberately sought to reduce the strength of the clan heads. But whether or not they did so, the existence of the chiefs appointed by themselves, without which there could have been no centralized government, created a situation in which lineage membership was no longer the individual's only source of security and assistance, and so automatically reduced the importance of lineage authorities.

*

If we assume that at some time in the past the peoples of the present Bantu states were divided into autonomous lineages, we are bound to agree that in the development of government by the state the importance of lineages has been reduced. I have suggested that it may be useful to think of this as a process in which new types of authority undertake activities that are themselves new, rather than as a struggle for power in which the lineages are defeated. There remained certain fields in which lineage membership was of prime importance and is so to this day. I refer not merely to the rules regulating marriage, inheritance, and behaviour towards the members of one's own and allied lineages, but to those contexts in which lineage membership is important in relationships with the ruler.

One example comes from present-day Buganda. When a man is appointed a chief – nowadays this means an official of the Buganda civil service – or succeeds to the ownership of land, he is formally presented to the Kabaka by the head of his clan, and he makes a declaration naming himself, his father and grandfather, and the divisions of the clan through which he reckons his descent from the common ancestor of all the clan.

In the past the significance which the clans or lineages never lost was in the field of public ritual. Much of this has vanished with the formal acceptance of Christianity. But traditional rites of accession are still carried out, and still bring into action some of the many people who in the past had each his own indispensable contribution to make in some act which only a member of his descent group could properly perform.

Among the Shilluk the senior lineages – those whose ancestors are believed to have come into the country with Nyikang – have a share, through the position of their heads as settlement heads, in the actual choice of the Reth. During the accession ceremonies one clan provides a girl to be the royal wife, married with cattle from the sacred herd of Nyikang. Others provide objects that are used at different points of the ritual, silver and cloth – traded or raided from the Arabs – ostrich feathers to deck the effigy of Nyikang, antelope skins for the Reth's ceremonial cloak, palm fibre to make other robes, new spears and drums, cattle for sacrifice, and some are responsible for the buildings in which the rites of installation are performed. The claims of the different clans or lineages to make their special contributions are held to go back to the origin of the kingdom, when the ancestor of each 'first performed' the action, whatever it is, that one of his descendants repeats at the beginning of every new reign. Thus, at the accession rites not only is it recognized that to make a king calls for the participation of all the leading descent groups, but they and all the populace are reminded of the original divine ordering of these divisions as the basis of Shilluk society.

Alur ritual gives a special place to the clans whose ancestors are believed to have been associated with the chiefs before they emigrated to their present country. Southall enumerates the duties which they shared. The Alur are among the peoples where a new chief is expected to be surprised that he has been chosen and reluctant to accept office. While the succession is being discussed the likely candidates go into hiding, and the successful one has to be found and captured with a show of force. This is the duty of the elders of two of the senior clans; when they have found the new chief they carry him on their shoulders to the shrines of his ancestors. Before his installation he is secluded for three days in the company of old men who tell him the secrets of his ritual duties; five clan heads are among these. When he leaves the seclusion hut he has to step over a man lying on the threshold; this must be a member of Panywer, one of the five, and it is said that once Panywer had also to provide a man to lie in the dead chief's grave for the corpse to rest upon. Another of the five is responsible for extinguishing and re-lighting the fire in the chief's homestead, and another for preparing skins to be used by him and dressing him in these before he is finally presented to the people. The fifth provide a man to stir the first dish of milk and millet eaten by the new chief.

Other clans are responsible for tending the shrines of past chiefs, just as the settlement heads of the Shilluk are responsible for those shrines of Nyikang which are situated within their boundaries.

The most elaborate record of royal ritual is that obtained by Roscoe from the Ganda elders who remembered it from the past; doubtless there was just as much elaboration at other courts. This account is peppered with titles which designate a special role played in the accession ceremonies; occasionally Roscoe mentions the clan to which the title belongs, still more rarely he mentions that some title did not belong to a particular clan. All these men were called chiefs, which may imply that they held fiefs in return for their services. If the analogy with other kingdoms is valid most of these offices were probably hereditary in clans or lineages.

After the new king had been formally chosen from among his brothers, the chief Walukaga – his *was* a hereditary office – produced spears and offered them to anyone who might wish to challenge the choice. The priest Semanobe – and most priests were hereditary – guarded Budo hill, the sacred place of the accession rites, against attack by rival claimants, and had himself to be defeated in a sham fight before the king could ascend the hill. He presided the next day over the installation of the new ruler. Kalibala of the Grasshopper clan produced a gazelle to be killed by the king in a ritual hunt. Chiefs of the Yam and other clans brought barkcloth to robe the king. The head of the Buffalo clan provided the two strong men who carried the king and his sister on their shoulders through the crowd to receive the people's obeisance.

After the accession ceremony the king visited various chiefs, and at the house of each performed rites that were believed to ensure him long life. These were the rites that involved the taking of others' lives. Most of the victims were found at random, but the chief of the Lung-fish clan had to offer a member of his own clan. Other persons had words to speak or actions to perform, as though in a play, which have little meaning now that it is too late to ask questions about what they symbolized.

One can, however, draw a distinction between these ritual responsibilities that people hold because they are believed to have a special relationship with supernatural beings and those that they hold, so to say, as laymen. The clans which make the barkcloth robe of the Kabaka, or provide the porridge-cooler for the Alur chief, do so in virtue not of any special sacredness but of the claim that their ancestors were associates of the ruler's ancestors.

The belief that the power to approach supernatural beings has been given only to members of particular descent groups has been shown to be in many places the very essence of the recognition of kingship.

In Buganda, however, kings did not make this claim. They endowed, by their regular offerings and by the provision of labour, temples that were under the care of specialist priests. There were many temples, and the largest of them had many priests; and from Roscoe's account, which is not very clear, it seems that each priest had to come from a particular clan. At any rate he says this expressly of the priests at the great temple of Mukasa, and on the whole it seems more likely that this was a general principle than that the great temple of Mukasa was unique.

At a sacrifice in this temple, which he describes, five leading priests took part, with many assistants, in the sacrifice of an animal. One of these carried a drum, one a spear, one the knife to kill the victim, one a stone to sharpen the knife on, and one a bowl to catch the blood.

This division of priestly functions has the same effect, of requiring the cooperation of many divisions of the people in rites essential to the general good, as the division of functions in accession rites. It is a field where descent groups are as important as they are in chiefless societies, perhaps even more so.

CHAPTER II

Primitive Government and Modern Times

IT is a long time since any of the peoples described in this book has been independent of external control. The Sudan became nominally subject to the Turkish rulers of Egypt in 1821, and in 1889 the agreement establishing an Anglo-Egyptian Condominium provided that it should actually be administered by British officials. Uganda was recognized as a British sphere of influence in 1890, and the British government undertook direct responsibility for its administration in 1893. The western boundary that was drawn at that time cut Alurland in two, so that part of it fell in the Congo Free State (later the Belgian Congo). Administration of this territory by Free State officials began in 1897. The Imperial British East Africa Company obtained a charter authorizing it to administer Kenya in 1888, and a British Protectorate over the country was declared in 1895. The German East Africa Company administered what is now Tanganyika from 1885; the German Government from 1890. In the peace settlement of 1919 German East Africa was divided into two mandated areas; the bulk of the territory was placed under British administration, but Ruanda and Urundi were allotted to Belgium as mandatory.

This rapid enumeration indicates the dates when Europeans first made themselves responsible for the government of different parts of East Africa. By itself it does not indicate how long particular peoples have been subject to external authority, since this authority was only gradually extended until it covered all the populations in each of the new political units. The Ganda were the first people of the Uganda Protectorate to have extensive dealings with Europeans, and they had the advantage of getting in first with their version of the extent of their kingdom. The re-modelling of their government on the lines approved by their new overlords began in 1895, and when it was done to the satisfaction of the latter they did their best to create an identical administrative system for each of the other peoples of the Protectorate.

The populations that were usually left to the last were those that actively resisted the new order, and were able to keep up their resistance because their country was difficult to get at and move about in. Troops would be sent there to suppress risings and punish raiding or attacks on persons travelling through the country, but only much later was any attempt made to alter the internal political arrangements of these peoples. Thus civil administration was not introduced to the Karimojong until 1921; it was theoretically established in Turkanaland in 1910, but the country was under military control from 1918 to 1926; the Nuer were not 'settled' until 1928, and Nuer individuals were not given authority as agents of government policy until 1942 (after the time when Evans-Pritchard lived in their country).

The policies of these governments were directed towards a number of different aims. They hoped by extending their authority over areas of Africa to secure advantages for their own nationals, or at least to prevent the exclusion of their own nationals from opportunities of gaining advantage. They believed that it was a moral imperative to develop the productive potentialities of all parts of the globe, and that this process was bound to benefit the peoples among whom it was undertaken; indeed, they perceived that these peoples were already interested in the goods to be obtained by trade. They also believed that there were certain absolute standards of good government which it was their duty to impose on peoples who had not worked these out for themselves. The individuals who put these policies into practice were sustained in the difficulties of their task, and in overruling opposition, by the dogma that civilization was a blessing that its possessors ought to spread; just as they civilized their own children by obliging them to do things they did not want to, and sometimes by punishing them severely. And nobody today is saying that they ought not to have spread civilization; today's complaint is that they did not spread enough of it, or the right parts.

The link between the African peoples and the new policy-making bodies was the administrative officer, a new kind of territorial chief with a much wider field of operations than that of any but the largest kingdoms. In East Africa he is typically the 'D.C.' or District Commissioner. He had little or no say in the making of policy – so little that one can find books written from the administrative officer's point of view which refer to the 'Government' as a separate entity presumed to be hostile. The D.C. was responsible for the good government of his District, and the implementation of central government policy insofar as this affected the people in his District. He was not responsible for the economic policies against which much of the criticism of colonial rule has been directed, although he was expected to admonish people to take up some kind of commercially productive activity. In the days when wage-labour was a novelty D.C.s were expected to encourage men to 'go out and work'. How much was expected of them depended on the demand for labour, which was greater in Kenya than in the other territories under discussion. But in the very first stages of European occupation the new rulers had to be able to get the labour without which they could not even make their occupation effective – to carry the D.C.'s tent and stores when he travelled and later to build roads. When administration was established, the D.C. was expected to encourage all those changes in African ways of life that were generally regarded as progressive – sending children to school, keeping villages clean, planting cash crops, limiting the numbers of stock, submitting to vaccination and so forth. But first and foremost the D.C.s were the custodians of law and order and the collectors of taxes, just like their African predecessors in the Interlacustrine Bantu states.

District Comissioners could not make themselves directly

responsible for every individual under their authority, any more than the Kabaka's saza chiefs could. They had to entrust responsibility to African subordinates, and where they found persons who already commanded authority and were willing to exercise it in furtherance of the policies of the European government, they naturally chose them for this position.

Sometimes, however, there were no obvious authorities, or what was perhaps worse, there was no single authority; much of the early part of this book has been concerned with societies of which this is true. Thus the influence of the D.C., and of European administration in general, was exerted in opposite directions according to the circumstances. In some places new positions of authority were created, and individuals enabled to dominate their fellows in ways that would earlier have been out of the question, while in others it was necessary first of all to reduce the power of existing rulers and then to seek to have them use it to new ends and through differently chosen instruments.

Different ideas prevailed, too, about how the African agents of the new dispensation should be chosen. In Uganda the organization of the Ganda kingdom so much impressed the early Protectorate officials that after streamlining it a little they made it the model for the whole of the territory. Both the southern Sudan and Tanganyika followed the principle that held the field in British colonial theory of the inter-war period, that the indigenous political system, whatever it was, must be utilized as the starting-point for any development. Kenya never accepted this principle, but found sometimes in practice that it was useful to rely on men whose status in their own society gave them influence over their fellows.

As we look back over the last sixty years, we can see that there was no one permanent principle which ought to have guided the colonial rulers in their dealings with the small-scale societies subject to their over-rule. Between the wars the argument most often heard was that the political systems existing before colonial rule were 'natural growths', to be fostered rather than destroyed for the sake of something deemed to be more appropriate to the contemporary world. Now we are told that the recognition of traditional authority was a mistake from the first, that it supported the influences which are most opposed to necessary changes, and that it entrenched the sentiments of 'tribal' separatism which are proving so disruptive in some of the new African states.

The truth is that there is no one course which would have been the correct one all through the history of colonial rule in Africa. The ideal would have been a flexibility such as is hardly possible for any large-scale organization. The explanation is really rather a simple one, though it does not provide a simple guide to action. When Africa was independent, traditional rulers commanded the respect of all their people, and to have set them aside would have created bitter resentment in the grandfathers of those who today condemn the policy of recognizing them. But under the new influences that colonial government brought with it, some Africans began to make the same criticisms of the traditional way of life that their European rulers made, and to temper their respect for the traditional rulers with criticism. If colonial governments had had superhuman wisdom, they would at exactly the right moment have given their backing to these forward-looking members of the populations under their authority. But could any ordinary human being have judged that moment aright?

Actually some colonial governments, of which Kenya is the principal British example, have begun by taking little account of traditional authorities, but have sometimes found it necessary to recognize the fact that traditional leadership and traditional ways of taking decisions continued to exist. Others – and this is more characteristically British – have begun by recognizing traditional authorities, and later found it necessary to recognize the fact that people who have no right by tradition to a share in government are demanding it on the ground of their understanding of modern ways. Whenever western values and techniques have been adopted by a significant minority, new leaders have appeared whose influence rivals that of the traditional rulers, and it is these new leaders who have won self-government for former colonial populations. But traditional rulers have nowhere lost their influence completely, and in the independent territories the new-style politicians have themselves had to decide whether to sweep them away in revolutions – the only possible way of destroying their influence altogether – or to assign them some place in the new order.

❦

The subject of the present chapter, however, is what has happened to the primitive political systems described in this book since they have become subject to foreign overlords with different ideas from their own about the purposes of government.

The western nations in the nineteenth century had long forgotten the times when their own kings had to contend with unruly feudal barons, and the still more distant times when these kings' subjects could only get wrongs redressed by private retaliation. To them the first step in the spread of civilization was to make private vengeance impossible, and insist upon the settlement of disputes before courts which not only pronounced decisions but executed them. The second was to prohibit armed conflict between the members of previously independent political communities who had now become subject to a single government and would henceforward be required to recognize a common rule of law. Under colonial rule, only the police, under the orders of the D.C. and such other recognized authorities as there might be, had the right to use force.

Their first contacts with the inaccessible pastoral peoples were limited to the periodical collection of taxes in cattle, and armed intervention to punish such raids or killings as came to their notice. Any more intensive administration,

reasons of which there is now no record – and died outside their own country. Shortly after this the Prince of Wales visited Kenya, and all headmen in the colony were summoned to meet him in Nairobi. Those from Turkana were so much afraid of what might happen to them there that they had to be brought in by force. Here is another dilemma of a superior government which is desirous of securing consent to its authority; it may be obliged to punish its subordinate agents, but the more local influence these men have, the more such punishment will arouse hostility and suspicion of the government's motives.

In the course of a generation, however, headmen have got used to their jobs, and the Turkana have got used to the presence among them of some fifty headmen and sub-headmen exercising authority in the name of the Kenya government. Each headman is in charge of a fixed area, and his main job is to collect the taxes due from the people in this area. The areas are supposed to be divisions of the country recognized by the Turkana themselves, but when people move to and fro as much as they do it does not mean very much to tell them that X is the headman of the people of area Y. Even if they think of Y as their home country they may be away from it more often than they are in it. But the headman must stay in it so that the D.C. can know where to get in touch with him.

Thus the headman is not well placed to be an instrument of official policies of the constructive type which seek to disseminate the techniques and values of western civilization. But in any case it is hard to see how the Turkana could adopt modern techniques and values in an environment which so harshly determines a mode of life that makes it almost impracticable to bring them under any territorial administration.

The appointment of headmen has nevertheless made a difference to the structure of Turkana society. It has created a new social class consisting of men with a regular money income – extremely small, but enough to give them a start in the economic race. They have a means of building up herds that other men do not have; one way of doing this is to buy cattle cheap from men who need money to pay their taxes. If there were more active interference by the Kenya government in Turkana affairs, no doubt the headmen would have other means of entrenching themselves by using their position as intermediaries between the government and the general population.

All over Kenya the colonial government had to deal with societies where no individual could be identified as the 'natural' leader, and everywhere it selected whatever men seemed best fitted to do the work of subordinate agents. Those who made the appointments were sometimes more and sometimes less concerned to select men with local influence; they weighed this, which they quite realized was an advantage, against the advantages of literacy, of some conception of the aims of the government, of trustworthiness proved in some other relationship, for example as a sergeant of police. But however they made their choice the effect of it was to create for their own purposes a quite new class of authorities; one might almost call them client-chiefs of the European government, since they owed to it alone their position and its rewards. Some of them became very unpopular. But this was not because they were 'the wrong chiefs'; it was because they were chiefs at all.

While the government deliberately created chiefs as its agents, in the settlement of disputes between Africans it tried to follow African custom. Its intention here was to recognize what already existed, not to create new institutions, and it conferred judicial powers – strictly limited in those cases which were now treated as criminal – on 'councils of elders constituted in accordance with native law and custom'. In fact, usually nothing as formal as this phrase suggests existed, as the descriptions in earlier chapters have shown. Some peoples had their village council tree, where the elders sat and talked over village affairs and were available if anyone sought their judgement or mediation. Others took their disputes to any elder whom they trusted and whose house was close at hand. The rules of the age-organization prescribed who *might* settle cases rather than who *must*. It is unlikely that bodies of fifty or more elders got together to try cases in the old days. However, the tribunals whom the government recognized did consist at first of elders who conceived of themselves as doing what they had done 'from the beginning of things'. Indeed they early got into trouble for condemning people to death for witchcraft. The sentence, one official report says, 'was carried out by the members of the council compelling the relatives of the deceased to set fire to a hut in which the condemned man had been placed'. This happened in Kikuyu country, and is clearly an example of the kind of treatment of a heinous offence that their neighbours the Kamba call *kingolle.**

From the beginning the Kenya government, like all colonial governments, sought to guide the procedure of the tribunals in accordance with its own ideas of the methods most likely to result in just decisions. They were expected to keep records so that the D.C. could supervise their activities, and, as the elders were illiterate, young men who had been to school were attached to them as clerks. In some cases the chiefs appointed by government were made presidents of the tribunals. The constitution of these bodies was defined by regulations which stated the number of members each should have, and sometimes provided that members should hold their office for a limited number of years. The tribunal members were appointed by the D.C., who might take into account different considerations, including the advantages of numbering among them young men who were at home in the new world of schools, wage labour, and cash crops. In principle they tried to make appointments that would be acceptable to the populace in general, sometimes even organizing informal elections. Thus the responsibility for settling disputes, or reconciling conflicting claims, no longer rested with the elders alone, nor were all the elders entitled

* See Chapter 1.

to perform this function. Their decisions were now enforced, not by the generality of younger men, but by paid police-men.

In Kenya the appointed chiefs were made executive agents of the new government in routine matters such as the collection of taxes, but for the local application of the kind of policy that nowadays is described under the general heading 'Development and Welfare' they were not enough. It was the general principle of most British territories in Africa that some part of the taxes paid by Africans should be earmarked for spending on local services in the places where it had been collected, and that the local taxpayers should have some say in the spending of this money. Where traditional chiefs have been recognized as 'Native Authorities', this money is paid into treasuries attached to their headquarters. In Kenya, however, funds to be spent on local services were provided from local rates paid in addition to the tax collected by the central government, and it was clearly desirable to consult some representatives of local opinion on the raising and spending of this money. This was done by setting up in each district a council consisting partly of men nominated by the D.C. and partly of men chosen by the population to be represented. The nominated members are usually 'chiefs' appointed by the government, but all the chiefs in a district are not always nominated to its council. The other members are chosen at public meetings held in each of the 'locations' into which every district is divided. Several thousand people usually attend such meetings; the candidates are present, and people show their support either by acclamation or by lining up behind the candidate of their choice. Chiefs who have not been nominated to councils sometimes get elected in this way; men with some schooling are often chosen. These councils, although they do no more than advise the D.C., who has the final say in the raising and spending of money, are nevertheless organs of government. As such they are wholly new to the peoples of Kenya, and no attempt was ever made to link them with any existing council. Like the chiefs and headmen in the executive sphere, the members of these councils are chosen, at least in part, for other qualities than those that would have given them influence in the old days. Within the councils, with their limited powers, they can hardly be spoken of as exercising leadership. Yet they are chosen as 'spokesmen', the word used by so many peoples of the leading men in the old days. What is interesting here is to see how a new type of man is held to be fitted for this part.

*

Where colonial governments found a state organization in existence, there was no difficulty in identifying men who exercised authority and could be required, as the condition of retaining it, to exercise it on behalf of the new ruler. The problem there seemed to be to improve the standards of government in accordance with western values. This meant, in the first place, limiting the power of persons in authority and imposing strict rules for its exercise, and in the second, expecting them to interest themselves in all the many improvements that western knowledge could make in the life of the people in general. The right to raise armies and make war was taken away from the rulers, who thenceforward had to depend upon the colonial government for protection against internal and external enemies. They lost the right to inflict corporal punishments of the kind described by Speke. Penal codes specified the actions which were to count as offences, and limited the punishments for them to fines and imprisonment.

Courts were set up under European magistrates to deal with the more serious cases. In this respect Buganda is exceptional; the Kabaka's court has power to try all offences except murder and manslaughter. The proceedings of all the courts were supervised by European officials, who were expected to intervene where there seemed to have been a miscarriage of justice by western standards. While their powers and activities were limited in this way, they were given the new duty of enforcing the laws made by the colonial government in matters such as public health, the control of sleeping sickness, the prevention of disease in cotton, and the organization of markets.

At the same time that chiefs became responsible to a government above and beyond their own ruler, and were expected by that government to interfere in all kinds of ways in the lives of ordinary people, their relations with the populations under their authority were changed in other ways. The aim of the European government was to make them the agents of policies that would be generally beneficial. In their eyes the office of chief should be one of public service rather than of privilege, and the early administrators thought this would not be the case without considerable reforms. Where they recognized the right of rulers to command the labour of their subjects, as they did notably in Buganda, they sought to have the labour employed in ways which corresponded to their idea of public works – for example in building roads rather than in building houses for chiefs. In spite of this, a good deal of the cotton that was grown when this crop was first introduced into Uganda was grown by men who were ordered to plant it in fulfilment of their obligation to give labour to a chief. But when the labour due was commuted for a cash payment, this did not go into the pockets of individual chiefs but into a central treasury. From this treasury, which was also fed from other sources, the chiefs received fixed salaries – in the case of the saza chiefs in Buganda, very handsome salaries. They now no longer received any form of tribute direct from the peasants under their authority; the peasants were protected from extortionate demands, but they also lost the personal protection of the chief and the hospitality that used to be offered to all who came to his court to pay their respects. The higher-grade chiefs, who do have good incomes, spend them in keeping up with the Joneses, and in more solid investments such as education for their sons and other young relatives, and those at lower levels simply cannot afford to take on the position of dispenser of largesse to the neighbourhood.

Senior chiefs do not now get their position as a reward for faithful services to the king. In Buganda, in virtue of the agreement made in 1900, the Kabaka formally appoints his saza chiefs, with the approval of the Protectorate authorities. This means that saza chiefs are not likely to be in sympathy with opponents of the Kabaka on any controversial issue that may arise in modern Buganda. But the most important requirement of a modern saza chief is that he should be good at office work, and the next that he should have 'progressive ideas' – *not* in the field of politics, where they might lead him to support nationalist movements, but in that of technical improvements in the standard of village life. When chiefs are promoted they cannot now take an army of followers with them (though they do sometimes take their office staff); and the chiefs of the next grade below the saza (called gombolola chiefs) are promoted or transferred pretty frequently. Thus they do not stay long enough in one place to get to know many people well, and they cannot spend what time they have in sitting on their veranda welcoming all comers and entertaining them with beer. Instead they must be holding court – now a formal occasion in a special building, on fixed days of the week – or sitting at the receipt of taxes (which gombolola chiefs now have to collect themselves at places where produce is bought) or making up returns relating to tax collections, court cases, beer-brewing permits, food crops, vermin destruction, and many other matters.* The chiefs on lower salaries cannot afford to give the hospitality that was made possible in the past by the gifts brought by the very people who received the hospitality. Taxes have replaced personal gifts, and, like tribute labour, are devoted to impersonal public purposes. More is done to direct the available resources to the improvement of general welfare, but less sophisticated people do not see the process as a reinterpretation in improved terms of

* J. H. M. Beattie, *Bunyoro, an African Kingdom* (1960), p. 44.

traditional political relationships. They only see the isolation
of chiefs from their people, and their new role as servants of
the foreign government.

The chiefs of higher rank are expected to move about
their territory, hold meetings, and explain to people the
measures for the improvement of hygiene, cultivation, and
the like that they are expected to further. But if people are
to adopt these measures they must be constantly reminded
of them, and this is the duty of the lower level chiefs, headmen of villages, and the grade above this known in Uganda
as miruka or 'parish chiefs'. Quoting again a description
from Bunyoro, it is these chiefs who 'inspect people's food
gardens, issue beer-brewing permits, supervise the clearing
of paths and tracks and the maintenance of roads, tell the
people where and what to plant, organize communal pig
and baboon hunts, summon people to attend at court, and
carry out an infinity of small day-to-day duties'.*

The ideal behaviour for these lower level authorities is
different from that expected of more important chiefs.
Though it is clearly wrong to think of the kings and great
chiefs of the past as having ruled by fear alone, it has been
shown that they were expected to inspire fear and that this
was an element in the dignity of their position. This is not
expected of chiefs of lower rank and lesser dignity, especially
of village headmen who hold their position because they are
lineage heads. The ideal for them is that they should maintain the peace of the village by reconciling inhabitants who
quarrel, and not that they should themselves disturb the
tranquillity of life by harassing their people with orders from
outside authorities.

Village headmen have been incorporated in the African
civil service in some parts of Uganda, but not in all. In
Bunyoro they receive from the revenues of the African
Local Government – as the kingdom of Bunyoro has now
become – salaries lower than the wages of some unskilled

* J. H. M. Beattie, 'The Nyoro' in *East African Chiefs*, ed. Audrey
Richards (1960), p. 119.

labourers. In Busoga the headmen have refused this, and so are still rewarded for their services by tribute – now a money payment of one shilling a year from every man in the village. This payment, as they themselves understand, expresses recognition of a personal relationship between themselves and the other villagers – their 'ownership' of the village, as they would put it. They recognize too that if they accepted the formal status of paid officials they would be liable to transfer, and that the special relationship of each with a particular village, and that village only, would be broken. In fact very few village headmen are moved, because the only reason for this would be to promote them to be parish chiefs. Those Soga headmen who are interested in furthering the progressive ideas of their superiors do in fact join the civil service as parish chiefs. Then they appoint a kinsman or client to take charge of their village; this is an arrangement that would not be possible if the post of village headman was part of a civil service establishment.

*

It was shown earlier how important in the Interlacustrine states was the right of a chief to say who should live on the land under his control. Chiefs still exercise this right, but in rather different conditions from those of the days before European rule. The present situation in Buganda is the result of the distribution of freehold estates that was made under the Uganda Agreement, mentioned in Chapter 8. As was explained there, Sir Harry Johnston recognized that the chiefs' estates were a source of revenue and that this was one of the rewards of office. He considered this reasonable; but as he intended to employ only the most senior chiefs as administrative authorities, he thought that only they should have estates. All the rest of the land would be managed by a sort of board of trustees, who would no doubt have decided what claims to the occupation of land were valid and what land was available to be alienated for plantations, since at that time it was assumed that this was the only way to develop the resources of tropical territories. Such a plan would have made nonsense of the fundamental principle of Ganda society, that every man was either a chief or the subject of a chief and that chiefs derived their position from the Kabaka. It is interesting to speculate what might have happened if it had been put into force, as it might have been if the Ganda leaders had not had their missionary friends to help them in the negotiations. An anthropologist, impressed by the toughness of traditional relationships in peasant societies, would guess that, unless there had been very active intervention in Ganda affairs, something like the previous system would have re-established itself; those critics of British administration who say it has been too conservative may think a chance to modernize the Ganda system was missed. The chiefs themselves saw the proposal as one that would abolish all distinctions between chief and peasant, and with the help of their missionary advocates persuaded Johnston that this would be intolerable.

Thus, a thousand chiefs – all it seems royal clients or *their* clients, and none the chiefs of clan estates – were given grants of land, and these grants were made in freehold; that is in perpetuity. The men who were to receive them were described as private landowners, and the land as 'the estates of which they are already in possession'. In addition, saza chiefs while in office had the right to areas of land surrounding their official headquarters.

But from the time when the promised grants were actually allotted – which took some years – the majority of the 'private landowners' whom the agreement had actually created were men who held no office in the administrative system. And more and more private landowners came into existence as the original ones sold portions of their land.

Logically, this system made the control of land – with the advantages to be derived from this – independent of any political responsibility. For the descendants of the original owners it was a happy accident instead of being a reward for services rendered. They soon learned to turn their position to profitable account, until a law was passed by the Kabaka's council which limited the rents and dues that landlords could charge.

Yet such is the tenacity of traditional values that the landlords are not only called chiefs but are expected to perform some of the political functions of chiefs, and their rent-paying tenants are said by Protectorate officials to hold their land on 'customary tenure' – a phrase which everywhere else in Africa would exclude the possibility of a landlord-tenant relationship. The chiefs whose existence as paid civil servants is officially recognized expect the landlords to do a part of their job for them, just as the saza chiefs expected this of their subordinates in the past. Landlords hear disputes between their tenants, and are expected to keep order among them and collect the taxes due from them. It is difficult nowadays to rise in the world through the official political system, since this now calls for formal education as well as mother-wit. It is much easier to buy land with the proceeds of a good season's cotton crop and let part of it to one or two tenants; then one is a chief, if only a small one, with one's own peasants under one. Conversely the people who are chosen as parish chiefs or village headmen in Buganda are landowners; no law requires this, but nobody who was not a landowner could exercise authority over others.

In the countries bordering on Buganda, Busoga to the east and Bunyoro to the north, people who might have put up the same case as the Ganda chiefs for the grant to them of freehold estates tried to get arrangements similar to the Uganda Agreement extended to them. But a later generation of Protectorate officials realized that, in giving final rights of disposal over land to the chiefs who had only held their land on condition of service to the king, they had misinterpreted the Ganda system. They also thought it unfair to the mass of the population that they should be required to pay rent for the land on which their existence depended. Accordingly they refused to make freehold grants elsewhere. But in Bunyoro they decided to secure the rights of the ordinary cultivator by issuing a 'certificate of occupancy' to anyone who wanted it, guaranteeing him the undisturbed occupancy of a holding as long as he was cultivating it. These certificates were intended only to apply to land that the holder was actually cultivating, and to give the farmer security against anyone who might claim the right to turn him out. At the same time any demand for rent was made illegal. In intention this was the exact contrary of the Buganda policy.

In practice it was made, as the Ganda system was made, to conform to pre-existing notions of the relationship between land, chiefs, and people. The Nyoro think, as the Ganda do, that a chief is a man to whom others attach themselves by coming to live on the land that he controls. They cannot conceive of a chief who does not have this relationship with *anybody*, and since in Bunyoro chiefs are not endowed with official estates as they are in Buganda, every man who gets a civil service post as chief at once secures from the ruler a grant of inhabited land, and a certificate of occupancy to secure his right to it. He does not want to get rich by collecting rent, as he cannot now do; he simply thinks it fitting that he should have some people under his direct authority – his men, to whom he and nobody else is 'the chief', whoever may be 'the government'.

At the same time other people have certificates of occupancy over land on which there are tenants, perhaps only one or two. Every such person is a chief in Nyoro eyes, though the civil service establishment takes no account of him. It is truer to say that he expects officials to approach his tenants through him than that they expect him to shoulder some of their responsibilities (and this may be the case with the Ganda too, although accounts of them do not happen to put the position this way). Like a village headman, he is expected to be on the tenants' side rather than on that of external authority; in the days when all the citizen's duties were not discharged by a single tax payment, it was his business to protect them from excessive demands for labour or for contributions of food for important visitors. The description by Beattie of Bunyoro in the earlier part of this century under British rule suggests that, in the days of independence also, the small fief-holders may have acted as a buffer between their followers and higher authority. These 'landlord-chiefs' convey government instructions to their tenants, and deal with disputes that arise between them, not as aloof outsiders but more like family heads (with whom they are sometimes compared); the senior men among the tenants sit with the landlord to judge the matter. They may fine people who offend, but the fine consists of the wherewithal for a feast which the whole community of landlord and tenants share.

In Busoga nothing was done by the Protectorate government to change the traditional system whereby the headman of a village allotted holdings to newcomers who asked for them. But circumstances have changed it, in the sense that nowadays it costs a good deal to get such a holding. It was characteristic of the Interlacustrine states, as of many other non-western societies, that anyone who approached a superior with a request was expected to bring him a gift. Just as the Hima in Ankole presented a cow to the ruler when he wished to become his man, so did the Soga, in a country of few cattle, present a barkcloth. As cash came into general circulation, people began to give money instead of other kinds of customary gift, and in some circumstances the recipient could name his price. This is what has happened in Busoga; it is good country for growing cotton and the demand for land is keen. The village headmen, who, as has been mentioned, have refused to become paid civil servants, have been forbidden by the government to collect tribute from their people. They consider this an injustice, and indeed they now receive little return for work that takes them away from their own farming. They recoup themselves as best they can by charging fees for the allocation of new holdings, and when they see an opportunity they jump on any holding that they can claim is vacant so as to allot it to a new holder. The demand for land is such that they no longer have to seek to attract and keep followers.

*

In Uganda the hereditary claims of rulers of the four largest states (Buganda, Bunyoro, Toro, and Ankole) have been recognized in formal agreements made with the Protectorate government, but elsewhere not much account has been taken of traditional rulers, and if they or members of their families have been appointed as civil service chiefs this has been as much because they were well placed to get secondary education as for any other reason. In Tanganyika, in contrast, the Native Authority system introduced in 1926 had as its basic principle that all traditional rulers must be recognized, so that their influence could be enlisted in support of improvement policies.

But in Uganda and Tanganyika alike, the small size of traditional political communities has proved an obstacle to policies that depend on raising and spending money. It was an essential element in the system which Sir Donald Cameron built on Lugard's theories that every Native Authority should have its own treasury, and thus control the spending of a proportion of the money that its people paid in taxes. In Tanganyika, in the depression years between the wars, the sums available to most individual Native Authorities were dismally small, and even today they are not princely. So the Tanganyika policy has been to federate groups of Native Authorities, which then pay their revenues into a common treasury. All the Native Authorities within an administrative district have a combined treasury, and meet in a 'council of chiefs' to decide how the revenues should be spent. In some cases the states represented are, like the Soga, political divisions of a population with a common language and culture, in others not.

The amalgamation of the Soga states into a single unit for the purposes of the Protectorate administration went much further. From 1906 to 1914 a Ganda chief, Semei Kakunguru, who had earlier led an army in Busoga and almost succeeded in making himself king, was put in charge of the District as 'Paramount Chief', at the head of a council of Soga rulers. At first the existing division into states was recognized, whatever their size; but gradually this was replaced by an organization into saza, gombolola, and muluka areas in a fixed hierarchy such as was now being established in Buganda, so that the smaller states became subdivisions of larger ones, and their rulers, if they were appointed to civil service chiefships at all, became subordinate to other rulers or to appointed chiefs, at first men who were brought in from Buganda. One or two rulers became saza chiefs, and for some time asserted the right to appoint their own subordinates. Most of them were no more than parish chiefs or village headmen.

Where rulers were appointed as saza or gombolola chiefs, it was assumed for a time that their heirs would succeed them, but gradually efficiency at office work came to seem more important, and the example of the larger states with their transferable chiefs was followed in Busoga too. Of course this did not have the effect of shifting rulers from one state to another, but of removing from rulers – though not from their near relations – any incentive to qualify for civil service chiefships.

Uganda was treated differently from Kenya, in that the courts which tried cases were not at first differentiated from the deliberative councils which were also recognized. Saza and gombolola chiefs had their councils, each consisting of chiefs of the next lower grade, which met regularly to try cases and were also used to disseminate messages and instructions from the Protectorate government; either the chiefs received these by letter, or D.C.s and technical officials came into the court-house and addressed those present. In the four 'Agreement States' the rulers' councils, which at first consisted, besides the Katikiro, a treasurer, and a chief justice (newly created offices) mainly of saza and gombolola chiefs, had limited powers of legislation in local matters;

these were wider in Buganda than elsewhere. When the Ganda officials were withdrawn from Busoga, the council of chiefs was left as a coordinating body for the district. In 1919 this body elected one of the Soga rulers to be its permanent chairman; he was a young man at the time, and held the office for thirty years. But he never succeeded in establishing a claim to pass it on to his heir.

Whatever had been the initial attitudes of British administrators towards African institutions, the fact that government was now directed to new aims and called for new skills made it into something different from anything that had existed before the colonial era. In the years just before the Second World War, when the great depression was coming to an end and colonial revenues had begun to rise, people interested in the development of local services in African areas – both European and African – became impatient with the rate of progress achieved by most traditional authorities. At the same time Africans who had had some schooling were beginning to take an interest in governmental policies and feel that they ought to have a share in making them, and the idea became current that a safe first step in this direction would be to extend the membership of the various councils associated with local authorities. In Tanganyika elected members were added to chiefs' councils, and in Uganda, outside the Agreement States, the constitution of the various councils was changed, so that they should no longer consist entirely of civil servants but should include persons without official position, representing *both* the traditional authority of clan heads *and* the new educated classes. Some of these were elected and some nominated; most councils included teachers and ministers of the most important Christian denominations in the council area.

After the war a new doctrine held the field: that a real advance in the development of local services could be expected if local government were made representative, and if such non-traditional councils as already existed were given much greater responsibility for the raising and spending of money. The new constitutional position in Kenya and in Uganda – outside Buganda – was that the civil service chiefs were the executive agents of the elected councils and not, as before, people who took their orders in a chain of command from the D.C. and so need not pay much attention to the other councillors. What had been called Native Administrations now became African Local Governments, and the kingdoms of Toro, Ankole, and Bunyoro were known thenceforward by this unromantic title.

Buganda was in a special position, for a state which covered a whole Province was too large to form a single local authority. It had been the intention of the Protectorate government to promote a devolution of power within Buganda, but this aim was not achieved, and Buganda remains a highly centralized kingdom. The rulers of the other Agreement States which constitute Districts of one Province are not unaware of this difference in status.

However, it is only in Buganda that demands for popular representation have come from within. The people expressed their dissatisfaction with the Kabaka's ministers – not with himself – in serious riots in 1945 and 1949, and the basis of membership in his council was changed step by step, until it now has a majority of elected members.

*

But in the years since the war, the focus of attention has shifted from the organization of these small political communities to the making of policy for these territories as a whole. African leaders in Tanganyika successfully claimed a majority of seats in the legislature and a corresponding share of ministerial portfolios, and in December 1961 attained complete independence. Similar developments are in train in Kenya. Uganda paradoxically, where there is no European population to claim a privileged position, lags behind.

Where do yesterday's leaders stand in all this? The answer – except in Uganda – is 'nowhere'. The people who have seen the world, and felt the wind of change turn against the colonial Powers, are not, most of them, aspirants to political office within the narrow field of any African state. A few of the latter, such as Chief Marealle of the Chagga in Tanganyika, have spent a good deal of time abroad, but they are exceptions. Most of them are commoners who have managed to go to Europe or America to study. Most of them are young, though here Jomo Kenyatta is the conspicuous exception.

Where their rebellion has been made by force, they have necessarily found themselves in opposition to chiefs who were government officials and whose duty it was to bring to justice breakers of the law. The attacks by Mau Mau terrorists in Kenya on 'loyal' chiefs were a logical part of their campaign, and were the less surprising in a country where these chiefs owed their authority solely to the alien government.

The position of hereditary rulers naturally differs from that of chiefs whose office is itself an alien creation, and the attitudes of their subjects differs according to the extent of their familiarity with western thought. Some politicians in Uganda believe that they merely 'exploit' their people, but the majority are unable to imagine their disappearance, and talk of making them 'constitutional monarchs' who take no part in politics. In fact this is already their constitutional position; they take no part in the legislative activities of their councils, and have even been persuaded to surrender to public service commissions their say in the appointment of chiefs. (But at any rate in Buganda, the members of the Public Service Commission are men very close to the Kabaka.)

The significance of the rulers as indispensable symbols of national unity and identity was never clearer than at the time when the Uganda government withdrew recognition from the Kabaka and sent him out of the country. The reaction of indignation was universal, and so great that he had to be brought back two years later, in spite of the repeated declarations of the government that this could not be considered. The real distress of the unsophisticated countrymen was as striking as the solid front of the political leaders. No doubt the emotions of these two sections were not identical. The simpler folk thought a necessary part of the existence of Buganda had been destroyed; the more sophisticated saw this occasion as one when 'imperialist' intervention could not be tolerated. But the person of the Kabaka was the focus of both attitudes.

Attitudes towards the civil service chiefs in Uganda are more mixed. Despite the fact that they have now been selected on their merits for quite a long time, and that no hereditary claims are allowed, a good many of them belong to the families of former chiefs, or in the small Soga states of rulers. They marry one another's sisters and daughters, and the senior chiefs are becoming a hereditary class, largely because their salaries enable them to give their sons the education that qualifies them for chiefship. In Buganda they have become an object of resentment to the new-style politicians, and the rioters in 1949 demanded that their position should be made elective. Their dominance in Buganda politics has been somewhat reduced by the introduction of an elected majority in the Kabaka's council.

In the performance of their duties chiefs are criticized from two directions by the different elements among their subjects. The westernized section considers that they are too autocratic and unwilling to listen to public opinion. Older and simpler people do not mind how autocratic are 'the Mukama's spears', as the people of Bunyoro call them. What they complain of is that the chiefs are out of touch with their people. They rush about the country in motor cars, instead of sitting at home ready to dispense hospitality to everyone who comes to pay his respects, and killing beasts from time to time to make a feast. The oldest men do not even like the principle of selection by merit. Chiefs, they think, ought to be aristocrats, otherwise they are just a particularly well-paid kind of wage-labourer.

It is clear that there is no longer any place in Africa for the type of government that met the needs of populations of herdsmen or subsistence peasants. Modern governments have evolved to deal with problems such as Africa never contemplated before the colonial era, and to do so they must be organized on a larger scale than any that have been described here. This technical necessity would be inescapable, even without the demand for new institutions that now comes from Africans themselves. There was a period when African rulers, if they chose, could be 'enlightened leaders' using their influence to persuade people to send their children to school, or be vaccinated, or grow cash crops. In some places they still can be. But since they are essentially the guardians of tradition, they must find themselves more and more out of sympathy with the young men who are now assuming the leadership of the African peoples. In Uganda, British administrations have gone further than they ever did in West Africa to reduce the power of rulers while preserving their dignity. But the rulers are interested in more than dignity, and they can be expected to keep what power they can as long as they can.

It is harder to predict the future role of civil service chiefs, at any rate where they cannot attach themselves to a powerful ruler. In the ideal polity envisaged when the local government drive began, they would all be local government officials, and central government would have no local agents. This now seems improbable. We are much more likely to see African District Comissioners than the abolition of District Commissioners. Perhaps the present civil service chiefs will become a lower grade in a single hierarchy, and the more successful ones will advance through its grades. Perhaps those local councils which have never attained in practice to more than an advisory status will remain as they are, and government policy will be made effective through the chiefs. Perhaps independent African governments will prefer to be sure of having party supporters on the councils, and so use them as the local instruments of their policy. It is pretty certain that government will be at least as highly centralized as it has been under colonial rule, and that the idea of local governments as balancing the power of central government will have little appeal. In these circumstances the civil servant chiefs will retain no vestige of the client relationship towards any ruler. But it may well be found that for a long time the sense of tribal differences is so strong that in the administration of districts or smaller areas people will not tolerate the authority of officials not chosen from among themselves, and that in that sense their chiefs will still symbolize their political separateness.

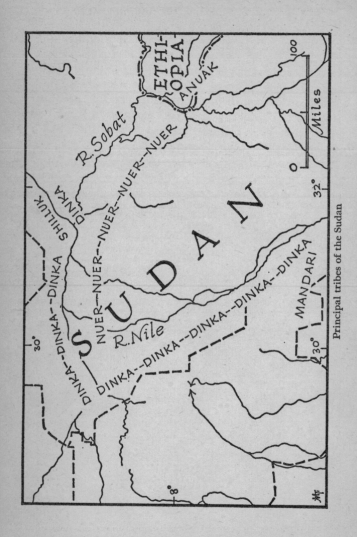

Principal tribes of the Sudan

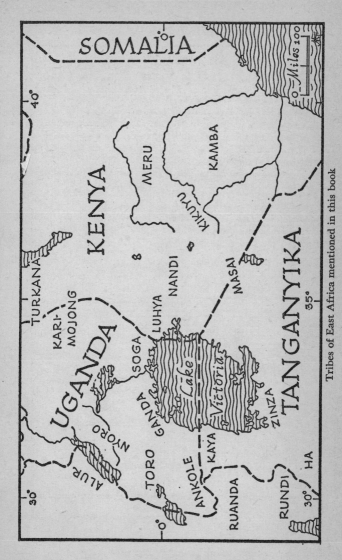

Tribes of East Africa mentioned in this book

Further Reading

The Nilotes

EVANS-PRITCHARD, E. E.,
The Nuer (Clarendon Press, Oxford, 1940).
Kinship and Marriage among the Nuer (Clarendon Press, Oxford, 1951).
Nuer Religion (Clarendon Press, Oxford, 1956).
The Political System of the Anuak of the Anglo-Egyptian Sudan (London School of Economics, London, 1940).
The Divine Kingship of the Shilluk (Frazer Lecture, University Press, Cambridge, 1948).

HOWELL, P. P.,
A Manual of Nuer Law (Published for the International African Institute, Oxford University Press, London, 1954).

SOUTHALL, A. W.,
Alur Society (Heffer, Cambridge, 1956).

The Nilo-Hamites

GULLIVER, P. H.,
The Family Herds (Jie and Turkana), (Routledge & Kegan Paul, London, 1955).

HUNTINGFORD, G. W. B.,
The Nandi of Kenya (Routledge & Kegan Paul, London, 1953).
Nandi Work and Culture (Colonial Research Studies, London, 1950).

PERISTIANY, J. G.,
The Social Institutions of the Kipsigis (G. Routledge & Sons, London, 1939).

The Kenya Bantu

BERNARDI, B.,
The Mugwe (Published for the International African Institute, Oxford University Press, London, 1959).

LAMBERT, H.,
Kikuyu Social and Political Institutions (Published for the International African Institute, Oxford University Press, London, 1956).

The Interlacustrine Bantu

BEATTIE, J. H. M.,
Bunyoro, an African Kingdom (Henry Holt, New York, 1960).

FALLERS, L. A.,
Bantu Bureaucracy (Soga) (Published for the East African Institute of Social Research, Heffer, Cambridge, 1956).

MAIR, L. P.,
An African People in the Twentieth Century (G. Routledge & Sons, London, 1934).

ROSCOE, J.,
The Baganda (Macmillan, London, 1911).

General

EVANS-PRITCHARD, E. E. AND FORTES, M. (EDS.),
African Political Systems (Published for the International Institute of African Languages and Cultures, London, 1940).

RICHARDS, A. I., (ED.)
East African Chiefs (Faber, London, 1960).

Index